The Discourse of Advertising

The Discourse of Advertising explores the language of contemporary advertising. The words of advertisements are not viewed in isolation, however, but in complex interaction with music and pictures, other texts around them, and the people who make and experience them.

This second edition considers advertising in the context of current changes in communication. All chapters have been fully revised and updated, and substantial new material has been added. The social functions and aesthetic effects of advertisements are comprehensively analysed across a wide range of media, from billboards to email and the Internet. Controversially, advertisements are contrasted and compared with literary texts throughout. The book clearly explains relevant concepts from semiotics, poetics, and linguistics, and can serve as an introduction to all of these disciplines. Practical exercises to stimulate further discussion are included at the end of each chapter.

This is a comprehensive and invaluable reference guide to all aspects of the language of advertising.

Guy Cook is Professor of Applied Linguistics at the University of Reading. He has published widely on discourse analysis and the teaching of language and literature. His previous books include *Discourse* (1989), *Discourse and Literature* (1994), and the winner of the Modern Languages Association Kenneth Mildenberger Prize *Language Play, Language Learning* (2000).

The INTERFACE Series

Language, Literature and Critical Practice
Ways of analysing text
David Birch

Literature, Language and Change
Ruth Waterhouse and John Stephens

Literary Studies in Action
Alan Durant and Nigel Fabb

Language in Popular Fiction
Walter Nash

Language, Text and Context
Essays in stylistics
Edited by Michael Toolan

The Language of Jokes
Analysing verbal play
Delia Chiaro

Language, Ideology and Point of View
Paul Simpson

A Linguistic History of English Poetry
Richard Bradford

Literature about Language
Valerie Shepherd

Twentieth-century Poetry
From text to context
Edited by Peter Verdonk

Textual Intervention
Critical and creative strategies for literary studies
Rob Pope

Feminist Stylistics
Sara Mills

Twentieth-century Fiction
From text to context
Peter Verdonk and Jean Jacques Weber

Variety in Written English
Texts in society: societies in text
Tony Box

English in Speech and Writing
Investigating language and literature
Rebecca Hughes

Language through Literature
An introduction
Paul Simpson

Patterns in Language
An introduction to language and literary style
Joanne Thornborrow and Shân Wareing

Exploring the Language of Drama
From text to context
Edited by Jonathan Culpeper, Mick Short and Peter Verdonk

Narrative
A critical linguistic introduction, second edition
Michael Toolan

The Series Editor
Ronald Carter is Professor of Modern English Language at the University of Nottingham and was National Coordinator of the 'Language in the National Curriculum' Project (LINC) from 1989 to 1992.

The Discourse of Advertising
Second Edition

Guy Cook

London and New York

First published 1992
Reprinted 1994 (twice), 1996

Second edition first published 2001
by Routledge
2 Park Square, Milton Park, Abingdon, Oxon OX14 4RN

Simultaneously published in the USA and Canada
by Routledge
270 Madison Ave, New York, NY 10016

Reprinted 2009 (twice)

Routledge is an imprint of the Taylor & Francis Group, an Informa business

© 1992, 2001 Guy Cook

Typeset in Times by Wearset, Boldon, Tyne and Wear
Printed and bound in Great Britain by the MPG Books Group,
Bodmin and King's Lynn

British Library Cataloguing in Publication Data
A catalogue record for this book is available from the British Library

Library of Congress Cataloging in Publication Data
Cook, Guy (Guy W.D.)
  The discourse of advertising / Guy Cook.– 2nd ed.
    p. cm. – (The Interface series)
  Includes bibliographical references and index.
  1. Discourse analysis. 2. Advertising–Language. I. Title.
  II. Interface (London, England)
  P302 .C625 2001
  659.1'01'4–dc21   2001019243

ISBN 978–0–415–23454–2 (hbk)
ISBN 978–0–415–23455–9 (pbk)

To Roxana

Contents

Figures

Acknowledgements

Two people deserve especial thanks for the invaluable help and encouragement they have given me in preparing this substantially revised second edition: Elena Poptsova Cook for her constant patience and support, and for pursuing the most elusive of copyright holders; Kieran O'Halloran for his meticulous reading of the manuscript, and perceptive suggestions on every aspect of it, from the most minor detail to the largest theoretical issues.

While writing this book, I have also benefited from discussion of contemporary advertising (and the global economy in which it thrives) with many students, friends and colleagues, in particular David Block, Lewis Glinert, Maisie Langridge, Greg Myers, Alison Sealey, Barbara Seidlhofer, Tony Smith, Henry Widdowson, and Malcolm Williams.

I also thank Ron Carter, the editor of this series, for his continued enthusiasm and support for this project, which is only a small part of his contribution to the study of language and literature. I am also grateful to Louisa Semlyen, Katharine Jacobson and Christabel Kirkpatrick at Routledge for their efficiency and endurance in dealing with my interminable queries about permissions and pictures.

There are many ads quoted and referred to in this book. Some manufacturers and advertisers were friendly and helpful; others were unfriendly, constantly unavailable, refused permission, or tried to persuade me to change what I had written. The former category were a pleasure to do business with, and will not, I sincerely hope, be at all dissatisfied with my comments.

The publishers and I would also like to acknowledge gratefully the use of copyright material in the illustrations and text from the following people and organizations:

Figure 1.2 May Day Celebrations: courtesy of the Hulton Getty Picture Collection; *Figure 2.2* Business 2 ad: Futurenet; *Figure 2.5* Times legal section ad: Times Newspapers Ltd; *Figure 3.1* Wonderbra ad: Playtex Europe; *Figure 3.2* Coca-Cola's Sprite soft drink ad: Coca-Cola Great

Britain and Ireland. 'Sprite' is a registered trade mark of The Coca-Cola Company, 'Sprite light' is a trade mark of The Coca-Cola Company and are reproduced with kind permission from The Coca-Cola Company. *Figure 3.3* Wrigley's chewing gum ad: stills by courtesy of The Wrigley Company Ltd; *Figure 3.5* VW Sharan ad: Volkswagen UK; *Figure 4.4* FCUK ad: French Connection Group Plc, reproduced courtesy of TBWA/London, UK; *Figure 4.6* Lypsyl ad: Novartis Consumer Health UK Ltd; *Figure 4.7* Kew Gardens ad: Kew Gardens; *Figure 4.9* Kattomeat ad: Friskies Petcare (UK) Ltd; *Figure 4.10* Maxwell House ad: Kraft Foods Inc; *Figure 4.12* Guiness ad: Guinness Great Britain, courtesy of AMV.BBDO; *Figure 4.13* Black Heart Rum ad: Allied Domecq Spirits and Wine ad; *Figure 4.16* AA Insurance ad: The AA; *Figure 4.16* TE TAO logo: Kuan Ltd; *Figure 4.17* Tiger Beer ad: Asia Pacific Breweries Ltd; *Figure 4.18* Kodak logo: re-printed courtesy of Eastman Kodak Company; Kellog logo: The Kellog logo is reproduced by permission of Kellog Company; *Figure 4.19* Giovanni Versace ad: Versace s.p.a.; *Figure 4.20* Natural History Museum logo: Natural History Museum; *Figure 5.4* Subaru ad: Subaru (UK) Ltd; *Figure 5.5* Nudity Sells Cars: courtesy of the Hulton Getty Picture Collection; *Figure 5.5* Armitage Shanks ad: American Standard Plumbing (UK) Ltd; *Figure 6.2* Cointreau ad: The Remy-Cointreau Group; *Figure 7.2* Philips cordless phones ad: Philips Consumer Communications; *Figure 7.3* Clearasil ad: Grey Worldwide; *Figure 7.4* Secret Weapon lipstick ad: Superdrug. Advertisement produced by Bates UK for Superdrug; *Figure 8.4* Ashtray anti-smoking ad: Health Promotion England; *Figure 8.5* Royal Navy ad: The Royal Navy; *Figure 10.1* Barnardos ad: Barnardos; *Figure 10.2* Benetton ad: photograph by Lucinda Devlin, reproduced by permission of Benetton Group s.p.a..

'In a Station of the Metro', by Ezra Pound, from PERSONAE, copyright ©1926 by Ezra Pound. Reprinted by permission of New Directions Publishing Corp: also by permission of Faber and Faber Ltd; excerpt from *The Great Gatsby* by F. Scott Fitzgerald, reprinted with permission of Charles Scribner's Sons; excerpt from *Bliss* by Peter Carey, reproduced by kind permission of Faber and Faber Ltd; two lines from 'Sunny Prestatyn' from *Collected Poems* by Philip Larkin, reproduced by kind permission of Faber and Faber Ltd; 'This Is Just To Say' from *Collected Poems* by William Carlos Williams, published by Carcanet Press Ltd. Reprinted by kind permission of Carcanet Press Ltd; words used in L'Oréal advertisement reproduced by kind permission of L'Oréal; 'I Shall Be Free', written by Bob Dylan, reprinted by kind permission of Sony/ATV Music Publishing Ltd.

1 Introduction

The genre of the advertisement

1.1 Why study advertising?

In contemporary society, advertising is everywhere. We cannot walk down the street, shop, watch television, go through our mail, log on to the Internet, read a newspaper or take a train without encountering it. Whether we are alone, with our friends or family, or in a crowd, advertising is always with us, if only on the label of something we are using. Given this ubiquity, it is strange that many people are reluctant to pay attention to ads. An ad is never the programme they are watching, never the letter they are waiting for, never the website they are seeking, nor the part of the newspaper they are reading. Despite all the care and skill in their creation, ads are flicked past, put in the bin, **zapped** (avoided by remote-control channel switching), or **zipped** (fast-forwarded on video) – some video machines even have a 'built-in ad-skipping facility'. People pay to see films and read books; they put paintings in galleries and sculptures in museums; but advertising is often regarded as a peripheral creation – except by those directly involved in it. This is odd, because a stranger to our society (the proverbial Martian anthropologist?) would probably be struck by the prominence and quantity of advertising, and might reasonably pay more attention to it than to the texts of literature, law, science and journalism, which we say we value more highly. Advertising is everywhere but nowhere. A major aim of this book is to explore the reasons for this paradoxical and ambivalent status.

Attitudes to advertising can be indicative of our personality, or social and ideological position. This is not equally true of all acts of communication, many of which are relatively uncontroversial. Few people, if any, have strong views about the need for recipes or car number plates. Other genres arouse stronger feelings. Some people feel that a university lecture is an authoritarian way of teaching, that Christmas cards are an unnecessary waste of paper and time, and that census forms are an intrusion upon privacy. In this respect, advertising is one of the most controversial of all contemporary genres, partly because it is relatively new, but also because it is closely associated with the values of the competitive high-growth global market economy in which it thrives. In a world beset by social and environmental problems, advertising can be seen as urging people to consume more by making them feel dissatisfied or inadequate, by appealing to greed, worry and ambition. On the other hand, it may be argued that many ads are skilful, clever and amusing, and that it is unjust to make them a scapegoat for all the sorrows of the modern world. Thus to ask someone their opinion of advertising in general, or of a particular ad, can be to embark upon an emotionally and ideologically charged discussion, revealing their political and social position, and their acceptance of, or alienation from, the status quo.

Indeed outsiders interested in advertising could be said – broadly speaking – to fall into two categories. In crude and unsympathetic terms I might caricature one category as amoral aesthetes mesmerized by its decadent beauty, and the other as over-serious moralists appalled at its materialism. The first group toy with ideas of working in a big ad agency, the latter believe that by understanding advertising they will neutralize its effects and improve the world. This simple dichotomy is clumsy and exaggerated. There are certainly many more delicate categories within these two bands. Nevertheless, it has a degree of truth. Advertising is a topic which both causes and reveals existing social divisions. For this reason, in an educational setting, advertising can be a stimulus – vying with the claims made for literature in a liberal education – for discussion of urgent issues: the destruction of the environment, the wealth gap (both within and between countries), the merits of socialism and capitalism, the growth of a world culture, the struggle of feminism and patriarchy, the status of art and popular culture, the consequences of mass communication and high technology. Few genres can generate so much controversy.

On the other hand, some of the sharpness of earlier differences of opinion may have abated. The presence of advertising now seems so unshakable and secure, even to its opponents, that the possibility that it could suddenly be swept away, by either revolution or reaction, seems to have retreated. Intense large-scale advertising now has a history almost everywhere. People grow up with it and grow used to it, so that even when it is perceived as an evil it is also perceived as inevitable and unremarkable. In addition, advertising itself has changed, becoming more subtle and more entertaining than the crude hard selling of the 1950s and 1960s (though this very subtlety can be seen as more pernicious). There has been an apparent change of attitude towards contemporary problems. Some ads make a show of environmental concern, of support for social justice, of wishing to improve public health. This apparent social conscience may give rise to three very different judgements. According to the first, advanced by some leading advertisers, it is possible for advertising to influence society for good as well as for bad. In the second view, advertising is amoral, and merely reflects states and changes in society, whether good or bad (White 2000: 252–65). In the third view, the apparent social concern professed in some ads is simply fraudulent, and ads are always bad: a veneer of feminism masks deeper sexism; superficial environmental concern cynically sells pollution. In its strongest form, this last view may argue that a growth economy, social exploitation and inequality, violence and the destruction of the planet are all inextricably linked to each other, and that advertising is both an expression of this apocalyptic unity and dependent upon it.

Ads use fictions, word play, compressed story-telling, stylized acting, photography, cartoons, puns and rhythms in ways which are often memorable, enjoyable and amusing. New ads evoke comment. The words and details of ads often come to people's minds more readily than those of novels and poems and plays, and they are often recalled with more laughter and enthusiasm. Yet it is often a love–hate relationship: one which frequently causes unease, and in which the love is often denied. It seems that with many ads, we suffer a split, contradictory reaction: involuntary spontaneous enjoyment, conscious reflective rejection. With other genres we usually know where our loyalties lie; with ads we are just confused.

These, however, are generalizations, both about ads and about people, and although advertising seems to be homogenous and increasingly international and cross-cultural, such generalizations immediately run into trouble. In some parts of the world, especially western Europe and North America, there is a long tradition of high-pressure advertising, and therefore perhaps more tolerance and amused scepticism about it, than there is in countries in which pervasive advertising is relatively new. In those places, concern about the damage done by multinational advertising to local cultural identity is felt more strongly, and opinion polarized. If tendencies towards globalization continue, as it seems almost inevitable that they will, then perhaps such differences will (sadly) matter less and less. If, on the other hand, different markets take their own directions, then the divergence may continue, or increase. Seeing how fast some critiques of advertising have become dated and irrelevant, I shall avoid the assumption that the status quo will last, or that I or anyone else can predict how it will change. If this book reflects a particularly British or 2001 attitude to ads, I hope it may yet stimulate readers in other places and later times to reflect on their own advertising in ways appropriate to them.

1.2 Advertising as discourse

The purpose of this book is to analyse ads as **discourse**. Although the main focus of **discourse analysis** is on language, it is not concerned with language alone. It also examines the context of communication: who is communicating with whom and why; in what kind of society and situation; through what medium; how different types and acts of communication evolved, and their relationship to each other. When music and pictures combine with language to alter or add to its meaning, then discourse analysis must consider these modes of communication too.

The breadth of this approach is justified by the belief that neither specific acts of communication nor the internal mechanisms of language can be well understood in any other way. Contrary to the theory and practice of some schools of linguistics, which treat language as a neatly isolated object, discourse analysis views language and context holistically.

As there is a good deal of dispute over the terms 'context', 'text' and 'discourse', I shall need to say more precisely how I am going to use them here.

Text is used to mean linguistic forms, temporarily and artificially separated from context for the purposes of analysis.

Context includes all of the following:

1   **substance:** the physical material which carries or relays text
2   music and pictures
3   **paralanguage:** meaningful behaviour accompanying language, such as voice quality, gestures, facial expressions and touch (in speech), and choice of typeface and letter sizes (in writing)
4   **situation:** the properties and relations of objects and people in the vicinity of the text, as perceived by the participants
5   **co-text:** text which precedes or follows that under analysis, and which participants judge to belong to the same discourse
6   **intertext:** text which the participants perceive as belonging to other discourse, but which they associate with the text under consideration, and which affects their interpretation
7   **participants:** their intentions and interpretations, knowledge and beliefs, attitudes, affiliations and feelings. Each participant is simultaneously a part of the context and an observer of it. Participants are usually described as **senders** and **receivers**. (The sender of a message is not always the same as the **addresser**, however, the person who relays it. In a television ad, for example, the addresser may be an actor, though the sender is an advertising agency. Neither is the receiver always the **addressee**, the person for whom it is intended. The addressees may be a specific target group, but the receiver is anyone who sees the ad.)
8   **function:** what the text is intended to do by the senders and addressers, or perceived to do by the receivers and addressees.

Discourse (in the sense used in this book[1]) is text and context together, interacting in a way which is perceived as meaningful and unified by the participants (who are both part of the context and observers of it). The task of discourse analysis is to describe both this phenomenon in general and particular instances of it, and to say how participants distinguish one type of discourse from another. To do this, it needs to pay close attention not only to human cognitive processes in general, but also to features specific to a given culture.

Understandably, discourse analysis is sometimes accused of being large and rather messy, for it cannot bring to analysis the precision of approaches which isolate one facet of communication from others. It is a premise of this book, however, that the precision of such methods is bought at the price of misrepresenting the complexity of human communication. The study of language must take context into account, because language is always in context, and there are no acts of communication without participants, intertexts, situations, paralanguage and substance. Denial of this may yield tidy descriptions and theories with pretensions to explain comprehensively 'how language works'. But unless such approaches are an intermediate stage of description, a temporary tactic preceding a reintegration of this fabricated object with context, it is not clear what is being analysed. Language only exists on its own in the invented examples of formal linguistics textbooks. There seems little point, however, to any theory which cleanly describes something it created for itself. Its conclusions are circular and illusory.

By refusing to ignore context, discourse analysis embarks upon a journey with no destination. Yet this is a necessary condition of its subject. Discourse – especially discourse as complex as advertising – always holds out more to be analysed, leaves more to be said. But this need not be a cause for despair. It would be both depressing and self-deceptive to believe that one could exhaust all the aspects of the genre, and present an answer to all the problems it poses.

Many studies of advertising do separate out components of ads, concentrate on one or a few, and ignore the others. Thus there are studies of the language of advertising which have little or nothing to say about its pictures and music or the people who create it, but there are also studies which describe the pictures of advertising without paying any attention to language. Research within the advertising business often concentrates solely upon receivers of ads, endlessly debating how best to divide them, inventing ever more delicate categories ('trendies', 'cowboys', 'puritans', 'drifters', 'utopians', 'traditionalists', etc.[2]), and assessing their reactions with ever more sophisticated techniques. Describing advertising as discourse is both more complex and more difficult than any of these approaches, for it means trying to describe all these elements, and their effects on each other. As a starting point, the approach may be summed up by Figure 1.1 (overleaf). An ad is an interaction of elements.

A problem is to decide whether we should put any of these factors at the centre of the diagram, and thus, by implication, at the centre of our approach. (In the diagram, the centre is the interaction of all the elements around, and in a sense there is nothing there.) One possibility, for example, would be to put the text of the ad (its words, and perhaps its music and pictures) at the centre, making a stable point to which all the other elements relate. This book attempts not to do this. Though the focus is on language, I shall try always to see language in relation to the other

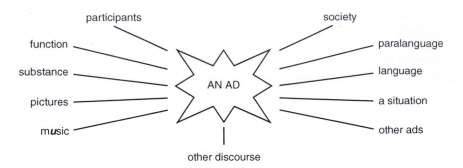

Figure 1.1 Interaction of elements in ads.

elements, remembering that a change in any one element usually entails a change in the whole. An ad is not a tangible or stable entity; it is the dynamic synthesis of many components, and comes into being through them.

This interdependence of elements is not peculiar to the element which happens to be at the centre of Figure 1.1 – 'advertisement'; it is true of all the other elements in the figure too. Each comes into existence through the interaction of the others. A society *is* its senders, receivers, discourses and situations. A participant is identified by his or her language, paralanguage, position in society, and knowledge of other discourses.

In addition to its existence in the here and now, each element of communication which makes up an ad or any other act of communication has a history. Figure 1.1 does not take this into account, but presents a **synchronic** snapshot of a moment in time and ignores the **diachronic** history of each part.

Although it is sometimes said that there have been ads at least since classical times – the earliest known ad supposedly being for a brothel in Ephesus (D. White 1988) – advertising in the era of colour magazines, television, and the Internet is a new phenomenon, both in nature, quantity and effect. Yet, although contemporary advertising is relatively young, it already has a considerable tradition. Each new ad is encountered against a background of thousands of earlier ads. The effect of reading in the context of tradition is well known in the study of literary discourse, and is what most university literature courses devote themselves to developing in their students, but it is often overlooked in discussions of ads, perhaps because a time when advertising seemed new and tradition-free is still well within living memory. Nowadays, we do not experience advertising as a new phenomenon, as was perhaps the case in the 1950s and 1960s. Many academic studies have been slow to realize this. They read ads in isolation from the past, discounting the effect of the growing tradition, and participants' detailed knowledge of it.

1.3 Genres

Both individuals and societies pour out discourse all the time, but it is not, for them, an amorphous and undistinguished stream. It is part of a person's cultural competence to divide the discourse of their society into units, to give those units names, and to assign them to categories. Some instances of discourse are perceived to be *conversations*, for example, others are *consultations, lessons, news bulletins, e-mails, brochures, prayers, squabbles, stories, jokes, plays, web pages, printouts, handouts, operas, soap operas, games, films*. There are hundreds of such categories (Dimter 1985), or **genres**, a term borrowed by discourse analysis from literary studies, and defined by Swales (1990: 58) as 'a class of communicative events which share some set of communicative purposes'.

> These purposes ... constitute the rationale for the genre. This rationale shapes the schematic structure of the discourse and influences and constrains choice of content and style. ... In addition to purpose, exemplars of a genre exhibit various patterns of similarity in terms of structure, style, content and intended audience.

Genres often merge into each other and defy exact definition. (Advertising, as we shall see, is a particularly slippery case.) A given piece of discourse may exemplify several genres at once. There is nothing mutually exclusive, for example, in the terms 'story', 'joke' and 'cartoon', and a piece of discourse could be all three at once. Genre identification also involves non-verbal forms of communication. Films usually have dialogue but not always, and even when they do the relative importance of words and pictures varies considerably, not only from film to film, but also from spectator to spectator. The same is true of ads. There are ads without language – or in which language plays a subordinate part.

The importance of genres in a theory of communication, and of the way participants recognize them, is another reason why discourse analysis cannot be limited to descriptions of extractions or idealizations (which is what single sentences often are), but needs to describe both whole texts and their contexts, including physical substance. In speech, genre identification may be influenced by whether the language is shouted or sung, whether it is beamed down from a satellite on to millions of television screens, or whispered in darkness to one person through the grille in a confessional. In writing, it may be influenced by whether the communication is scribbled in pencil, embossed in gold, flashed from giant neon tubes, or flanked by linking instructions and icons on the World Wide Web.

Genres may be described in terms of their social function, but equally societies may be categorized in terms of the genres they use. From 1945 until the end of the 1980s, the advertising of goods in Eastern Europe and the Soviet Union, though not altogether unknown, was strikingly rare. Its

Figure 1.2 A Communist Party *lozung*. May Day (International Labourers' Day) Celebrations in Red Square, Moscow 1971, courtesy Hulton Getty Picture Library.

absence struck visitors from capitalist countries very forcibly: bare walls in metro stations, unbroken print in newspapers, mail deliveries without circulars. There was however a genre (called in Russian the *lozung*) which was not found in the capitalist countries: a hoarding, neon sign or strip of red material bearing a communist slogan (see Figure 1.2), put in place by the authorities and addressed to the population in general. As the Eastern European societies changed, the *lozung* disappeared, and new, capitalist genres become more prominent. Pre-eminent among these was advertising – so that now, typical Eastern European advertisements are very similar to those in the West (Figure 1.3). Changes in genres are indicative of rapid social change. Throughout the 1990s and into the 2000s, advertising has both colonized new territories and become ever more prominent in its homelands. As such it can be an important key to the nature and direction of the changes of this period: globalization and the homogenization of markets and political systems.

Now, advertising is a prominent genre in virtually all contemporary societies, and I shall write as though you, the reader, like me, the writer, live in a society where it is already well established. It is this assumption which motivates my use of the word 'us'.

Figure 1.3 A contemporary Hungarian advertisement.

1.4 Defining advertisements as a genre

Defined very generally, advertising is 'the promotion of goods or services for sale through impersonal media' (the *Collins Concise Dictionary*). In this book, however, the term is interpreted both more broadly and more narrowly: more broadly because it includes ads which do not offer a product at all; more narrowly because it does not deal with everything which such a definition encompasses. With the advent of TV advertising in the 1950s, advertising was transformed in character, and became much more various than this simple dictionary definition suggests. The fact that such a definition will encompass everything from a market ticket offering goods for sale in the most straightforward terms ('Lovely bananas, 50p a pound') to a multi-million pound thirty-second TV mini-drama, or a pulsing 'pop-up' window on the World Wide Web, indicates that our vocabulary has not kept pace with change. Advertising at the beginning of the twenty first century is radically different from that of the 1950s and 1960s, though also in a direct line of descent from it. There is no clear point of change, but the recognition that there have been changes is essential.

The defining features of the modern advertisement as a genre are surprisingly hard to pin down – and I shall not try to do this until the final chapter. Many people decide, when faced with the problem of definition, that the crucial feature which distinguishes advertisements from related genres is their function, which is always to persuade people to buy a particular product. They may add that, whatever else it may say, an ad must always contain the name of a product. Yet there are a number of reasons to reject these popular definitions. Firstly, there are advertisements which do not sell anything, but plead or warn or seek support. Urging us, for example, to avoid heart attacks by eating more healthily, and drawing attention to the existence of The British Heart Foundation. Secondly, there are instances of other genres, such as poems or songs, which *become* ads by being used in a particular way (a process which may be reversible, allowing an ad to become a poem). Thirdly, even if the majority of ads have the function of persuading their addressees to buy, this is not their only function. They may also amuse, inform, misinform, worry or warn. It can be argued that these other functions are all in the service of a main function which is usually to sell; alternatively, even selling ads perform multiple functions which are more or less autonomous (whatever manufacturers may believe). Moreover, if an ad is defined by its selling function alone, then one might wonder what it becomes when the product is no longer available, or when the receiver is someone who cannot or will not buy the product. I can receive ads for cigarettes, bubble gum, tampons, denture cleaners and holidays in the Bahamas, though as a non-smoking adult male with my own teeth and limited funds, I know that these are not for me. I look at an ad in a magazine called *Petersen's Handguns* – which I bought in the USA – for 'Galco International Miami Classic Handguns' (Figure 1.4). It shows a handsome young male executive and his blonde, female, leather-mini-skirted secretary, leaning very close to each other across a desk, both wearing guns in shoulder holsters. His is heavy and masculine, hers is lightweight and feminine. But I, living in England, have neither the intention nor the legal right to buy the product. This does not mean that the ad says nothing to me.

The issue is further complicated by the fact that the term 'function' can be understood from two perspectives. The function which the sender intends the discourse to have may not be the same as the function it actually does have for the receiver. The sender may intend the gun ad to persuade people to buy Galco guns (I do not flatter myself that I am one), but the reader may use it in a discussion of gun laws, or as an example in a book. With ads, as with certain other genres, there is the further complication that there is no single sender, because ads are not the creation of an individual. Instead, there are many strata of senders, ranging from the manufacturer through the agency and its creative department, to actors and camera crews. For each stratum, the intended function may be different. Though the manufacturer may seek only to persuade people to buy, the writer may seek to impress other colleagues, or realize an aesthetic aim.

One way out of this definitional quagmire would be to insist that,

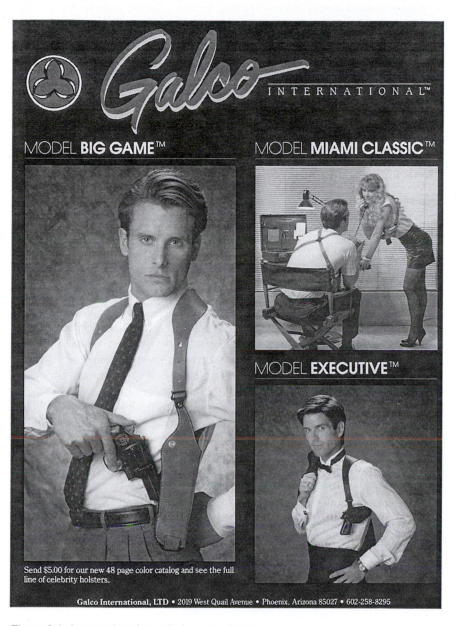

Figure 1.4 A gun advertisement from the USA.

despite awkward cases, the overriding defining factor is nevertheless the function of persuading to buy, and that discourse described as advertising which does not do this is misclassified. This seems wrong for two reasons. Firstly, the term *is* used more broadly. Secondly, to be satisfied with this simple characterization distracts from the variety of ads, and from the points of contact they have with other genres. Ads draw upon, and thus share features with, many other genres, including political propaganda, conversation, song, film, myth, poetry, fairy tales, soap operas, sitcoms, novels, graffiti, jokes and cartoons.

1.5 Defining 'definition'

Attempts to define ads as a genre run into severe trouble when they look for textual or contextual features, or combinations of features, which all ads have in common, but are not present in other genres. The problem here, however, may be the kind of definition we are looking for: the definition of 'definition' itself.

One way of defining a word is to look for 'components' of meaning which it brings together and which describe properties of the entity or concept to which it refers. Thus, for example, the word 'stallion' has the components 'adult', 'male' and 'horse', and all adult male horses can be described by this word. If meaning is a statement of equivalence, then the meaning of the word is its equivalence to these components, and this, in one sense, is 'what the word means'. Broken down into components, words can be described as entering into various **sense relations** with each other according to components they do or do not have in common, and these relations can be described hierarchically (see Figure 1.5). A 'stallion' is a kind of 'horse', which is a kind of 'mammal', which is a kind of 'animal'. In **semantics**, there are technical terms for different types of relationship within this hierarchy. 'Mammal' is the **supernym** (term above) or **superordinate** of horse; conversely, horse is a **hyponym** (term below) of mammal.

While this **componential definition** systematizes the meaning of certain words, it has a number of severe drawbacks. It cannot cope with **connotations** (the vaguer associations of a word for a group or individual) or metaphorical uses, both of which are particularly important in ads.

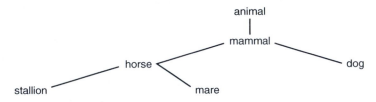

Figure 1.5 Semantic relations: horse and dog.

(Imagine the implications of calling a perfume for men 'Stallion' or 'Bull', or a perfume for women 'Mare' or 'Cow'.) Although componential analysis works well enough with a word like 'stallion', and differentiates it from related words, it is less successful with words whose meanings are different to different individuals or groups, and merge into related words in a fuzzy intermediate area. The component of words denoting political creeds ('fascism', 'communism', 'parliamentary democracy'), for example, are very different to their supporters and their opponents. There are also word meanings whose boundaries merge, even for an individual. What are the components of the word 'love', for example, and how do they differ from those of 'like'? Other words, though reasonably fixed, do not lend themselves to this kind of definition at all. 'Game' may refer to activities as diverse as a toddler throwing pebbles into a puddle, and a world championship chess match. Different games have only what Wittgenstein (1968: 32) described as a 'family resemblance', a connection which needs tracing through several intermediate instances, rather than any shared components.

A more satisfactory approach to meaning, which may help us to define 'advertisement', is that of **prototype theory** (Rosch 1977), which suggests that we choose or understand a word by reference to a mental representation of a typical instance.[3] Whether a given entity is a bird, for example, will depend on its resemblance to our prototype of a bird. This will vary from person to person and culture to culture. For many Europeans a typical bird may be the House Sparrow, for many North Americans perhaps the American Robin. The less like our prototype an instance is, the less likely we are to identify it with the word for that category, but we are still willing to tolerate fuzzy, borderline, and dubious cases.

If we apply this approach to the problem of defining the genre of advertisement, then instances which are described as ads, but do not share the components of a typical ad, need no longer trouble us. The prototypical ad will vary between individuals, cultures and periods, but probably, for most British people, it is a soap-powder commercial in which a housewife praises the product for making her family's clothes so white. In the USA it is likely to be an ad showing a satisfied family eating an instant dessert. Like most prototypes, this is likely to be derived from a specific instance (a Persil ad in the UK, a Jell-O ad in the USA) encountered in the past. (Interestingly, television programmes on advertising frequently repeat these instances: thus perhaps establishing the prototypes for those too young to have encountered the originals.) The further a given instance moves from this yardstick, the less likely it is to be classified as an ad (although even ads for political parties have something in common with eulogies of soap suds). Because it tolerates fuzzy and indeterminate areas between concepts, prototype theory is also very helpful when dealing with the hybrid genres created by advertisers' frequent and ingenious attempts to disguise their ads as something else.

A weakness of both componential analysis and prototype theory is their concentration on a word or what it refers to, rather than its environment. Yet with an 'ad' (as with 'stallions' and 'birds') it is sometimes nothing intrinsic which helps us in identification, but rather the immediate surroundings (Myers 1999: 115–31). We tend to view anything which occurs at a given position in a television schedule, or in a certain position in a magazine, as an ad, quite irrespective of components which can be ticked off on a checklist, or the way it can be related to a prototype.

1.6 Categories of ad: medium, product, technique, consumer

The issue of defining 'ad' is closely linked to that of defining categories of ad. But here again the issue is anything but simple.

I shall use the term **medium** as the singular of the term (mass) media, to refer to such different means of mass communication as the printed book, newspapers and magazines, radio, television, and the Internet. As such, a medium is partly but not wholly distinguished from others by its use of a particular technology, such as radio waves, print, or computer networks, which in turn limits the modes of communication available to it. Yet the distinction between one medium and another is not always so concrete, and can also be situational or functional. Books, newspapers and magazines, for example, all use print, but are nevertheless distinct.

One might reasonably claim that the medium in which an ad appears is an important parameter of difference, and that ads in magazines are quite different from those on television or roadside hoardings. It is certainly true that many ads are affected by, or take advantage of, particular media and situations. ('In the future there will be a faster way to work' says a hoarding ad alongside a London road notorious for its rush hour traffic jams.[4]) Ads on trains and platforms often have longer copy, or demand reflection, on the assumption that their receivers, in the enforced idleness of awaiting or riding on a train, are likely to scrutinize the ad more carefully. An example on the London Underground was an ad for Clinomyn Smokers' Toothpaste. It showed Humphrey Bogart holding a tube of toothpaste and saying: 'If this gives smokers gleaming white teeth then I'm not Ingrid Bergman.'

Television ads rely on music and moving pictures in ways that magazine ads cannot. Yet despite these differences, many campaigns run the 'same ad' concurrently in many media, so that each one reminds us of the others. Print ads, for example, may keep some part of the words and images of a television ad in front of people, even when they are away from home. Other ads may direct people from one medium to another, as is most noticeably the case when print and television ads direct their receivers to a World Wide Web site for more information on the product.

Another way of categorizing ads is by product or service. Luxuries like spirits, perfume and chocolate demand (and get) different advertising techniques from those used for household necessities like soap and eggs, and both of these categories have expensive counterparts: holidays and sound systems (perhaps perceived as luxuries), or cars, computers and fridges (usually perceived as necessities). Not all ads, however, sell products or services: as well as **product ads**, there are also **non-product ads**, including, for example, those for charities and political parties.

Another possible means of categorization is by technique. One well-established distinction is between the **hard-sell** and the **soft-sell** ad. Hard selling makes a direct appeal. My personal prototype of a hard-sell ad involves a man in a suit, standing in front of a pile of carpets, talking loudly and directly to the camera about low cost, limited availability and guaranteed reliability. Soft selling relies more on mood than on exhortation, and on the implication that life will be better with the product. The possessor reflects the possessed: this is a major unspoken premise of all soft-selling ads. A typical soft sell was a cinema ad for Bacardi rum, in which slim and athletic young men and women in revealing swim-wear were shown diving from a yacht into blue water and basking happily on a tropical beach. The implications hardly need spelling out, though perhaps their extraordinary reversal of the effect of using the product does, because it is so complete that it may pass unnoticed. Drinking large quantities of spirits makes people fatter, less fit, less sexually potent, and poorer; in direct sunlight it also gives people headaches. It is not prototypically the activity of muscular young men or slim young women in swim-wear, but of fat, stressed middle-aged men in suits!

Another enduring classification of technique is that between **reason** and **tickle** (Bernstein 1974: 118). Reason ads suggest motives for purchase. Fairy Liquid, for example, is said to be a better buy than other washing-up liquids because – squirt for squirt – it washes more dishes. Tickle ads, on the other hand, appeal to emotion, humour and mood. Cigarette ads (with the exception of those stressing a low tar content) are of necessity ticklers. (What reasons could they give?) But the reason/tickle distinction is not just the hard/soft distinction with a new name. A soft sell often implies reasons for purchase without a direct appeal. An early 1990s ad for Audi cars, for example, showed a prosperous and conventionally handsome man receiving an urgent phone call during the night, waking his small son, wrapping him in a blanket and putting him in the car, then driving swiftly but carefully through dawn streets to a maternity hospital where his wife has just given birth. In the early-morning half light, a milk float, whose driver presumably expects the streets to be empty, emerges suddenly from a side street. The Audi responds quickly and swerves efficiently without skidding. The implication is that this manoeuvrability is a reason for purchase – though this is never directly stated. The ad also implies (softly) that possession affects the possessor, for the driver is good-looking, loving, responsible and alert. Like products themselves fashions for desirable qualities may change. The responsible family man is far less prominent in car ads of the 2000s than he was in the 1990s. A 2000 ad for the Ford Focus, demonstrating the same easy control in an emergency, has the driver swerving to avoid a moose in a wildlife park! However, the basic soft-sell technique – associating product, person and lifestyle – has hardly changed at all.

The techniques of **slow drip** and **sudden burst** refer not to the content of an ad, but to the frequency of its release (Brierley 1995: 116). Another important and self-explanatory difference is that between **short copy** and **long copy** (i.e. ads with few words and ads with many).

Choice of technique, however, clearly relates to product, to media, and to copy length. It is easier to reason in the long copy of a magazine ad than in the twenty or thirty seconds of a television commercial. Luxuries lend themselves to soft, tickle selling. More expensive items, whose purchase merits longer consideration, are prone to reason selling, and therefore to longer written copy. Similarly, there is an aura of respectability about slow-drip campaigns which suggest product reliability and durability. For this reason they are commonly used both with big buys like cars and for cheaper domestic purchases like baked beans, whose markets are less susceptible to seasonal variation than, say, toys and perfumes, both of which scramble wildly for attention before Christmas and then diminish in January.

As far as advertisers themselves are concerned, the most important categorization of ads is by consumer (Brierley 1995: 25–41; Myers 1999: 52–167). The advertising industry expends enormous effort on attempts both to categorize people effectively and then to target the categories. Techniques range from the more traditional surveys or inclusion of coupons (which show who has read the ad) to more recent innovations such as focus groups and the notorious Internet 'cookies' which (unknown to the user) send back information about sites visited and routes followed. Fashions in categorizing consumer behaviour change as fast as ads themselves and there is endless discussion about whether the best divisions are those of lifestyle, socioeconomic class, point in the life cycle, neighbourhood, personality type, or of something else altogether. Again, there is overlap with the other types of categorization suggested above. Certain products are more likely to be bought by men than by women, by the rich, by a certain age group and so on. Tickle may work better on one group than on another.

None of these categorizations allows us to separate off one kind of ad distinctly from another. The factors of medium, product, technique and copy length all interact. There is also an additional hazard. The chronic frustration to all attempts to typologize ads is the advertisers' striving to grab attention through surprise. The fact that a particular targeted group, or a particular product, associates with a particular medium or technique is in itself often a good reason for change.

1.7 Ads and literature

One of the aims of this book is to assess poetic creativity in ads, and to relate this to creativity in literature, as a way of problematizing both. For this reason there is frequent discussion of literary as well as advertising texts. But there is as little consensus about what constitutes literature as there is about the status and morality of advertising. Though people use the term 'literature' quite successfully, and know what kinds of text they will find in the 'literature section' of a book shop or the reading list of a 'literature course', attempts to define the term have been notoriously unsuccessful. Whatever criteria are used – whether linguistic, semantic, functional, social or psychological – there are too many exceptions: works classed as literature which do not display the cited characteristics, and works not classed as literature which do. New 'sub-literary' genres have intensified the problem, for they share a great deal with 'literature'. Language play and patterning can be found in ads; fictional worlds in sitcoms and soap operas; social and personal significance in pop songs.

Yet literature – despite disputes over individual works – undoubtedly is a recognizable category of discourse. As I need to talk about it, I shall adopt three working hypotheses as a starting point: the first is that literature is what people call literature; the second that it is a group of written texts not fully accounted for by any other category; the third that it is accorded considerable acclaim and value by individuals or by a society as a whole.

One explanation of the acclaim of literary texts, especially in schools and universities, is their supposed social and psychological insight. The value attached to them, however, is not solely utilitarian or ideological. For most people, literary texts are neither useful texts, nor texts with which they necessarily agree. There is also the notion that literary language is both distinctive and valuable in itself. This **formalist** view, however, runs into severe difficulties when it tries to posit specific linguistic characteristics of literariness. On the one hand, there are many literary texts whose language seems 'unliterary', on the other hand there are non-literary genres (such as advertising) whose language seems (at least superficially) literary. We are stuck, it seems, with imprecision, circularity and the indefinable.

1.8 The structure of this book

Despite the difficulty of precisely defining the word 'advertisement' and its relationship to literature, this book is structured around the notion that ads are a distinct genre. It views them as much more than an act of communication whose sole purpose is to sell a given product. Such a characterisation is too simple – whether we are in love with ads or hate them. Ads are more complex than this, and deserve far more attention.

Taking this as a starting point, the purpose of this book is to provide a principled framework for the description and analysis of individual advertisements and of advertising in general. It also uses advertising to introduce concepts from discourse analysis, semiotics, stylistics, and linguistics. There are three parts to this book, each one divided into three chapters. They examine the textual and contextual features of ads one by one and **bottom-up**, although the overall aim is to show how these layers interact and combine.

Part I deals with the materials of ads.
Chapter 2 examines their substance and surroundings.
Chapter 3 examines choices and combinations of music and pictures, writing and speech.
Chapter 4 examines paralanguage, and the uses of phonology and graphology.

Part II deals with the texts of ads.
Chapter 5 examines the connotations of words and phrases on their own and in context.
Chapter 6 examines linguistic parallelism in ads and its relationship to poetry.
Chapter 7 examines the linguistic features which create cohesion in the texts of ads, and their communicative effect.

Part III focuses upon the participants in advertising communication, and tackles problem of evaluating and assessing advertising as a whole.
Chapter 8 discusses the senders of ads and the stance they take up towards their addressees.
Chapter 9 examines ways of hearing ads; it discusses the observers of ads and their judgements upon them.
Chapter 10 returns to the issue of defining advertisements as a genre (the subject of this introductory chapter) and discusses their psychological and social function.

Using the metaphor of discourse as a series of layers with a top and a bottom, this structure can be represented diagrammatically, as in Figure 1.6. A rich analysis of any advertisement or group of advertisements will need to pay attention to all of these layers, and the interaction between them.

At the end of each chapter, there are exercises and suggestions for further reading. Some of the exercises deal with the chapter they finish, others look forward to the issues in the following chapter. If you want to use this book in an active way, and explore your own opinion on each topic before being exposed to mine, then I suggest that you look at each set of exercises before reading the chapter.

D				
I	Part III	(PEOPLE)	social/psychological function	'TOP'
S			observers and addresses	
C			senders and narrators	
O	Part II	(TEXT)	connected text	
U			grammar and prosody	
R			words and phrases	
S	Part I	(MATERIALS)	paralanguage	
E			music and pictures	
			substance	'BOTTOM'

Figure 1.6 Hierarchy of discourse and chapters in this book.

1.9 Terminology and notation

The theoretical basis of this book, and its terminology and approach, derive then from a combination of linguistics, discourse analysis, literary theory, and semiotics. The book does, however, aim to be accessible to a reader who is a newcomer to these disciplines – and could indeed form part of an introduction to them. For this reason, technical terms are in bold type on or near first mention, and a brief explanation of them is given. All emboldened terms together with the page reference of this explanation will be found in the index.

Necessarily, in some analyses, there is grammatical notation.[5] For this I use the convention of marking off phrases with round brackets ( ), clauses with square brackets [ ] and co-ordinated constructions with angle brackets < >. The following abbreviations are used for grammatical functions:

S = Subject; Od = direct object; Oi = indirect object; C = complement;
A = adjunct; o = object of a preposition; VOC = vocative; P = predicator

The following abbreviations are used for forms:

NP = noun phrase; VP = verb phrase; AjP = adjective phrase;
PP = prepositional phrase; AvP = adverb phrase; cj = conjunction

The following abbreviations are used for clauses:

MCl = main clause; NCl = noun clause; ACl = adverb clause;
RCl = relative clause

The symbol Ø indicates an ellipted word.

Exercises

1   Try to characterize the genres (written down the side of Figure 1.7), by identifying the features of context (written across the top) which are peculiar to them. The first one has already been done. Add some more genres of your own in spaces 8, 9, 10.

  Are the features you identify essential or optional to the genre? Could a road sign, for example, be any of the following: whispered (physical form); to a doll (addressee); by a six-year-old child (sender/addresser); as an expression of love (function); in a bus queue (situation)?

2   Is it possible to characterize the genre 'advertisement' by features or combinations of features? Who or what are the

  participants _____
  function _____
  intertexts _____
  co-texts _____
  situation _____
  paralanguage _____
  substance _____

3   Consider the following. Do they fit the description of ads you have given in Exercise 2?
  a The Family Planning Association wanted to remind students of the consequences of unprotected sex. Students in halls of residence were sent a plain white envelope containing a nappy with a sticker saying: 'It's a lot easier to put on than a condom.' Inside the nappy was a condom and a number for the FPA's confidential helpline.
  b Magazines for advertisers (such as *Campaign*) carry advertisements for magazines, websites and radio stations with copy such as the following:

    Fantastic! Virgin Radio's listening figures are up a massive 12%. Chris Evans' Breakfast show just got bigger by 8%. '10 great songs in a row' has upped daytime listening by 18%.
      Carltonactive. Add more to your ads. With Carlton Active, television works harder for everyone. Consumers get more about programmes and channels, accessing additional screen-based content whilst they watch. Similarly, advertisers benefit from being able to build more into their TV ads.

  c A poster displays the words: 'Your best friend is the one who won't buy you a drink – when you're driving.'

Context	Participants		Function	Intertexts	Co-texts	Situation	Para-language	Substances
	sender	receiver						
Type			warm	other	none			
1 Road signs: transport	motorist		inform	road		roadside	large	metal
ministry				signs			letters	board
2 Catholic mass:								
3 Web page:								
4 University exam:								
5 Driving licence:								
6 email:								
7 Poem:								
8 Credit card:								
9 _____								
10 _____								

Figure 1.7 Features of genres.

d A television programme about an expedition to the Arctic showed explorers with the brand name GORE-TEX written on their coats. This was not *just* an endorsement. The explorers had chosen Gore-Tex as the best clothing for their purposes.

e Leech (1990) analysed a poster in a Kentucky Fried Chicken restaurant which was positioned in such a way that it was visible to the staff serving behind the counter, not to the customers.

> There was a man who had a dream ... a dream that involved hard work, dedication and integrity. Where other men would have given up, this man made that dream a reality. His dream was Kentucky Fried Chicken ... and his name was Colonel Harland D. Sanders 1890–1980

f A direct mail company pays people to include advertisements in any email they send.

g The pressure group ECPAT ran a series of cinema advertisements alleging that loopholes in the British Sex Offenders Act allowed convicted paedophiles to travel to Britain. The advertisements showed mini dramas in which such men gained easy access to small children.

4 Consider the following advertisements and list ways in which they differ from modern advertisements.

a from *The Spectator* on the 12 March, 1711.

> The number of silk gowns that are weekly sold at Mrs. Rogers' in Exchange Alley (though not much above a month since she has undertaken it) makes it very evident that her Gowns are very cheap as well as nice Fancies, for she does not heap a great deal of rubbish together, but chooses the most proper silks and suitable

Linings: and for the future will keep such Choice, that all Persons of quality and other may be furnished with varieties of Fancies and all Sizes.

b A 1940s cigarette advertisement.

The thorough test of any cigarette is steady smoking. Smoke only Camels for the next thirty days ... And see how mild Camels are, pack after pack ... how well they agree with your throat as you steady smoke. See if you don't find Camel more enjoyable than any other cigarette you've ever smoked.

c A 1940s advertisement for Feluna pills.

What makes a Woman Nag?
Men just cannot guess how those wearisome headaches, pains, 'nerves' and domestic worries gradually wear a woman down almost beyond endurance. They cannot understand the gloomy depression of a woman's 'grey days' and the 'nerviness' that turns to irritation and impatience. And yet Feluna Pills make a woman's suffering – YOUR suffering – all so unnecessary. Feluna Pills are specially compounded to correct the physical weaknesses of women and girls. Away goes listlessness and irritability. Anaemia is conquered and with the thrill of new blood comes zest for life. You become your REAL self.

5   Advertising is both part of, and has helped to create, a new global culture which ignores national boundaries. To what extent does it also reflect differences between cultures, even among the richest nations? Consider the Japanese ad for a marriage agency (Figure 1.8) and the ways in which it differs from ads for introduction agencies in the West.

Further reading

(Full references to further reading suggestions can be found in the bibliography at the end of the book.)

On advertising in general

Three very useful and accessible introductions to advertising in general are:

*   Brierley, S. (1995) *The Advertising Handbook*.
*   Myers, G. (1999) *Ad Worlds*.
*   White, R. (2000) *Advertising* (4th edition).
*   Wilmshurst, J. and Mackay, A. (1999) *The Fundamentals of Advertising* (2nd edition).

Figure 1.8 A Japanese advertisement for a marriage agency. In this ad the woman is saying: 'As I would like to have a bright child, maybe I should meet a graduate from Tokyo University . . .' the columns on the left list men already registered with the agency: their age, height, company, hobby and university.

There is also a good deal to read and watch on ads apart from academic analyses and textbooks:

- The journals of the advertising trade, such as *Advertising Age* (in the USA) and *Marketing* and *Campaign* (in the UK).
- Television programmes on ads, both serious and humorous.
- Codes of advertising practice such as the *British Codes of Advertising*

Practice and Sales Promotion (produced by the Advertising Standards Authority).
- Frequent items and articles about advertising in the daily press.

Some of the earliest academic analyses of advertising are still well worth reading. Particularly recommended are:

- Goffman, E. (1979) *Gender Advertisements.*
- Leech, G.N. (1966) *English in Advertising.*
- McLuhan, M. (1964) 'Keeping upset with the Joneses', in *Understanding Media.*

On the language and semiotics of advertising. Particularly recommended are:

- Godard, A. (1998) *The Language of Advertising* (a sourcebook of activities and commentaries.)
- Myers, G. (1994) *Words in Ads.*
- Nava, M. *et al.* (1997) *Buy this Book: Studies in Advertising and Consumption.*

Part I
Materials

2 Substance and surroundings

2.1 The substance of ads

All communication relies on physical substance. Communication involving language uses a number of different kinds. Spoken language is carried by sound waves originating from the human vocal tract (or occasionally a speech synthesizer). Written language is carried by marks on a prepared surface such as paper or painted metal, by points of light on a screen, or by three-dimensional letters, such as those used in neon signs. The sign languages used by the deaf (which are as complex as any spoken language) are carried by movements and configurations of the hands. These **primary substances** of language can be relayed by **secondary substances** such as celluloid film, computer disc, electric cable, magnetic tape or radio waves. Particular genres are often associated with particular choices and combinations of substance. A 'chat', for example, is carried by sound waves and may be relayed by telephone, but is not printed on expensive paper or carved on stone. A 'television news broadcast' is first written, then relayed by auto-cue, then spoken, then relayed by cable or by radio waves. A 'novel' is printed on paper and bound or glued between covers – and even if it is read aloud, recorded, broadcast, or stored electronically, the book as a physical object remains somehow its prototypical home.

Choices of substance matter. In a broad sense, they affect the 'meaning' of discourse, though the impact of particular choices varies between cultures. The significance of the choice of primary substance – sound waves, slate, paper, screen – will depend on the state of literacy and technology. All languages use speech (or signing in deaf sign languages), and only later, if at all, develop writing. As the use of writing spreads in a society, it comes to be associated with public and formal communication, and with important acts of commitment and obligation. The spoken undertakings of orality give way to the signed documents and contracts of literacy. Literate societies generally accord more status to writing than to speech, though there are some notable exceptions – such as liturgies, lectures, marriage ceremonies, inaugurations and legal proceedings which have survived the shift and are still oral, even if the words used are often read, learned from, or prompted by writing. Within a culture which uses both handwriting and print, it is the latter which usually carries more status, with word-processed documents somewhere between the two.

Even more distinctions accompanied the advent of sound recording, and broadcasting, which effected a new transition, sometimes referred to as a 'secondary orality' (Ong 1982). In some ways, these new media seem to return us to orality, while preserving the advantages of writing. Language is preserved in time and disseminated across space, but comes to us as sound, in the voice of an individual. Word-processing, electronic mail and mobile phones have introduced yet more changes, and again seem to mix the features of both speech and writing. On screen, a good deal of writing, like speech, disappears without trace. It has none of the finality of print, for what is written can be endlessly altered. Email and mobile-phone text messages use writing, yet they have many of the features of conversation. Computer and telephone technology has reintroduced behaviour reminiscent of an oral culture. Promises are again made without signatures and documentation.

Advertising is very much a child of this secondary orality. Even when printed, it assumes the style of personal spoken communication. Most ads are short television and radio broadcasts, magazine pages, roadside hoardings, World Wide Web banners, or junk mail. As such they use a wide array of primary and secondary substances. The choice of substance affects the nature of the ad and is an integral part of its identity, although the variety of substances in ads means that the genre of the advertisement cannot be identified with any one. (It is looser, for example, than the connection between 'road sign' and paint on a metal board, or between 'credit card' and embossed plastic.) Yet the choice of substance in a particular ad is an essential part of its identity. This intimate relationship of an ad with its substance presents a marked contrast with literary discourse. For although literature, like advertising, is carried by a variety of substances, it is usually described as though it were independent of them, existing in some incorporeal region of the mind. The essence of *Hamlet* is felt to remain the same, whether it is a television production, a live performance, the quarto manuscript, a dog-eared paperback, or a calf-bound gold-tooled edition, and no imperfection in any of these substances would alter opinion of this essence. People talk about such different instances as though they were essentially the same work. This is not so much the case with advertising.

Ads make use of all sorts of objects and surfaces in all sorts of ways. Araldite once advertised their glue by sticking a complete car to a roadside hoarding, and, rather less expensively, there have been ads written on the side of cows grazing alongside the London to Brighton railway line (R. White 1988: 96–8).There are ads on buses, book matches, milk cartons, T-shirts and – less commonly – on vapour trails and firework patterns in the sky. There are also ads which, though printed on paper, make that paper appear burned, smudged or ripped (as in Figure 2.1). In the fcuk ad

Figure 2.1 A Dutch ad for hamburgers.

in Figure 4.4 the corner of the magazine page was folded over as though there were an error in the cutting and binding of the magazine.

At Grand Slam tennis tournaments, the bottles and cans seen on the umpire's stand between games, though rarely used by the resting players, *become* ads for the products. This raises the issue of whether every product has a dual and ambiguous identity. By having its own brand-name written on it, every product is both itself and an ad for itself. Nor can this issue be dodged by drawing a distinction between contents and wrapping. In many products, such as chocolate and soap, the brand name is not only written on the wrapping, but also cut into the object, making the substance which carries the name the same as the substance to which it refers. If we assume, as seems likely, that the drinks displayed in tennis tournaments are not those actually drunk by the players, then there is justification in saying that their role as ads supersedes their existence as drinks. It is almost impossible to separate the advertising from the advertised. One morning, through my letter box, I received a miniature sachet of *Vidal Sassoon Wash-and-Go Salon Shampoo and Conditioner All in One*. Even though I did not use it, it was still an ad: for itself.

Ads can also make use of smell. Magazines carry samples of perfume to be released by lifting or peeling off odour-impregnated paper. Scratch-and-smell food ads use a similar device, and at least one also gave the time of a television commercial for the same product, enabling the reader to watch and sniff simultaneously. The Cue Cartoon cable television network advertised itself by distributing 'smelly telly' cards which children were then asked to rub at particular points in the programmes so that they could experience the same odours as the characters.

A list of all the different substances used by ads would be vast, and is no doubt growing every day. Ads use any of the substances available to language – and follow close on the heels of language into each successive, new technology: film, telephone, radio, television, the Internet, interactive television. They also adapt substances which language does not normally use – such as soap or vapour.

Such variety fulfils several purposes. Firstly and most obviously it is attention-getting, and can compensate for an intrinsic lack of interest in the message itself. In December 1990 Absolut Vodka, at a total cost of $1.4 million, placed a talking microchip in every copy of *Vanity Fair*, so that, when the pages were opened, it said 'Merry Christmas' in four languages. The technology was novel and memorable, though the message itself ('Merry Christmas', etc.) was unoriginal. The appeal of novel substance, however, unlike that of novel text, is intrinsically short lived. With every repetition, effectiveness diminishes. Secondly, certain choices of substance, or combinations of them, help to fix the product more firmly in the memory by actively involving the reader. This is particularly the case with the exhortation to scratch-and-smell while watching television. The talking chip, activated by opening and closing the pages of the publication, was also likely to stimulate repetitions of this action in the reader. Toys in cereal packets make children rummage. People buy recordings of pop songs which are featured in ads (often bringing them commercial success). Lastly, an innovative use of substance may poach some of the intrinsic interest and prestige associated with another medium or event: firework displays, tennis matches, quality clothing, pop concerts.

2.2 The Internet

Undoubtedly, from the mid-1990s onwards, the most popular new medium for advertising has been the Internet, whose primary substance (the screen) is the same as television, but whose secondary substance (the phone lines linking computer terminals) is different. It is, however, as yet unclear whether this new medium will offer advertisements the same exposure and success as the older media of television and print. The very size of the Internet, the greater control which its users have over the material they look at, and the diversity of ways in which it is used, make it harder in some ways for advertisers to target consumers. On the other hand, the web offers advertisers unique opportunities to access particular groups and specialised demands. Yet that too can have a fragmenting effect. As Internet use grows, and for some groups begins to overtake television as a source of entertainment, the advertising culture in which the 'big campaign' was ensured a period of exposure to virtually everyone in a given society is seriously threatened. The impact which television had on advertising in the 1950s, taking campaigns out of specific publications or locations and putting them into everybody's sitting room, is likely to be thrown into reverse. This fragmentation derives not only from the Internet, but also from television technology – cable, satellite and digital television – which is ending the domination of the relatively few channels which were once a sure and unproblematic choice for advertisers. And even this distinction – between Internet and television – is unlikely to survive as the two become ever more closely integrated.

It is this mixture of advantage and disadvantage, and uncertainty about the direction and pace of change, which has thrown advertisers into some considerable confusion. Despite widespread enthusiasm for web advertising, and tremendous energy in pursuing it, there are also many cautionary voices, and the advertising press, while devoting many pages to the phenomenon, is also full of warnings that it may not be selling the goods. The messages emerging from this heated discussion are mixed. Consider for example the following views expressed in the advertising journal *Campaign* in the space of one month (June 2000). First, a study by the advertising agency CDP concluded that 'much of the £100 million spent on dotcom advertising in the past six months has been to no real effect'. Then another study,[1] reported in the same journal only two weeks later, concluded that 'banner ads are the marketing medium of the future', and

Figure 2.2 'Eight Seconds': advertisement for Business 2.

claimed that 70 per cent of British Internet surfers click on banner ads. The week before that, however, an article in the same journal (ironically placed above an ad reading 'real online advertising = real sales'!) had wondered whether

> the banner is dead ... click-through rates for banner ads on the Internet may be as low as 0.5 per cent and not higher than 3 per cent. Add to this that click-throughs rarely make a sale, according to research, and the picture does look fairly bleak.

Yet another article reminds advertisers that in Britain around 15 million people (over 25 per cent) make no use of the Internet at all. A similar uncertainty is manifested in the standard textbooks produced for students on marketing and advertising courses (Wilmshurst and Mackay 1999;

White 2000), now in their second and fourth editions respectively. White (2000: 211) describes web advertising in the UK as 'as yet insignificant', though unlikely to remain so, noting that in the USA, it already accounts for an annual $500 million turnover. Wilmshurst and Mackay give similarly brief and contradictory comments.

Clearly there is real confusion and anxiety about whether the latest medium is to be as significant as, say, the move on to television in the 1950s. The worries, however, reflect broader problems relating to technological changes in general (Brierley 1995: 226–53). In general the diffusion of media and the greater control offered to users in interactive media such as the Internet presents advertisers with a serious problem. It may well be, as many clearly suspect, that they are safer with posters ads and television commercials. Although many of these more traditional ads prominently offer a related web page address, in many cases its function may be to attract to the product the *kudos* of the Internet, rather than to persuade people to take the trouble to note the address down and follow up the lead. An advertisement for car insurance may give its web address as an essential part of its message; an advertisement for an alcoholic drink – though there is a web page to be found – gives it more as an extra. Perhaps there is another reason why virtually all contemporary advertisements now include a web address. As is evident by its popularity, the suffix 'dotcom', when spoken, has an aesthetically pleasing rhythm and resonance!

2.3 The situation of ads

It is not only the substance or medium itself which matters, but its social meaning. An image called up via the Internet is not just a picture on a screen but resonates with connotations of global communication and technological potential. In a similar way, the effectiveness of more traditional sites for ads cannot be accounted for in merely physical terms. The buildings in New York's Times Square are not just bricks and mortar; the shirt of an Olympic champion is not just cloth. The substance of an ad which is a vehicle for its own linguistic and pictorial messages also exists in a situation composed of other substances which carry other meanings of their own, and the interaction of ad and situation can create a third meaning which is quite different from either. This third meaning may undermine or enhance the advertiser's intention. It may derive from contrasts between the world of the ad and the world around it, as in Figure 2.3.

2.4 Accompanying discourse

In many ways, ads are **parasitic** upon their surroundings and other genres. Just as the substance of an ad is often stuck to some other significant

Figure 2.3 People and ads: an ad and a passer by, Leeds 1989.

substance, so its discourse both occurs within other discourse and also imitates it. (I use the term 'parasitic' rather than 'symbiotic', because even though many magazines and television channels depend on ads economically, ads are not needed in the communication effected by the host to which they attach themselves.) There is nothing inherently negative in such a description however. Many other genres are parasitic. Literary criticism is parasitic upon literature, sports commentary upon sport. Just as many parasitic organisms may be beneficial if not necessary to their hosts, the same may be true of parasitic discourses.

Among the elements of context listed in Chapter 1 are situation and intertext. Although these categories adequately describe the linguistic and non-linguistic environment of most genres, they are not sufficient for a description of ads. This is because ads typically occur together with, or embedded in, other discourse, to which they make no direct reference. An ad may occur in the middle of a television news broadcast, together with, yet isolated from, other ads. A printed ad occurs in the middle of a magazine article to which it makes no reference. These other genres are not covered by the term 'situation' (the non-linguistic environment), nor by the term 'intertext' (texts which are related by some thematic link). Consequently, we need another term, and I shall refer to them as **accompanying discourse**. As with situation, the interaction between ads and accompanying discourse creates new meanings, either by chance, through manipulation by the advertiser, or, more rarely, through subversive intervention against ads from outside.

Thus it was by unlucky chance that, in July 2000, an ad showing a silver Ford Mondeo appeared close to news coverage reporting the abduction of an eight-year-old girl, possibly in a silver Mondeo. Given the unpredictable contents of news broadcasts, such unfortunate coincidences are almost inevitable in their advertising breaks. A notable case was an ad showing a Vauxhall car dodging through collapsing construction work, appearing immediately after news coverage of the car-crushing collapse of a two-tier freeway during the 1989 San Francisco earthquake. In 1999, Barclays Bank ran television ads boasting the easy accessibility of its services on the same day that it announced large scale closure of smaller branches. On television such contradictions must be difficult to avoid. More surprisingly, however, such coincidences also occur in print ads, where far more time for planning is available. The *Observer* magazine has featured an ad for *Birds-Eye Menu-Master Tandoori Chicken Masala* immediately before a photograph of emaciated children in Auschwitz. *Marie Claire* placed an ad for Max Factor make-up opposite a photograph of amputee children from the Sierra Leonean civil war. The ad showed the smiling face of a beautiful young woman resting on her elegant hand ('Vibrant lips, strong cheeks. It's going to be a colourful spring.'); the photograph showed children with depressed faces and the stumps of mutilated limbs.

Yet equally, chance may also work to an ad's advantage. I have seen ads interspersing a magazine article about photography awards, and felt my attention drawn to the excellence of the advertisements' photography, which I preferred to that of the winning entries. There are times when such contrasts are not accidental, but deliberately intended to subvert. The wittier graffiti on ads fall into this category (see Figure 2.4 overleaf).

One of the strangest aspects of the relationship between ads and their accompanying discourses is the rarity of any cross-reference between the two. Ads even occur without comment in programmes about advertising. In this situation, an ad used in the programme may immediately precede or follow an ad in the advertising break! Rather than refer directly to the advertisements which interrupt them, television programmes pause with euphemisms such as 'We'll take a break' or 'See you in a minute'. Magazines interleaf ads and articles without comment. Deliberate exploitation of this alternation is so rare that it suggests publishing and broadcasting guidelines which forbid cross reference. Occasional transgressions of these written or unwritten rules only emphasize their force, as when the television chat show host Clive Anderson said, in the middle of one programme: 'We've got to stop for a bit now while people try to sell you things you don't want.'

Such interventions are rare: hardly surprisingly, given the financial dependency of most accompanying discourse on the ads which live within

Figure 2.4 A graffito on an ad.

it. It is for this reason that, while programme producers do not even see the ads which punctuate their shows, advertising agencies can buy space in specific programmes and exercise considerable control over the interaction between the two. Usually, this amounts to no more than an attempt to match the audience of a programme with the target market for a product, or exploitation of desires aroused by a programme or article, but it may also extend to imitation of the accompanying discourse in an attempt to blur the boundary between the two. This not only attracts attention to the ad, but also tries to invest it with some of the authority of the accompanying discourse. In newspapers, some ads are presented in the print and format of the news around them, a tendency which is sometimes combatted by explicit editorial labelling with the word 'advertisement'. On television in the USA (though not in Britain) sitcom celebrities appear in ads punctuating their own shows, in settings very like those of the show itself. As the screen does not go blank for a fraction of a second between each ad (as it does in Britain) this generates momentary confusion. The history of television ads in Britain, however, has been dotted with more humorous attempts to confuse or break the boundary between themselves and the programme in which they appear. A Hamlet cigar ad (in the days when smoking materials could still be advertised on television) began with the **logo**[2] and music of its host, Channel 4, as though the advertising break were over and the next programme about to start, then rearranged the strokes of the numeral '4' to form a face which started smoking a cigar. An ad for Kellogg's Corn Flakes appeared to be a news broadcast, until the camera drew back to show a couple watching it, and the newsreader remarks on their odd habit of eating cereal in the evening. A television showing of Shakespeare's *Romeo and Juliet*[3] included an ad showing Juliet on her balcony and Romeo below. 'Wherefore art thou Romeo?' says Juliet with her stomach rumbling from hunger. 'Juliet,' answers Romeo, 'Didst thou not have Shreddies for breakfast?' Immediately following this ad was the real balcony scene in the film.

On television, such imitation is often humorous and unconvincing. Real confusion, however, is sought by junk mail, which, mindful of its unopened destiny in the rubbish bin, frequently poses as something else. Thus there are circulars which look like postcards, telegrams, invitations, and so on. I recently received, for example, through the post, a set of holiday snaps – as one might do after returning from holiday and sending off a roll of film to be developed. The only difference was that the family in the photographs were not mine, nor the place one which I had ever visited. Their purpose was to inform me of the kind of holiday I might have, if I took a loan from The Bank of Scotland! Such discourses are more than parasitic, attempting to take on, and take over, the features of another type. One award-winning[4] example, left in the back of taxi cabs, looked like a crumpled $20 bill which someone had dropped. When opened it revealed an ad proclaiming the virtues of investing money in a Fidelity ISA. The direct mail shot in Figure 2.5 (overleaf), sent out to 50,000 lawyers to advertise *The Times* legal section, appears to be a summons to court. (In this it was aided by the fact that both *The Times* newspaper and an actual summons use a royal coat of arms.) Such tricks, however, may backfire, not only on the public, who may overlook important communications, but also on the firms themselves, as they likely to annoy. Though 'Summons' also won an award,[5] this was not based on knowledge of whether the recipients were actually amused by it, or persuaded to buy *The Times*.

A different kind of merger with accompanying discourse occurs in sponsored television programmes. This has been a feature of US television from its outset (Myers 1999: 117), and increasingly common in Britain since legalisation in the late 1980s. A similar phenomenon in print ads is the **advertorial**: lengthy entries in magazines and newspapers which attempt to combine article and ad, using the publication's house style, and providing the reader with information or discussion which is more substantial and wide ranging than that in the majority of ads. In these sub-genres of the ad, the stretching of the limited span of time and space usually available can be quite catastrophic to the interest and effectiveness. It is a relationship in which the parasite destroys its own host. The best ads are successful bandits, raiding the borders of their accompanying discourse, but with the sense not to stay too long.

THE TIMES

Publisher's fees only

SUMMONS

To our learned friend

Date of Information: 01/09/99

CASE NUMBER 4325

Date of Summons: 07/09/99

YOU ARE HEREBY SUMMONED TO APPEAR BEFORE YOUR NEWSAGENT AND PURCHASE YOUR 30p COPY OF THE TIMES FEATURING THE NEW EXPANDED 'LAW' SUPPLEMENT ON TUESDAY THE 7TH DAY OF SEPTEMBER 19 99

INFORMANT: TIMES NEWSPAPERS LIMITED,
P.O. BOX 495,
VIRGINIA STREET,
LONDON E1 9XY

STATEMENT OF FACTS

1. ON 07/09/99
AT YOUR NEWSAGENT, THE TIMES NEW 'LAW' SUPPLEMENT WILL FEATURE AN EXPANDED DIARY SECTION, KEEPING YOU INFORMED OF ALL THE NEWS ON CURRENT CASES AND LAWYERS MAKING THE HEADLINES.

2. ON 07/09/99
AT YOUR NEWSAGENT, THE TIMES NEW 'LAW' SUPPLEMENT WILL FEATURE A BULLETIN BOARD OF FORTHCOMING CONFERENCES/SEMINARS/LECTURES TO ENSURE YOU ARE FULLY AWARE OF THE LATEST EVENTS.

3. ON 07/09/99
AT YOUR NEWSAGENT, THE TIMES NEW 'LAW' SUPPLEMENT WILL CONTAIN THE LATEST NEWS ON THE NET, WITH RICHARD SUSSKIND'S GUIDE TO ON-LINE LEGAL DEVELOPMENTS. PLUS REVIEWS OF WHAT'S NEW IN THE BOOKSHOPS.

4. ON 07/09/99
AT YOUR NEWSAGENT, THE TIMES NEW 'LAW' SUPPLEMENT WILL FEATURE AN EXPANDED RECRUITMENT SECTION, AND NEWS REGARDING THE LATEST MOVES BETWEEN LAW FIRMS & CHAMBERS.

5. ON 07/09/99
AT YOUR NEWSAGENT, THE TIMES NEW 'LAW' SUPPLEMENT WILL CONTINUE TO PROVIDE YOU WITH THE POPULAR THOUGHTS AND COMMENTS OF REGULAR COLUMNISTS DAVID PANNICK QC, AND EDWARD FENNELL.

WHAT TO DO ABOUT THIS SUMMONS

1. In order for this case to proceed, you are required to attend your newsagent on the date shown above and collect your copy of the aforementioned publication, then complete the questionnaire overleaf (blue copy) and submit your details in the enclosed pre-paid envelope. The first fifty questionnaires received will be rewarded with a free copy of Queen's Counsel III - The Times' latest book of cartoons featuring the ever-optimistic tenants of 4 Lawn Buildings.

2. If you have not received one of the fifty free books by October 18th, you are still eligible to call The Times Bookshop on 08701 608080, where a copy of the Queen's Counsel III will be available to you at a discounted price of £6.99 plus free P+P, rather than the usual price of £7.99.

TIMES NEWSPAPERS LTD. LONDON

KEEP THIS SUMMONS. YOU MAY NEED TO REFER TO IT.

1st White – Reader
2nd Blue – Publisher
3rd Green – Editor

THE TIMES

This summons is only valid if sealed by the Publisher
If it is not sealed it should be reported to the Publisher.

Figure 2.5 Direct mail: 'Summons', an ad for *The Times* legal section.

2.5 Parasite discourse

This chapter has emphasized the way ads exist through other genres and culturally significant artefacts, either by attaching themselves to them (sometimes quite literally), by co-occurring with them, or by imitation. Ads make use of substance which is already being used for some other purpose, including the substance and wrappings of the goods they advertise; they find a place in the time and space of other discourse, and are seldom alone (magazines and programmes consisting only of ads are both rare and unsuccessful); they borrow so many features from other genres that they are in danger of having no separable identity of their own. Yet, as already remarked, being a parasite discourse is not necessarily a negative quality, nor is it unique to advertising alone. It is rather that advertising is an extreme example of a tendency apparent in all discourse. Many modernist literary texts achieve effect through **bricolage,** the borrowing and inter-weaving of material from other genres. James Joyce's novel *Ulysses*, for example, is an assembly of a range of styles – newspaper, romance, catechism and many others – none of which, in isolation, can be identified as the voice of either the author or the book. John Dos Passos's novel *USA* uses various genres in a similar manner. To denigrate such techniques as inferior to their sources implies a belief in both the possibility and the virtue of original and autonomous discourse: an idea which, like many others in contemporary attitudes to literature, derives from the Romantic stress on literary discourse as the vehicle of an isolated and extraordinary individual identity. An alternative view, often associated with postmodernism, regards all 'new' discourse as to some degree the reworking of existing discourse, and finds virtue in the complexity of writing which can tolerate many voices and influences at once, without seeking to simplify by silencing some at the expense of others. In this view it is no longer the self-assertiveness of the writer which is admired but, rather, his or her receptiveness and lack of individuality. Parody and comedy thrive on such tolerance and imitation, and many literary works regarded as classics re-work existing plots, while allowing the voices of other genres to enter into them with an accompanying potential to subvert the ideology which the original enshrined. Thus *Hamlet* may be seen as a revenge tragedy invaded by philosophy, *Crime and Punishment* as a detective story mixed in with a parable of religious salvation. Their stature comes not from originality in the narrow and impossible sense, but from a deeper originality of selection, combination and tolerance of contradiction. If advertising is parasitic in this positive sense, drawing blood from virtually every source from which it is not legally barred, then it is not this parasitism which disqualifies it from the acclaim accorded to literature, but some other features. The task which we must set ourselves is to understand what these differentiating features may be.

Exercises

1   Consider the effect of the following places for ads:
    a facing the lanes of a swimming pool
    b on a hot air balloon
    c on a t-shirt
    d on the back of a bus.
    Do they enhance or diminish the effect of an ad? Make a list of
    unusual situations in which you have encountered ads.

2   February 12, 1999 – A marketing campaign for Youth News Network
    (YNN), a news network aimed at high school students, is prompting a
    national educators' group to warn parents of the dangers of advert-
    ising in the classroom. The Canadian Association of Media Education
    Organizations (CAMEO) says that funding cuts to education have
    made Canadian schools an easy target for YNN. YNN provides
    schools with free audio-visual and computer equipment needed to
    access the network. In return, classrooms must tune in to daily
    news broadcasts, complete with advertising (http://www.media-
    awareness.ca: Media Awareness Network).
    a Are there television programmes in which the appearance of ads is
       undesirable?
    b Are there TV programmes in which astute advertisers would not
       want their ads to appear?
    c Consider the positioning of ads in television broadcasts of live
       sport, religious worship, news of major disasters and state funerals.
       What is the policy of television networks on this?

3   What happens to an ad when it is taken away from its accompanying
    discourse, or when it is sought out and bought by the receiver? There
    are, for example, series of ads which have been sold as videos, post-
    cards whose picture is an ad, television programmes which are compi-
    lations of amusing ads from different countries.
        How do you react to the following advertisement for advertising,
    sent unsolicited by email?

Guy

From:	\<gotmilk00@2die4.com\>
To:	\<gotmilk00@2die4.com\>
Sent:	28 September 2000 12:05
Subject:	LET MASS E-MAIL WORK FOR U! IT REALLY CAN GET U EXPOSED

We offer some of the best bulk e-mail prices on the Internet. Bulk e-mail can get you the best exposure on the net. What makes this kind of advertising so effective is the fact that you go to the potential customer. Not like search engines or print ads that the potential customer has to do all the searching. Dollar for dollar bulk e-mailing is also the most economical. We do all the mailing for you. You just provide us with the ad! It's that simple!

What we offer:

*General AOL Lists or other ISPs
$200.00 for 1-million e-mails sent.
$400.00 for 3-million e-mails sent.
$600.00 for 5-million e-mails sent.
$800.00 for 7-million e-mails sent.
$1000.00 for 10-million e-mails sent.

WE ALSO HAVE LARGER PACKAGES!

*Targeted Lists:
$400.00 for 1-million e-mails sent.
$700.00 for 2-million e-mails sent.
$1,000.00 for 3-million e-mails sent.

Call for bigger packages! ORDER NOW!!!AND GET THE RIGHT EXPOSURE!

So why not give us a call and see what it is that we can do for you. Call anytime 209-656-9143, we are in California. METHOD OF PAYMENT, CASHIERS CHECK MONEY ORDER OR BANK WIRE.

Sender:
Cybernet Enterprise 209-656-9143
go to gotmilk00@2die4.com to be removed. Please no mail bombs, legit removal.

Figure 2.6 An email ad.

Further Reading

- Overviews of issues related to the choice of different media are pro-vided by Myers (1999) *Ad Worlds*, Part 2; Brierley (1995) *The Advert-ising Handbook*: 107–15; White (2000) *Advertising* – the last of these very much from the advertiser's point of view.
- The effects of unusual substance and of accompanying discourses are generally neglected in linguistics and discourse analysis. See, however, the final chapter of Kress and van Leeuwen's (1996) *Reading Images: the Grammar of Visual Design.*
- For discussion of some implications of the changing technology of com-munication, see Walter Nash (1998) *The Biro and the Word Processor*, and David Morley and Kevin Robbins (1995) *Spaces of Identity: Global Media, Electronic Landscapes and Cultural Boundaries.*

3 Pictures, music, speech and writing

3.1 Introduction

The term **mode** is used in this book to refer to the choice between three means of communication: music, pictures and language.[1] Each may be further subdivided in various ways. Music may be orchestral or solo, amplified or acoustic; pictures may be still or motion, cartoon or photographic; language may be sung (in which case it overlaps with music), spoken, written or signed – and each of these divisions may be further subdivided. I shall refer to these further subdivisions as **sub-modes**. This chapter examines the effect of the selection and combination of the different modes in ads, and of three sub-modes of language: song, speech and writing.

Any analysis of the language of ads immediately encounters the paradox that it both must and cannot take the musical and pictorial modes into account as well. It must do this because there are many ads in which picture and music are the essence of the communication: creating mood, imparting information, persuading and making claims so strongly that, if language features at all – and there are many ads in which it does not – it is often only in a peripheral or auxiliary way. Even in those ads where language is the dominant mode of communication (perhaps a minority), it is still deceptive to look at it in isolation, because it rebounds against both picture and music, gaining and giving new meanings and connections. Yet analysis cannot adequately cope with music and pictures, because they are different from the mode of the analysis itself, which is language. While the words of this book can put the words of an ad on the page, they can only hint at the nature of its music and pictures, for these cannot be written down 'as themselves' but only as something else – words or frozen stills. This problem is more serious with television ads than with printed ones. On television, pictures move, music plays, and language comes in changing combinations of speech, song and writing; on paper, pictures stand still (and can even be reproduced), and there is no sound. Yet even in analyses of printed ads the problems are legion. Reproduction is unlikely to do justice to such factors as size and colour, and the relation of the ad to its accompanying discourse.

Figure 3.1 Wonderbra. The power of pictures to distract. The model's eyes are pointing to the text on the facing page. The words in the centre read 'Interesting Article?'

Many analyses of advertising solve this problem by ignoring it. Few make mention of the effect of music and song. It is just too difficult to handle. Where pictures are concerned, they either ignore television and limit themselves to printed ads where the pictures can be reproduced, or – if they do select from both print and television – relegate pictures to a secondary role, even when in the original, it was the pictures which predominated, and the language which was secondary.

I do not see a way of overcoming these problems – but neither do I believe they should be ignored. The obstacle which they pose enables advertising to keep analysis at bay, for it can shift its ground constantly, emphasizing now one mode and now another. There is a danger of dilution in analysis which attempts to tackle too much, and no individual analyst will feel equally at home in all modes and all media; but I believe that the converse fault – of fragmentation and incompleteness – is worse. Advertising, unlike analysis, operates in all modes and media at once, and must be treated accordingly. Therefore, though the focus of this book is on language, it also considers the effect on language of the other modes. Music and pictures are part of the discourse of ads, and to ignore or downplay them is a serious distortion.

3.2 An example: *The Perfect Combination*

These problems and pitfalls are best illustrated by an example. Let us take a fairly ordinary television ad, firstly as words only, and secondly as words in interaction with music and pictures. The example raises two quite separate problems: how to transcribe music and pictures on the page; and how to analyse their interaction with each other and with language. The ad is a television commercial for the soft drink Sprite[2] (screened in Britain in 1990, but representative of a type of ad which has persisted from the 1970s to the present). The words of the song are:

> When the heat is on,
> And the pace is slow,
> There's a cool fresh world
> Where you can go:
> Clear, crisp and light,
> It tastes of Sprite.
>
> A twist of lemon
> For a taste sensation;
> A squeeze of lime
> Is the perfect combination:
> Clear, crisp and light,
> Sheer taste of Sprite;
> Clear, crisp and light,
> Sheer taste of Sprite.

During the course of the ad two small written texts appear briefly at the bottom of the screen. The first says:

> Sprite and Diet Sprite are registered trademarks of the Coca-Cola company.

and the second:

> Diet Sprite can help slimming or weight control only as part of a calorie controlled diet.

In addition the words 'Sprite' and 'Diet Sprite' are visible on the product itself. The jingle, the small print, and the brand names are the only language. Along with these words go eighteen camera shots of four separate locations (see Figure 3.2); and the words are sung – rather than spoken – by a man's voice (with inevitable cheerfulness!).

The music and singing pass through four phases, distinguished by marked changes in speed and beat. The first phase conveys a sense of urgency building to a climax; the second phase releases the tension of the first with a bouncy and regular rhythm; in the third phase this rhythm disappears, and the beat is replaced by sound effects creating an air of magic and mystery; finally, the fourth phase repeats the second, confident and animated as before.

The relation of the words to accompanying pictures and to these phases of the music is set out, approximately, below – and I hope also provides a model for presenting and relating pictures, words and music in any TV ad.

Song words	**Pictures**

SCENE ONE: THE TRAFFIC JAM
MUSIC BUILDING TO A CLIMAX

Song words		Pictures
When the heat is on,	1	Couple in an open car in a traffic jam at the entrance to a coastal road tunnel. The driver of the lorry behind has left his cab to try to see the cause of the jam. Every-
And the pace is slow,		one is hot and frustrated.
There's a cool, fresh world	2	Close up of hands reaching into a cool-box containing ice, Sprite and Diet Sprite.
Where you can go:	3	Close-up of couple in the car. The man (the driver) looks at the woman.
	4	Both swig from their cans.
	5	The camera takes us through the opening in the top of the can, and into the Sprite inside!

Song words	**Pictures**

SCENE TWO: THE TOBOGGAN RUN
MUSIC INTENSIFIES, SPEEDS UP, LOOSENS

Song words	Pictures
Clear, crisp and light,	6 A professional toboggan run as seen from a high-speed toboggan emerging from a tunnel.
It tastes of Sprite.	7 Close-up of yellow helmet of the tobogganer.
	8 Toboggan run as seen by tobogganer.
A twist of lemon	9 The track is blocked by a giant slice of lemon.
For a taste sensation;	10 We see the lemon reflected in the visor of the approaching tobogganer.
	11 Close up of the slice of lemon: drops of juice are oozing out of it.
	12 We now see there are two riders on the toboggan, the pillion rider is holding on tightly. The toboggan smashes through the lemon and enters a tunnel.

SCENE THREE: IN THE TUNNEL
MUSIC SLOWS, LOSES BEAT, GROWS WHIMSICAL

Song words	Pictures
	13 An underwater shot inside the can of Sprite. We are moving through ice cubes towards the surface.
A squeeze of lime	14 On the toboggan run, the camera comes to a slice of lime at the other end of the tunnel, and breaks through.
Is the perfect combination:	15 The two tobogganers are out in the open again. Their toboggan is approaching another tunnel.

SCENE FOUR: MOVING TRAFFIC
MUSIC RETURNS TO REGULAR CONFIDENT BEAT

Song words	Pictures
Clear, crisp and light,	16 The toboggan enters the tunnel.
Sheer taste of Sprite;	17 Close-up of couple back in the car, moving fast.
Clear, crisp and light,	The woman is drinking from a can of Sprite.

Figure 3.2 'The Perfect Combination': advertisement for Sprite. (*Sprite* is a registered trade mark of the Coca-Cola Company, *Sprite light* is a trade mark of the Coca-Cola Company and are reproduced with kind permission of the Coca-Cola Company.)

Sheer taste of Sprite.   18   The car emerges from a tunnel on a
                                                coastal road. The man and woman
                                                are cool, happy and relaxed.

Taken together with the pictures in these four scenes, and the four corresponding phases of the music, the words of the jingle, which are so one-
dimensional in isolation, take on new meaning, and contribute to a
complex set of visual metaphors and parallels. A number of words,
phrases and clauses become puns. Thus

> When the heat is on

no longer has only its dead metaphorical sense of 'when life is difficult'. It
also refers literally to the uncomfortable heat experienced in the waiting
vehicles. By the same process

> And the pace is slow

refers literally to the traffic jam, as well as, idiomatically, to a dull period
of life. The pictures reinstate the lost force of the dead metaphor from
which its idiomatic sense derives. In the line

> There's a cool, fresh world

'world' in the context of Scene Two refers to the fantasy world of the
toboggan run which is apparently inside the can; the words

> Where you can go

accompany the transition shot in which we see the can from the point of
view of the person drinking from it, who then appears to shrink and enter
into it. In this fantasy world, inside the Sprite, all the undesirable qualities
of the world in the opening scenes are reversed. There is cool snow and fast
movement. In the lines of the bouncy chorus which accompanies these new
pictures, 'it' refers to both to this fantasy world, and to the Sprite itself:

> Clear, crisp and light,
> It tastes of Sprite.

The visually created puns continue.

> A twist of lemon

is also a twist in the toboggan run, and a twist in the tale – for who would
expect to find either a toboggan run inside a soft-drink can, or a giant slice

of lemon on a toboggan run? The lemon, appearing on the track, is both a fantasy within a fantasy (and thus at even further remove) but also, because Sprite tastes of lemon, the beginning of a transition back to the opening scene, for on the other side of the lemon we are back in the can, and as we emerge from it, the car emerges from the tunnel in Scene Four. Perhaps it is far-fetched to say that

A squeeze of lime

refers punningly to the squeezing of the front rider by the pillion rider, but it does seem reasonable to say that the words

is the perfect combination

occurring with the picture of the two tobogganers, refers simultaneously to their athletic teamwork, to the relationship of the couple in the car (who are presumably also the tobogganers), to the combination of cold Sprite with hot weather, and to the combination of lemon and lime flavours in the Sprite itself.

These complex relations between the three worlds (road, toboggan run, Sprite can) are all aided by the image of the tunnel, which occurs in each one, and whose darkness effects the transition from one world to the next. Connections between the worlds are reinforced by the puns, but separated in mood by changes in the music, allowing the ad to make two suggestions – both frequent in ads. The first is that the product is a solution to a problem, the second that the product will bring people together. In this ad, the couple (good-looking, young, affluent, happy, heterosexual) have a problem. They are stuck in a traffic jam on a hot day. Perhaps this symbolises a rather dull or stressful period in their life ('The heat is on ... the pace is slow'). They drink Sprite and enter its magic world. Within that world, the problems of heat and inertia do not exist; but when they return from that world these problems have ceased to exist in the everyday world too. We do not see what started the traffic moving, but we feel it was Sprite.

The young man and the young woman are, like the flavours in Sprite, 'the perfect combination'. They are also dressed in the Sprite colours of yellow and green – both in the car, and on the toboggan. As they drink, they look at each other. The product appears to contribute to their perfect compatibility!

What I have tried to show by this analysis is that the effect of the ad is not to be found in any of the three major modes alone, but only in their combination. Each mode gains from the other. In this ad, the message is distributed fairly evenly between music, pictures and (sung) language. (The least powerful sub-mode of language in this ad is writing, used in the reminder of trademark registration and the caveat imposed by the Independent Television Commission[3] (ITC) code of advertising practice, neither of which is part of the story, and both of which are emasculated by their small print and brief duration. Not all ads distribute their attention so evenly between modes, and in the remainder of this chapter we shall examine examples with varying degree of emphasis on music, pictures, speech and writing.

3.3 Music and connotation

Like language, music has discrete units (notes) which can be combined in different ways along a time-line (melody). Yet unlike language, the resulting combinations cannot be interpreted with any degree of consensus as referring to specific states or events in the world. In this sense, music has a syntax, but no semantics. Music, however, is greater in its combinatory power than language. For, though music moves forward in time, it can also combine notes at any instant on that line as harmonies, and additionally vary those harmonies by using different combinations of instruments and voices. In addition, the degree to which music can vary the pace and duration of notes, and exploit pitch variation, far exceeds that of language.

A piece of music can be transcribed as a score with enough accuracy for one interpretation of the transcription to yield results very much like another. Yet the formal structures captured in the score – the timing, melody, harmony, rhythm and combination of instruments – are not what matters most in the use of music in advertising. For, although music may have no semantics, in the sense of making reference to the world in a way which will be understood similarly by all members of a community, it does have, as language also has, connotations. For an individual, or for a group, a given piece of music may evoke a certain mood, or associate with quite specific places, events and images. Such connotations are at once both predictable and also vague and variable. A certain type of music might, for example, be described in the broadest terms as signifying or creating 'cheerfulness' or 'gloominess'. More specific reactions will vary not only between social groups, but also between and within individuals. To give an example of a group-specific connotation, one which is much exploited by advertisers, it is likely in contemporary Western society that indulgent nostalgia can be induced by playing middle-aged people the pop music of their youth.

A further problem is that connotations in music, as in language, are indeterminate even to a particular individual in a particular situation. They cannot be paraphrased into language with any precision. A piece of music has an effect on me, and means something to me, of that I am sure: but the nature of that effect is beyond words – a truism whose triteness is itself verbal, and self-reflexive, for my retreat into this cliché is an illustration of the very limitation of language which I am trying to describe.

These aspects of music endear it to most film-makers, and especially to advertisers. The connotation of music can create or overshadow both pictures and words. (There is a simple experiment in illustration of this. Watch a section of film with different musical soundtracks and you transform its mood completely. The menace and foreboding of a horror film, for example, is generally musical, and can be destroyed by an inappropriate choice.)

Advertising favours any mode of communication which is simultaneously powerful but indeterminate in this way. This also applies to its use of language (see Chapter 5); for, although there are semantic meanings on which a certain agreement can be reached, any discourse also has connotations as elusive and as personal as those of music, and it is on the manipulation of these that advertising concentrates. To search advertising for fixed meanings and then to challenge them, as most critics and litigants do, is to miss the point, and to treat the discourse of advertising as though it were law, business or science – all of which aspire to more precise meanings. Like poetry, advertising thrives on meaning which is both predictable but unprovable. The effect achieved, and its appeal to the advertiser, can be illustrated by analogy with sexual suggestiveness in pictures. Suppose that a picture of a young woman inserting a chocolate bar into her mouth makes one person think of fellatio, but someone else says that this meaning says more about the observer than it does about the picture. This kind of dispute, with its assumption that meaning resides in a text quite independently of individual and group preconceptions, is depressingly common in discussions of advertising. As the picture does not in fact depict fellatio, but something else, what the dispute comes down to is whether everyone, a substantial number of people, a few obsessed individuals, or one particular person, understand it in this way. Without an opinion poll, the dispute is unresolvable, but it is really quite improbable that such an interpretation will be individual. It is more likely to be the interpretation of a sizeable group, and, if the ad is well prepared, this will have been predicted and assessed as an interpretation which will happen in, and be likely to increase sales among, a target audience. Yet the fact that it is unprovable on a personal level, that each addressee may consider it as possibly an individual rather than a group interpretation, and that members of this group may thus be unwilling to express it either to each other or to another group, will make it more powerful.

Music makes its impact in a similar way. It is not, in this case, an unwillingness to express its effect which keeps people silent but, rather, an inability to formulate the impression in words. Its formal structure ('the score') is quite beside the point (as irrelevant as the literal behaviour of the woman with the chocolate bar). What matters is connotation, a vague and indeterminate world of associations quite alien to any description with pretensions to scientific rigour. Yet if such descriptions have to leave music aside because they cannot reduce it to precise formulation, they are avoiding a mode with a power extreme enough to overbalance those of both pictures and language. I have no answer to this problem, but I intend to describe the music of ads, where relevant, in impressionistic terms (as I did for the Sprite ad) always remembering that such descriptions may be idiosyncratic, peculiar to a limited section of the audience, or attempts to describe the indescribable.

3.4 Telling tales: music with pictures and talk (The Peugeot 306)

Song words		Pictures and dialogue
Take one fresh and tender kiss.	1	A man of about 60 is arriving home to his villa by the sea.
Add one stolen night of bliss.	2	Inside the villa, a young man and young woman are making passionate love. In their passion they knock a bedside photograph on to the floor. The glass shatters. It is a picture of the older man.
(sweet, sweet the memories you gave to me)		
	3	A fierce guard dog is barking outside.
One girl, one boy,	4	The door bell rings. Putting on a robe, the young woman descends hurriedly to answer the door. 'Frank!' She sounds worried and surprised. 'So where is he?' demands the older man.
Some grief, some joy,	5	Clutching his clothes, the younger man is jumping over the balcony, to escape.
Memories are made of this.	6	The young man reaches the car and gets in. He imagines the younger woman, writhing erotically in the passenger seat. Suddenly the older man bangs angrily on the car window. 'Come on. Get out of the car!'
	7	The young man gets out. The older man hands him a pair of running shoes. 'Put 'em on. We're running this marathon together, father and son.' The young woman is seen approaching, smiling, carrying a child.

8   The Peugeot symbol. Written
    underneath:
    Peugeot. The drive of your life.
    www.peugeot.com
    Voiceover: 'The Peugeot 306. It's
    a family affair.'

The song in the background is Dean Martin's 'Memories Are Made of This'. Given that, on a first viewing, the audience is likely to read the opening events as a classic tale of discovered adultery, its jolly, crooning tone seems anomalous, in contrast to what is seen. It sets a mood which does not match the story, with its likely ending of violence and revenge. Elements in the images: the older man's dark complexion and Italian accent, the apparently much younger wife, the setting by the sea (Sicily?), the guard dog, suggest a mafia family, and add to the sense of foreboding. Not until the final events, when it becomes clear that the older man is the young man's father rather than the woman's cuckolded husband, does the song retrospectively seem appropriate. And when this reversal comes, every earlier event – in memory or on subsequent viewing – is changed. The photograph by the bed was of a parent not a spouse, the man left hurriedly to avoid running in the race, etc. In this context, not only do all the events and lines of dialogue take on new meanings, the final line also becomes a pun:

The Peugeot 306, it's a family affair.

In one sense this means simply that the car is suitable for a family, but in addition the word 'family' echoes the mistaken impression that this was a story of the mafia. The word 'affair' refers both to the apparent adulterous love affair and, in a more general sense, to the disagreement over where to run the marathon.

This story is told in thirty seconds, through pictures and very sparse dialogue. As such it is representative of a particular kind of television advertisement. These are mini-dramas which compress a large number of narrative events into a very short space of time making use of highly skilled and stylized acting. As such they make the fullest use of music, song, images and dialogue together, though it is interesting to note that they revert in their final moments to a more traditional reliance on writing and speech. The ad ends with the product symbol and logo, combined with a spoken summary in a benevolent and complacent male voice, speaking – unlike the characters – with a standard English pronunciation.

3.5 Pictures alone

Pictures, however, do far more than carry a story. In a classic essay on advertising from the 1960s, 'Keeping upset with the Joneses', Marshall McLuhan wrote

> The copy is merely a punning gag to distract the critical faculties while the picture ... goes to work on the hypnotised viewer. Those who have spent their lives protesting about false and misleading ad 'copy' are godsends to advertisers, as teetotallers are to brewers, and moral censors are to books and films. The protesters are the best acclaimers and accelerators. Since the advent of pictures, the job of the ad copy is as incidental and latent as the meaning of a poem is to a poem, or the words of a song are to a song. Highly literate people cannot cope with the nonverbal art of the pictorial, so they dance impatiently up and down to express a pointless disapproval that renders them futile and gives new power and authority to the ads. The unconscious depth, messages of ads are never attacked by the literate, because of their incapacity to notice or discuss nonverbal forms of arrangement and meaning. They have not the art to argue with pictures.
>
> (McLuhan 1964: 246)

The foresight of these remarks, published at a time when both ads and analyses of them tended to be quite rudimentary, is striking. Advertisers rely more and more upon pictures, while their critics still harp on the literal meaning of copy. (Even a quick glance through the *British Codes of Advertising and Sales Promotion*, or the case reports of successful complaints against ads to the Advertising Standards Authority (ASA), reveal that a great deal of official criticism centres upon wording, despite its demonstrably subsidiary role in many cases.)

McLuhan, publishing at a time when television advertising was still in its infancy, and ads were far more reliant upon words and literal meanings than now, might have been excused for misjudging the relative power of different modes. Forty years later, not only have pictures gained ground, but also language, where it is used, leans further and further toward meanings it derives from interaction with pictures. In addition, many ads create powerful and complex messages – entirely or almost entirely through pictures and music, and are virtually language-free. In illustration of this, I shall examine one such ad in detail.

This is 'Last Stick' (a television and cinema ad from 1991) for the internationally best-selling chewing gum[4] Wrigley's Spearmint (Figure 3.3). Like the Peugeot 306 ad (from 2000) it too is a narrative. It uses thirty-six frames in sixty seconds. But it is not for its skill in compressed story-telling that I wish to analyse it here, but for its extraordinarily rich use of symbolic imagery. The tale unfolds to the music of 'All Right Now' by Free, a pounding pop song of 1970 (successfully re-released at the same time as the ad). Though the words of this song also concern a meeting between two strangers, I shall treat this ad, its message and its method as fundamentally non-verbal, as I believe they are, though I also briefly refer to the mood of the song in the analysis. In order to discuss the significance of the different images used, I shall first need to give an outline of the story.

The ad begins with a broad panoramic shot of a bus – *The Westerner* – making its way in bright sunlight past high mountains through prairies full of ripe wheat (Figure 3.3a). The camera shifts to the interior of the bus where a young man and a young woman sit across the aisle from each other, on the inner seats (see Figure 3.3b). Both are blond, white, conventionally good-looking. They are clearly attracted to each other, but shy. She glances at him, but as he looks back she looks away. Behind the couple, we glimpse the other passengers: a Hispanic couple holding a bunch of flowers, another white couple, an older 'country couple' (the man wearing a cowboy hat). There are alternating close-up shots of the young man and young woman (Figure 3.3c). She is reading a magazine. She looks at the young man again. He looks away, out of the window, but seems pleased. The scene shifts back to the prairie outside: telegraph wires along the road, distant mountains, a heat haze. The next shots are extreme close-ups – just the eyes and nose of each main character in turn (see Figures 3.3d and 3.3e). He glances sideways; she looks back. The scene changes back to the exterior again: a combine harvester, a man on a horse riding past in the other direction. Back inside, the young woman is fanning herself with her magazine. The young man reaches into the pocket of his shirt. We see a close-up of his hand taking out a packet of Wrigley's Spearmint Gum. He takes out a stick of gum and then looks back into the packet. It was the last stick. He hesitates – then offers it to her and she accepts. From the seat in front, a small boy looks round curiously, until the hand of the invisible adult beside him descends firmly on to his head and twists him back towards the front. We return to the young woman who is reading the Wrigley's wrapping paper. The camera shows her hand in close-up as she breaks the stick in half, and offers one half back to the young man. There are alternating shots – again very close – of the two main characters looking affectionately towards each other. In a longer shot of the interior of the bus, she shifts her body closer towards him. He does the same.

The bus stops outside a building called 'The Rosebud'. Outside, there is a van parked and a horse tethered, a cartwheel leaning against the wall. An 'old-timer' with a large white beard is sitting on the porch whittling a piece of wood. The young man is leaving the bus. He turns and raises his hands in a gesture of resignation. We see the young woman's face close up. She looks down sadly. Inside, the young man sits down, while outside the bus pulls away. As the young man sits dejected, the young woman enters behind him. She has got off the bus to be with him.

Figure 3.3 Wrigley's chewing gum ad: 'Last Stick'

The final shots show his hand with half a stick of Wrigley's gum, and her hand with the other half. The two halves join and fit perfectly; they merge into one, then transform into a whole, full packet. Words appear on the screen:

GREAT TO CHEW. EVEN BETTER TO SHARE.

A male voice says: 'Cool, refreshing Wrigley's Spearmint Gum. Great to chew. Even better to share.' The hands disappear, and we see the packet on its own.

In this ad, there are four distinct pictorial perspectives. There is the broad sweep of the outside world of nature – sunlight, corn, mountains – a benign, fertile, agricultural world at harvest time, in which the traditional (horses) and the new (combine harvesters) are in harmony. Moving in more closely, there is the social world of the bus and the bus station. This too is harmonious, with a cross-section of American society: the old man and the little boy, the rural couple, different ethnic groups. Moving in even more closely, there are shots in which we see the young man and woman, within this social context, forming a relationship. Lastly, closest in of all (Figure 3.3d), we see their faces from so short a distance that the image is one of complete intimacy. Only in an embrace would one see someone so close. The most dominant image is the middle perspective: the young man and young woman forming their relationship in a social context.

The overriding impression, then, is of a young man and woman meeting in a beautiful landscape, as part of a harmonious and approving society. It is also a very American world: the prairie, the old-timer, 'The Rosebud' (the same name as the sled which symbolizes lost childhood in *Citizen Kane*). It centres upon the monogamous heterosexual relationship of a man and a woman, which in turn centres upon the product – chewing gum. The bus, the social world, moves through the world of nature. A further harmony between the human and natural world is effected by the echo of the colour of the corn in the colour of the young woman's hair. In the shots of the interior of the bus, the couple are at the middle, moving, but apparently still, with the agricultural world visible outside the window. Like any couple, they have both a social identity (as they appear to, and with, the other passengers) and a private identity, as they appear to each other (the close-ups). At the very heart of this image is the stick of gum, passed from hand to hand, which brings them together and forms the bond between them. These concentric levels of detail are best represented dia-grammatically (Figure 3.4).

I have been using the word 'aisle' deliberately. The view of the bus is reminiscent of a wedding viewed from the altar: a young man and woman coyly sitting on either side of the aisle, the guests in the pews behind them. (Only the little boy – like a choirboy – is in front of them.) The woman immediately behind the young woman is holding a bunch of flowers like a

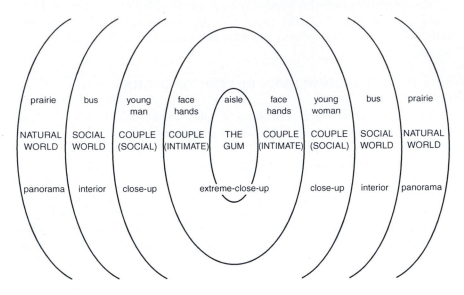

Figure 3.4 Concentric worlds in 'Last Stick'.

bridesmaid. There are other parallels too. The young man reaches in his pocket for the gum as a groom reaches for the ring. He gives it to her, and it is a symbol of their union. In the final shots, we see an image of joined hands (another symbol of marriage) and also – in the only merged shot of the whole sequence – a transformation in which two become one. On the other hand, the casual nature of the encounter is emphasized by both the words and the period of the song. (The slow and significant placing of the gum in the mouth suggests both oral sex and the communion service.) There is a tension between this image of holy matrimony and the story of a casual pick-up, between a sexual union sanctified by society and one quite outside its institutionalized constraints.

This ad is a classic example of a common advertising theme: the product bringing people together. It is presented at the centre of a sweeping view of the cosmic, social and sexual world, drawing to it the most powerful American ideological images: the Midwest wheat fields, the plural society, the marriage ceremony, and (if the wheaten-haired woman symbolizes fertility) a marriage of man and harvest, man and mother. All this in one minute, and without words!

3.6 Speech and writing

> When you really have something to say – say it in text.
>
> (Vodaphone ad)

The drift away from language towards music and pictures is paralleled by a preference within the language of television ads for the sub-modes of song and speech over writing. Both tendencies reflect a general preference for orality; sound and vision are the vehicles of face-to-face interaction, while in writing we neither see nor hear our interlocutor.

Further evidence of advertisers' belief in the greater power of speech is provided by the universal tendency in television ads to use writing for those parts of the message which are thrust upon it from outside. In Britain, control is theoretically voluntary. Two regulative bodies, the Advertising Standards Authority and the Independent Television Commission, lean heavily on advertisers to comply with codes of practice. One of the results of regulation, whether legal or voluntary, is the appearance on screen or page of disclaimers such as

1   Rates (variable, correct at 2.7.00) are 4.4% Gross PA/AER for balances over £1, 6.4% PA/AER for balances over £25,000.
2   Past performance is not necessarily a guide to future performance.
3   Cards normally replaced in 24 hours, or less in exceptional circumstances.
4   Some studies suggest that a high-fibre low-fat diet may reduce the risk of cancer.
5   All products and services available at most stores.
6   Subject to availability.

In theory the purpose of such caveats is to rectify, unambiguously, any false impression which might have been given by the ad, or provide factual information which it has not mentioned, but which the consumer might require. In practice, this is often not the case. Even for those who know what 'PA/AER' means, caveat (1) is hardly processible in the ten seconds it is given on screen, especially when shown in conjunction with an entertaining and distracting story. Caveat (2), about share prices, seems only to state the obvious. It is anything but clear in (3) quite how long one has to wait for a credit card to be replaced, or in (4) whether there are other studies expressing the opposite opinion, while (5) is a considerable conundrum. Sometimes there is apparent – if not literal – contradiction between the small print on the screen and the words being spoken at the same time. In (6), the written words 'Subject to availability' seem at odds with the more confident spoken line, 'Now available at Boots'. The assumption that the viewers' attention is on the pictures and sound is almost certainly correct, and is borne out by empirical research using 'eye trackers' which monitor a subject's attention to different parts of a screen at any given point during an ad. In children's ads this knowing camouflage of the disadvantages of purchase can be particularly deceptive and cruel, for pictures which show lavishly detailed smoothly functioning toys and games are belied by such unnoticed reservations as

7   Some assembly needed.
8   Vehicles sold separately.

The paradoxes presented by obligatory caveats are not only present on television. In radio advertising, where processing is of necessity linear, caveats cannot be hidden. They have to be spoken up front like everything else. In print ads, in contrast, they are traditionally downplayed by being tucked away in small print at the bottom. In the USA, however, this is not always allowed, with some amusing consequences. Ads appear with claims which seem blatantly undermined by large obligatory additions.

KIM LOST 50 LBS

boasts one advertisement for a slimming product.

RESULTS NOT TYPICAL

adds the regulator, in equally big letters, immediately underneath.

A particularly interesting case of the relation between pictures and words including those of obligatory caveats, has been evident in British cigarette advertisements. Subject to increasingly strict legislation forbidding any suggestion of personal or social advantage in smoking, and demanding ever larger and blunter warnings of the health dangers, the ads resorted to unusual strategies. A famous series of ads for Silk Cut cigarettes named the product by using pictures only, and made this act of naming the content of the ad. Each ad showed a piece of silk and a cut (for example, a piece of silk which has been cut by scissors; a silk cloth and a poodle which has just been trimmed; an iron with spikes near a piece of silk on an ironing board[5]). Despite widespread acclaim for the originality of this strategy, it draws in fact upon a well established technique with a long history. This is **rebus writing** in which each syllable of a compound word is evoked by a picture relating to a **homophone**,[6] so that

In a modern rebus, 'Fancy' can be created by a fan and then the sea, or 'mumble' by a chrysanthemum and then a bull.

(Bolinger 1975: 485)

These ads were widely believed not to name its product. Nothing could have been further from the truth, for in fact they consisted entirely of an elaborate and roundabout naming. In the wordless pictures, a piece of silk stood for the word 'SILK'; another object or action stood for the word 'CUT'; the two combine to form the composite 'SILK CUT' which in turn named the cigarettes. The ads also used a distinctive colour (in this case purple) to signify the product itself. This association, which we have already encountered in the Sprite ad, is another means of wordless reference to a product, which is widespread in the marketing of major brands.

There was, as already remarked, no writing in these Silk Cut ads, but there was, of course, writing *with* them. Each one carried a statutory health warning, written in large clear letters (black on white) and occupying a substantial space, saying for example:

SMOKING CAN CAUSE HEART DISEASE

Nothing could testify more strikingly to the advertiser's faith in the superior power of pictures over words than their evident belief that it was still worth advertising in these conditions. One might even go so far as to say that the warning was a help, serving to identify the ads (which carried neither the written name of the product nor its picture) as one for cigarettes.

3.7 Language in the service of pictures

Visual puns and metaphors have become a common and complex feature of much contemporary advertising (Forceville 1996). Examples abound. In one ad a bottle of J&B whisky which might be described in words such as 'fine grain' stands on a table top whose wood has a visible fine grain, in a different sense. A bottle of Gordon's gin and a glass in which it has been poured 'over Jaffa' (i.e. orange) stands on a balcony with a view over the city of Jaffa. In these ads the punning phrases are written and the two senses illustrated. In other advertisements, a word or phrase can be evoked wholly pictorially. Many dead metaphors are revitalized by this technique of evoking words by pictures. Thus an ad for Ultra Bold washing powder showed money 'pouring down the drain'; an ad for one insurance firm showed another literally 'stealing the shirt from someone's back'.

This last type of visual metaphor (the drain and the shirt) has dispensed with both speech and writing, though they do evoke exact idiomatic phrases. In this they manifest an atavistic tendency in ads to return to pre- or quasi-literate forms of communication, and particularly to a stage in the evolution of writing between the use of pictures and the first logograms (a written sign which signifies a whole word). Though pictures may refer to an event in the world, they cannot be sure to evoke the same words in every speaker. A representation of a man hunting a deer 𐤷𐤷 may yield many different sentences, such as 'the deer died', 'the man killed an animal', etc. The first 'real' writing may be said to occur when a picture or combination of pictures is linked not to an entity or event in the world – and thus to all of the many linguistic signs and sign combinations which may refer to it – but to a word.

It is to this complex issues of the nature of linguistic signs, and the relationships they enter into with non-linguistic signs, that we shall turn in more detail, and more theoretically, in Chapter 4.

Exercises

1   Comment on the use of words and picture in Figure 3.5 and the relationship between them. What does it tell you about the car, the target audience, the advertiser?

2   A 1970s ad for Rothman's cigarettes analysed by Williamson (1978) showed only a man's forearm resting on a car door. The following elements in the picture might be interpreted as meaningful:
  • gold braid stripes of a naval officer on the sleeve
  • a muscular hand and hairy wrist
  • an expensive watch

The Sharan. Power in disguise.

Figure 3.5 'Shark': advertisement for the Volkswagen Sharan.

- a helicopter is reflected in the wing mirror
- the Rothman's coat of arms
- the word 'Rothman's' imposed on the picture
- a packet of Rothman cigarettes imposed on the picture.

What do these elements mean, how do they achieve this meaning, and is the kind of meaning the same in each case? This ad would now be illegal in Britain. Do you agree that such ads for cigarettes should be banned?

3   Choose an ad which tells a story through pictures and music rather than dialogue. Video it and transcribe it using the same format as Sections 3.2 and 3.4 (This is much easier if you have a freeze-frame video.) What meanings emerge from the transcription which you missed on a first viewing? If they are only evident when the ad is 'frozen' and studied, why were they included?

Further reading

Seminal works on the relation of music and words are Roland Barthes' 'The grain of the voice', in *Image, Music, Text* (1977); Leonard Bernstein's (1976) *The Unanswered Question;* Robert Hodge's (1985) essay 'Song'. More recently, relevant readings are Theo van Leeuwen's (1999) *Speech, Music, Sound*; the section on song in my own (1996) essay 'Language Play in English', and on music in my book *Language Play, Language Learning* (2000: 14–23).

On the pictures of ads, the last chapters of Goffman's (1979) *Gender Advertisements,* Chapter 7 of Berger's (1972) *Ways of Seeing* and Durand's (1987) 'Rhetorical Figures in the Advertising Image' are all thought-provoking and entertaining, making their points by the juxtaposition and correlation of images with the minimum of commentary. Though written some time ago, their insights are still relevant today. More recently, Kress and van Leeuwen's (1996) *Reading Images* provides an introduction to the ways in which images communicate meaning; and Charles Forceville's (1996) *Pictorial Metaphors in Advertising* provides analysis of how images interact with or substitute for words.

4 Language and paralanguage

4.1 Language and paralanguage: dimensions of the sign

Language is usually carried by marks on a surface or sounds in air: **graphetic** and **phonetic** substance. Each of these give rise to two kinds of meaning simultaneously. On the one hand, the substance is perceived as the sounds or letters of a particular language (the **phonology** or **graphology**) which in turn[1] form words and word combinations (the **morphology** and **grammar**) which are in turn perceived as meaningful (the **semantics**). But the substance which carries language is also the vehicle of another kind of meaning, conveyed simultaneously by voice quality, or choice of script, letter size and so on. This latter kind of meaning, occurring together with linguistic meaning, is paralinguistic (see Section 1.2) – a term which also embraces other meaningful behaviour which accompanies language but does not carry it, such as gesturing, facial expression, body posture, eye contact, or the way writing is bound or displayed.

Paralanguage has been neglected in twentieth-century linguistics. This stems in part from the work of the Swiss linguist Ferdinand de Saussure (1857–1913). The next section critically examines some aspects of his theory, partly because it *is* useful in the study of both advertising and literature, but also as a way of approaching the many types of paralinguistic and discoursal meaning which it neglects. From there the discussion moves on to the semiotic theory of the American philosopher Charles Sanders Peirce (1839–1914), and a critique of semiotics in general. The description of these theories in the first half of this chapter will involve some digression from the analysis of advertisements, but one which I believe is important, and whose relevance will be clear in the second half of the chapter.

4.2 Semiology and semiotics

The word **'semiology'** (which translates the French 'sémiologie') is associated with de Saussure. The word **'semiotics'** was used by Peirce. Both refer to the study of signs, but a difference is sometimes drawn between the approaches of these two leading theorists. I shall use the term 'semiotics' to cover both, though when talking specifically of de Saussure's theory refer to it as 'semiology'.

4.2.1 Saussurean semiology

In his theory of **semiology**, published posthumously in 1915,[2] de Saussure (1974: 65–78) described a language as a system of signs which have meaning by virtue of their relationships to each other. Each sign comprises a **signifier** (a word) and a **signified** (a concept). Each **sign** has meaning only by virtue of its place in the system, and the fact that this system is known and shared by its users. A language is a 'social fact', a convention. Within larger linguistic units such as sentences, meanings are created by choices and relationships of signs. A sentence – a combination of signs – is itself thus a complex signifier for a complex signified, and may be treated as a complex sign. Saussure was primarily interested in speech, regarding writing as derived from it. As speech unfolds in time, with only one sign occurring at each moment, there are two ways of creating meaning. The first is the **syntagm,** in which signs create meaning by their relationships to the signs before or after them – by their order. Thus

I see what I eat

is not the same as

I eat what I see

(as the Mad Hatter observes in *Alice's Adventures in Wonderland*). The second is the **paradigm,** in which a given sign creates meaning by virtue of its relationship to other signs which might have occupied the same slot, but did not. Thus

I love Pepsi.

does not have the same meanings as

I love Coke.

There is a set of words which can fill each slot in this Subject–Verb–Object sentence, and substitution of one for another will change its meaning. This idea of meaning through combination or choice is not limited to language. If we consider clothing, for example, as the expression of a semiotic system with social meaning (Barthes 1985) – rather than just a means of keeping warm – then we can say that, paradigmatically, the meaning of a top hat is different from that of a baseball cap. This paradigmatic meaning created

	FEET	LEGS and	WAIST	UPPER TORSO	HEAD
1	shoes & socks		trousers	shirt	0
2	sandals	0	jeans	T-shirt	baseball cap
3	high heels	tights	skirt	top	0
4	wellingtons	0	shorts		top hat
5	slippers	0	kilt		beret
			pyjama	pyjama	crash helmet
			trousers	jacket	

Figure 4.1 Paradigmatic selection and syntagmatic combinations of clothes. The overall effect and meaning derives not only from each element but from their combination. Some combinations are conventional, others bizarre.

by choice will be affected by syntagmatic meaning created by combination (Figure 4.1). A top hat has a different signification when worn with evening dress than it has when worn with a swimsuit.

These notions of paradigm and syntagm may be extended to the pictures of ads. In 'Last Stick', for example, a blond, white, young man is chosen instead of a black man, or a woman, or an old man (i.e. paradigmatically) and placed in combination with (i.e. syntagmatically) a blonde, white young woman, in a bus (not a Cadillac) in a prairie (not the Bronx). Different choices and combinations yield different meanings.

Paradigmatic and syntagmatic choice also have a particular relevance to marketing and distribution. The layout of shops and the grouping of products within them are generally paradigmatic rather than syntagmatic (Kehret-Ward 1987). In a supermarket, we encounter all types of cheese in one place, of tomato paste in another, of pizza bases in another, of wine in another and so on. We select one of each to fill a particular slot. If, however, the shop was arranged so that mozzarella cheese, and one kind only of tomatoes, one kind of pizza base, and one kind of wine occurred together, forming the combination 'pizza margherita with Chianti' this would be syntagmatic. At times some stores have experimented with syntagmatic marketing, trying to set out products in 'clusters', for example pre-shave lotion + razor + shaving soap + after shave lotion. Yet the approach to both advertising and marketing remains paradigmatic. Products are presented as alternatives to their competitors, rather than as complements to their accompaniments.

In de Saussure's view, linguistic signs are arbitrary. There is a connection of meaning, between a signifier and a signified, but it is not motivated by any resemblance between the two;[3] it holds only because it is known to hold by people who use the system. Though the meanings of signs change over time, it is not within the power of any individual to change them: they are both mutable and immutable. The history of a sign, its diachronic development, is not part of its meaning; all that matters is its present position in the system, and the synchronic relationships it enters into with other signs.

Saussure's description of the sign as

<u>SIGNIFIED</u>
signifier

can be extended to describe such figures as metaphor, in which one signifier refers to two signifieds by virtue of a shared component in the signifieds[4] though not in the signifiers, and puns, where by chance one signifer relates to two signifieds. Figure 4.2 gives examples of a metaphor from the Sprite ad, and a pun from the Peugeot ad (both discussed in Chapter 3).

Metaphor

<u>DIFFICULTY</u> (shares features with) <u>HEAT</u>
'heat'

Pun

<u>EXTRA-MARITAL RELATIONSHIP – EVENT</u>
affair

Figure 4.2 Metaphors and puns expressed as relations between signifiers and signifieds.

In de Saussure's semiology, meaning is a matter of encoding and decoding. By making appropriate choices and combinations, a person who knows the system (the *langue*) encodes his or her thoughts into words and transmits them to another person (in possession of the same *langue*) who decodes them, thus recovering the original meaning. This view of language is sometimes referred to as the **conduit metaphor** (Reddy 1978) – or more bluntly as the 'drainpipe view' – because it views language as a kind of pipe through which encoded meanings flow from one mind to another, like water. The conduit metaphor presents language and thought as quite separate, and this – despite some protestations to the contrary (1974: 112) – is what de Saussure does. Thought is locked in the head of each individual, to be moved from one head to another by words (see Figure 4.3).

The idea of communication as a simple decoding process is prevalent in some semiotic approaches to advertising. The popular phrase *Decoding Advertisements* was first used by Judith Williamson as the title of a book published in 1978, and it has been echoed widely in courses and publications ever since. The essence of Williamson's approach is to unveil through analysis what she calls the 'real' meaning of the words and images of an ad, and the 'real world' to which the 'unreal' images of the ad refer (1978:

Figure 4.3 Talking heads (de Saussure 1974: 11).

47). (In this there is a clear assumption that 'reality' is not only quite distinct from 'fiction' but also morally superior.) Thus, for example, at the outset of her book, while examining two ads for two varieties of Chanel perfume (Chanel No. 5 and Chanel No. 19), one showing Catherine Deneuve, the other Margaux Hemingway, she 'discovers' that both women are signifiers, the former signifying 'flawless French beauty', the latter the essence of being 'young, American, way out' (1978: 26). Although such decoding techniques do yield interesting insights (in practice often rather obvious ones), a drawback of the approach is its hasty satisfaction that such equivalences constitute a complete analysis. This leads it to jettison all consideration of what is particular to the surface of discourse, or of a particular signifier, and thus miss much of complexity, skill and humour.

The influence of de Saussure's theory of language has been immense. Even rejections or modifications (like this one) remain dominated by it, defining themselves in opposition. Despite their shortcomings, de Saussure's categories provide a useful starting point, a way of coming to grips with the complex and elusive nature of human communication. Though linguistic communication is not effected solely through a code, it does involve knowledge of a code, and the Saussurean approach provides a way of describing how that code works.

Yet if the study of a message involves three areas – the psychological, the textual and the physical (a tripartite division which itself owes much to de Saussure) – and the relationship between these areas, then it is fair to say that de Saussure deals well with the textual area, but badly with the other two. His description of the psychological status of language relies too heavily on a dubious division between thought and language (1974: 111–14), and on the assumption that the thought (concepts) of all who use the same code are sufficiently similar for the meaning of a text to be substantially the same for each person. An alternative view is that thought, especially thought about the kind of messages handled by language, is too closely conditioned by that language to be separated from it. And if internalized meaning is inseparable from the language which handles it, then it can hardly be said to be internal at all, for language is realized outside the individual in interaction with others. Our very identity may be outside ourselves, in our interactions with others. (For further discussion see Chapter 8.)

Nor is thought (or language) so uniform among the speakers of a language that it will allow the kind of straightforward decoding procedure described by de Saussure. Speakers of English, receiving the same ad, may interpret it in substantially different ways, depending on whether they are children or adults, women or men, rich or poor, and so on. A combination of linguistic decoding with non-linguistic knowledge creates an interpretation, perhaps *resembling* the intention of the sender, but by no means *identical* to it.

Although language, in de Saussure's view, depends upon substance for transmission, his interest in this substance is very limited. He even proposed that linguistics should not concern itself with particular utterances (*parole*) or acts of communication at all, but only with the code (*langue*)! In de Saussure's semiology, and many other schools of linguistics, the role of substance is only to provide enough clues to identify a particular sign, and other aspects of it can be disregarded. Each word – each sign – is identified by a particular combination of **phonemes** or **graphemes** derived from the stream of sound or the marks of writing. The word 'rat', for example, is a succession of three phonemes /r/ /æ/ /t/ in speech, or three graphemes R–A–T in writing. It is important that the shapes or sounds are such that they will be assigned to a particular grapheme or phoneme and not cause confusion with other phonemes or graphemes; but, other than that, it matters neither what they are made of, nor what their exact shape or sound is. The English phoneme /r/ may be trilled by a Scottish speaker, lateralized by someone from England or the United States, or pronounced as a voiced labiodental approximant (a lippy 'w') by speakers who cannot make either of these; it may have a higher pitch in a child's speech than in an adult's; but from the Saussurean point of view none of these variations alters its semiotic function. All that matters is that it be recognised as a token of the phoneme /r/ and thus contribute to the composition of the signifier 'rat'. Similarly in writing, a ⌐ or ⌐ or ℛ or ℬ, written or printed, on gold or paper or chocolate, needs only to make a shape which will enable a receiver to perceive it as the grapheme R. From this perspective, in de Saussure's view, letters and sounds have no intrinsic importance. Their function is only, through syntagmatic combination, to realize the signifier, which once realized, can start entering into meaningful syntagmatic combinations with other signs.

Figure 4.4 Mixing up the signifiers: an advertisement for 'fcuk' (French Connection UK).

4.2.2 Language and paralanguage

The Saussurean approach, in dealing with the relationship between language and substance, leaves a great deal out of account. In communication, language always has physical substance of some kind, and though this substance – sound waves or marks on paper – serves as a trigger for the assignation of phonemes or graphemes by the receiver, allowing him or her to build the signs which create linguistic meaning, it carries other kinds of meaning too. In face-to-face communication, important meanings may be conveyed by eye contact, gesture, body movement, clothing, touch, body position, physical proximity, voice quality, volume, pitch range and laughter; in writing, the same is true of page and letter sizes, fonts and handwriting styles. These and many other factors also carry meaning which may reinforce or contradict the linguistic meaning of the signs which they accompany. They are examples of paralanguage.

It is not enough to say, as some linguists do, that such behaviour is best understood as another semiotic system, separate from language. Firstly, the two modes of meaning are not separate. Paralanguage interacts with language and on occasion outweighs it. (To see that this is true, one has only to imagine the effect of someone sobbing while saying: 'I am not upset'.) There is a good deal of experimental psychological evidence to support this view of the power of paralanguage. In one classic study (Argyle *et al.* 1970; 1971) undergraduate subjects, under the false impression that they were taking part in a quite different experiment, were told one of two things after the experiment: to leave quickly so as not to waste researchers' time, or to stay and chat, as the researchers were always pleased to meet students. One of these two linguistic messages were combined with one of two opposed paralinguistic messages. Either the experimenters shook the subjects' hands, smiled, and looked them in the eye while speaking; or they avoided eye contact and touch, and wore unfriendly facial expressions. Each subject thus experienced one of four possible combinations of behaviour (Figure 4.5). When subjects were asked, some time later, to recall whether they had been treated in friendly or unfriendly manner, their replies correlated only with the paralinguistic behaviour. It did not matter what had been said to them, but only what had been done.

Verbal behaviour	Paralinguistic behaviour	Overall effect
+	+	+
+	–	–
–	+	+
–	–	–

(+ = friendly, – = unfriendly)

Figure 4.5 Paralinguistic and linguistic effects.

Secondly, although paralinguistic behaviour signifies, and is thus in a broad sense semiotic, the nature of its signification is quite different from that of language. The linguistic sign, as we have seen above, is a discrete phenomenon, a case of being *either* one thing *or* another. In linguistic terms, a sound is perceived as one phoneme or another; there are no intermediate cases. (Though one could create a continuum of sounds between, say, /b/ and /p/, in a stream of speech a speaker of a language with this distinction would perceive a sound along that continuum as one or the other.) Words, composed of phonemes, inherit this absolute quality of their components: a word is either 'bat' or 'pat' or another word, but there are no intermediate cases. A similar either/or quality pertains with letters. Many paralinguistic phenomena, on the other hand, are graded. They are a case of more or less, not either/or. If I smile at you while speaking, squeeze your hand, or laugh, I may increase or decrease the breadth of my smile, the strength of my squeeze, or the loudness of my laugh, thus signifying more or less of whatever it is I mean by these actions. This has two important consequences. Firstly, there are an infinity of different degrees in any paralinguistic phenomenon. One cannot specify the number of different smiles and squeezes and laughs available in one person's repertoire. Secondly, one cannot equate graded paralinguistic phenomena with language by translating or paraphrasing it into words. Paralanguage is literally beyond complete description in language, because it belongs to a different kind of communication from language (Cook 1990). That is why, when talking about these acts, I had to use the vague phrase 'whatever it is I mean by them'. This is not to say that one cannot describe something like a laugh in an approximate way. One could say that a laugh in general is a sign of amusement. One could go on to categorize laughs into various types (titters, giggles, guffaws, etc.) and attribute different meanings to these categories. But this is not to say that one can describe all types of laugh or fully translate their meaning into words. The same is true of the paralanguage of writing: consider the meaning of a scrawl, as opposed to copperplate script, and the number of intermediate possibilities.

In these respects, human paralanguage maintains the graded signalling used by animals. The bark of a dog creates meaning in much the same way as a human smile, by varying intensity. The difference is that some human paralanguage also carries linguistic meaning. If you hear my voice, the sound waves carry the information you need in order to perceive the syntagmatic relations of the signs of my message, and set about decoding and interpreting them; but you will also know, from the volume, pitch and intonation of my voice, something about my emotional state and social identity – whether I am angry, or bored, or excited, and that I am an adult middle-class English male. For this reason human communication is sometimes characterized as utilizing a 'double channel' (Ellis and Beattie 1986: 16–77). Every utterance carries both linguistic and paralinguistic meaning. That is not to say, however, as some 'evolutionary psychologists' have tried to argue (Brown 1991: 23–7, 52–3) that the substantial basis of paralanguage is instinctive and universal. There are also well-documented variations (Morris 1977; Morris *et al.* 1979). In this respect the analogy with animal communication is misleading, for while the communicative behaviour of an animal is, generally speaking, common to all members of that species, human paralinguistic communication varies considerably. Contrastive cultural analysis reveals many cases of the same paralinguistic action having widely different meanings in different cultures. A particular kind of touch, proximity, eye contact, laughter or voice volume may mean nothing, or something quite different, when transferred from one culture to another. This causes considerable problems for advertisers organizing international campaigns, who must realize that it is often more than the words of an ad that need translation (Usunier 1999). The term **copy adaptation** has been coined to emphasize this difference from translation.

The signification of paralanguage is generally quite as arbitrary as that of language. Yet, although a good deal of paralanguage is neither natural nor culture-free, many aspects of it are beyond conscious control. A laugh or a smile may be used deliberately (not necessarily hypocritically) to send a particular message; at other times they may emerge spontaneously against the will of the communicator, as when people 'cannot help' laughing or smiling. Many paralinguistic features communicate relatively permanent features of a particular individual, including sex, social class and age. Language is much more under conscious control. Thus one of the most distinctive features of human language use is lying (Lyons 1977: 83).

It is possible to argue, as many linguists do, that paralanguage is of no concern to linguistics, because language is best understood when it is rigorously isolated from such distracting phenomena. This is an odd view, for language never occurs without paralanguage. The two constantly interact, and communicative competence involves using both together – but it is a view which has mesmerized and impoverished later linguistics. (Chomsky (1965: 3–4), though differing from de Saussure by describing language as a psychological rather than a social phenomenon, is in agreement on the exclusion of paralanguage.) There are however, alternative views. The Russian linguist and philosopher Mikhail Bakhtin (1895–1975), in a critique of de Saussure (first published in 1929 under the name of his colleague Volosinov), suggested that this dogmatic divorce between the study of language and paralanguage derives from an overemphasis on written discourse (Volosinov 1988: 52–62). Though linguistics professes belief in the primacy of speech (Bloomfield 1935: 21; de Saussure 1974: 23), what it actually analyses is most usually writing: transcriptions of speech, or written invented examples. This has led to both an underemphasis and distortion of the role of paralangauge in communication – for although writing has its own paralinguistic features, they are commonly less potent than the paralanguage of spoken interaction.

In literary studies, paralinguistic features are, with rare exceptions, considered to be of no significance at all. (Imagine the unorthodoxy of saying that the effect of a novel was altered by its binding or the size of its print.) Yet literature is in this – and in other respects – an unusual discourse. Certainly, an analysis of advertising will not get far with a linguistics which excludes paralanguage on principle; for advertising, like many other types of discourse, carries a heavy proportion of its meaning paralinguistically.

4.2.3 Peircean semiotics

The semiotic theory of Peirce provides categories which supplement those of de Saussure. Defining a sign very broadly as

> Something which stands to somebody for something else, in some respect or capacity.

> (Peirce [1931–58])

Peirce suggested further types of sign in addition to those of a purely arbitrary conventional nature.[5] Two of these, which are particularly useful in analyses of advertising, are the **index** and the **icon.**

An index is a sign which points to something else by virtue of a causal relationship. This category can include such natural co-occurrences as smoke and fire, dark clouds and impending rain, a human footprint and the presence of a human being, but it can also encompass more consciously controlled meanings. The imprint of a signet ring is an index of the ring itself, and of its wearer (though its signification of the wearer's approval is arbitrary). A wedding ring is both an index of marriage (because we assume the ring was first put on during a wedding ceremony), possibly iconic of marital union (!), and also an arbitrary signifier (because the connection of wearing a ring and being married is purely conventional). An ad, in a current magazine or TV programme, is an index of the existence and availability of a product. The notion of the index is particularly useful in the description of paralanguage. A slurred voice is an index of drunkenness, for example; expensive clothing is an index of wealth. Yet the interpretation of an index is not a process of decoding. It depends on knowledge of the world, and will vary from one language-user to another. Sweaty palms may have quite different indexical meaning to a doctor than to a person with no skill in diagnosing illness. (It is the idiosyncrasy and sensitivity of indexical interpretation, incidentally, which is the skill of Sherlock Holmes.)

An icon is a sign which means by virtue of resemblance to what it signifies. Maps and photographs are good examples. Yet this type of sign is almost always more complex than at first appears. Most icons resemble their signified only in some respects. A blue and white photograph of Elvis Presley having his famous GI haircut (used in an ad for Stubbs watches) is in a degree an icon of the person Elvis Presley (or our concept of him); but this does not entail that he was four inches tall, two dimensional, motionless or blue. The meaning of photographs, moreover, despite the widely held view that they show life 'as it is', is also created by arbitrary semiotic paradigmatic choice and syntagmatic ordering (Barthes 1977a, d). (Who is Elvis seen with? Who was he chosen instead of?) Many signs are believed to be iconic because the perception of a connection between signified and signifier is so habitual that it begins to seem natural. (Does the ⚦ on a lavatory door really look more like a man than a woman?) For a sign to be truly iconic, it would have to be transparent to someone who had never seen it before – and it seems unlikely that this is as much the case as sometimes supposed. We see the resemblance when we already know the meaning. This is especially true with onomatopoeic words which supposedly imitate the sound of their referent. The Russian words *puknut'* and *pyornut'* for example are regarded as onomatopoeic by Russian speakers, but it is not possible for someone who does not speak Russian to work out their meaning from the sound alone. (Both mean 'to fart': the first refers to a short, explosive fart, the second to a long and loud one.) It is not a question of a sign or combination of signs being wholly iconic, indexical or arbitrary. Many signify in all three ways at once.

4.2.4 Shortcomings of semiotics

A weakness of the semiotic approach is its exclusive devotion to similarities, and then an air of finality once these similarities are observed, which blinds it to what is unique. Under the influence of semiotics, **structuralist** analyses of culture and language devoted their attention to those features of phenomena which allow one instance to be seen as equivalent to another; and then concentrated on those features to the detriment of others. Fifty years ago, the method was a revolutionary one, and justly captured the intellectual imagination, not only for the added complexity it could bring to analysis but also for its political and philosophical implications. Its vision of cultures and cultural artefacts, no matter how superficially different, as fundamentally similar, reflecting abstract structures universally present in human cultures, was a powerful weapon against racism and cultural chauvinism. More recently, a similar concentration on the universal aspects of human culture, though with very different premises, has resurfaced in evolutionary psychology, which attempts to describe all facets of human behaviour as characteristics of the species, rather than as the products of particular times and places. Drawing upon Darwinian theory, it has attempted to characterise literature (Carroll 1995) and art in general (Dissanayake 1988) as activities conferring evolutionary advantages upon humans. Such universalist approaches undoubtedly have their strengths, and can reveal much of interest about cultural artefacts, including advertisements. Yet although analysis of an ad may benefit from consideration of what it has in common with the myths of earlier cultures, or with other genres from its own time and place, or with other ads, there are also important elements which are unique in advertising, or in a given ad, as there are in any genre or instance of it.

For all its benefits then, the semiotic approach also runs a danger of simplification and partial analysis. Its insights are useful but incomplete. Meaning is always seen as an equivalence between a surface signifier and something else. Words are seen as equivalent to their **denotation**. Utterances are reduced to **propositions** (declarative statements about states of affairs in the world) and discourse to the logical connections between these propositions. Narratives and myths are reduced to formulaic patterns. These reductions are then seen as the 'underlying' meaning. In linguistics, the work of Chomsky inherited this concentration on what is 'underneath' language. In earlier versions of the theory (e.g. Chomsky 1965) the search was for the so-called 'deep structure' of sentences; in later versions, for the computational programme of which sentences are evidence (Chomsky 1995).

Such concentration on underlying structures – whether in semiotics or linguistics – neglects the fact that there may also be surface forms which are important in themselves. There is moreover a contradiction in such an approach. Talk of 'deep' and 'surface' meaning is metaphorical and also pejorative. What is on the surface – 'superficial' – is trivial, false and empty-headed; what is 'deep', is serious, genuine and thoughtful. Ironically, in both semantics and linguistics, the claim that deep structures are the most important is insinuated through this purely surface metaphor. If we 'transform' the metaphors 'deep' and 'surface' to some underlying representation, this value judgement within them disappears!

One area of surface form often simplified or neglected is paralanguage.

4.3 Exploiting the double channel

Writing, of its nature, makes less use of paralanguage than speech. The physical substance of some written texts exists only to realize linguistic form. This tendency is accentuated by the high esteem accorded to the written word, and the belief that its function is to relay information objectively and impersonally. The function of paralanguage is more often to express attitudes and emotions, to regulate and establish social relations, to mediate between words and a particular situation. Paralanguage is also more concerned with facilitating the process of communication, rather than with its product: the meanings which literate people believe are somehow stored in a written text, quite independently of situation and speaker. A literate culture typically believes in, and elevates, the importance of 'objective scientific facts', regarded as persisting independently of speakers and situations. As such, many written texts aspire to eliminate all traces of either the situation in which they were composed, the process of composition, or the person who originated them. The nature of writing makes this possible, for it displaces language from the time and place of its composition, enabling the sender to work upon it as an object. You, the reader, do not see me, the writer, as you read this book, or know anything about the circumstances in which I am writing. You do not know what changes I have made in this sentence, when I added it to the manuscript, or whether I paused to have a cup of coffee between these dots ... and these. ... And by the conventions of our culture you do not care. You read this book for the information or ideas it carries, not to communicate with me as an individual physical presence. Writing makes the language here no longer dependent on me and my situation in any way. You can read this book in any order, when and how you want: and I will not even know. I may even be dead. As far as the paralanguage of this writing goes – the shapes of the letters and so on – it is considered so immaterial that I, typing these words on to the screen, do not even know how they will appear to you. Nor is that considered to be my business, but that of the publisher, whose choice of typeface will be influenced more by the desire for clarity which aids linguistic decoding than by any other considerations.

This perceived unimportance of paralanguage varies from genre to genre, however, even in writing. It is also very much a feature of contemporary scientific culture. In illuminated medieval manuscripts, and in traditional Chinese and Japanese calligraphy, the shape of writing has an intrinsic importance beyond the linguistic signs they realise. Though academic books may aspire to an ethereal impersonality, there are also anxious love letters in which everything is considered important: the paper and its perfume, the fact that it is handwritten instead of typed, and 'sealed with a kiss' (or as the Lypsyl ad in Figure 4.6 says, 'LYPSYLed with a kiss').

What has the computer done to this relation between written text, the immediate situation of the writer, and the relevance of paralinguistic detail? Very often (as in email) we are very aware of when and where the writer is, and of the processes of composition, revealed in the unedited and on-line nature of the result. In addition, word-processing software increasingly enables amateur writers (without the intervention of a publisher) to make significant use of the paralinguistic paraphernalia of writing by varying fonts, colours and layouts, and adding tables, graphs and illustrations. Yet to date, computer mediated communication, like handwritten letters, remains in a limbo somewhere between the impersonality of print communication, and the immediacy of face-to-face interaction. Perhaps it will move closer to the latter, but for the moment it retains some of the advantages and disadvantages of each.

Figure 4.6 Lypsyl lipsalve slogo: 'LYPSYLed with a kiss'.

4.4 Paralanguage in literature and ads

In the exploitation of written paralanguage, literature and advertising differ considerably.

Etymologically the word 'literature' is very closely associated with written language. It derives from the Latin word *littera,* meaning a letter of the alphabet, a root which it shares with the words 'literate' and 'literal' (Williams 1983: 183–8). In a phrase like 'the biology literature', it is still used simply to mean 'written material', and despite all difficulties of definition, whatever else a contemporary literary text may or may not be, it is always written. It is true that in its most usual contemporary sense – the sense which is so hard to define, but which refers, let us say for the sake of argument, to highly esteemed verbal art – literature appears to include *both* written and spoken material: novels and short stories which are primarily written texts, but also poems and plays, which are often recited, read aloud, or performed. Poetry, however, has been increasingly treated as written rather than spoken. The importance attributed to exact wording is possible only when poems are written down. It is hard to imagine a poem or play being accorded literary status in the twentieth century on the basis of performance only. However, the reverse situation – high acclaim for a written text which has never been performed – is quite feasible, and indeed common. Certainly, in academic study, the merits of a poem or a play are judged to be those of the written text; these may include a perceived potential for oral performance, though not the merits of any particular rendering. Such a bias, however, like the notion of 'literature' itself, is a relatively modern phenomenon. Many works now regarded as literary classics, such as *The Iliad* or *Beowulf* were performed orally before being written down. The modern partiality for writing is revealed by the tendency to assimilate spoken verbal art to writing. In contemporary culture any oral creation which is valued is immediately written down: highly esteemed pop songs and film scripts quickly appear in books.

Yet despite this tendency immediately to shift valued speech towards writing it remains true that poetry and drama, especially away from the clutches of academics, preserve features peculiar to speech, and only realizable in speech.

One feature which literature of all kinds preserves in common with spoken discourse is its affective role, its strong association with emotion rather than with fact. Literary discourse is commonly perceived as the expression of some extraordinary individual personality, whose ideas, experiences, memories and emotions are somehow transmitted to us through the text. (Such a view clearly shares the 'conduit' view of language, described in 4.2.1, seeing it as a channel between one mind and another.) This displacement of writing from the circumstances of its production disposes literate societies towards a depersonalization of the text, a divorce from individuals and situations, and a belief in objective scientific fact. Literature, when perceived as the expression of individuality, is at odds with this. The popular association of a literary text with the individual voice of its creator persists strongly, despite the efforts of various schools of literary theory throughout the twentieth century to undermine it. Russian Formalism and the New Criticism insisted on the autonomy of the text and the irrelevance of the writer's biography or the circumstances of production. Psychoanalytic and Marxist criticism, despite their differences, have in common a tendency to believe that writing reveals the struggle of forces (in the mind or in society respectively) of which the author was unaware.

Just how unsuccessful such critical movements have been in affecting the popular view of literature is witnessed by the fact that everywhere – in bookshops, schools, universities and casual conversations – literature continues to be classified by author. ('Have you got any Marquez?'; 'We're doing Balzac this term'; 'I am reading another Helen Dunmore'.) Nor has interest in the lives of authors diminished. In some respects, this obsession with literature as the expression of a unique personality, and the conception of the self which is necessary to it, is a relatively modern phenomenon, dating from the Romantic emphasis on an artist's extraordinary personality and powers (Foucault 1979). In another sense this intensely personal emphasis in literary communication is rooted in the pre-literate past. It preserves the individual nature of oral communication which can never be divorced from a particular speaker. This is perhaps part of the appeal of literature, for the transition from oral to written communication is a feature of **ontogenetic** (i.e. our personal individual) development as well as of **phylogenetic** (i.e. the history of human) change. We all lived in an oral, personal, affective world in infancy. This kind of communication remains powerful and pleasurable throughout life, while the depersonalized voice of objective facts remains somewhat alien. Advertising identifies itself with the former, while its opponents, by trying to associate it with incorrect facts, identify it with the latter.

Like literature, advertising inhabits a borderland between writing and speech, though in a different way. Although the language of TV ads is predominantly speech, while that of magazine and poster ads is writing, this difference exists only in reception, not in production. The words in contemporary ads are always carefully scripted and subjected to so much scrutiny and rewriting that in this respect they stand comparison with the drafting of laws or poetry. This has not always been so. Some early TV ads in the 1950s and 1960s contained ad lib and improvised passages (Geis 1982: 130–62). Now, the notion of anything unscripted appearing in an ad seems unthinkable. Yet although the scripts of spoken ads are carefully prepared, they are not, unlike those of poems and plays, either available to their audience or required by them. In this respect ads are closer to oral communication than to literature.

Recognition of the author, however, is less widespread. Outside the confines of the advertising world itself, ads are not commonly linked to an individual creative personality. Though exceptionally innovative talents, like those of Adam Lury or Trevor Beattie, are known to other advertisers, their names are virtually unheard of elsewhere, and the general public certainly does not identify ads by author.[6] This may be partly because an ad is not an individual creation, but involves many people. Joint authorship in literature, by contrast, is so unusual that exceptions (like the dramatists Beaumont and Fletcher) stand out. Another reason may be that creators of ads often feel too constrained by their brief to describe the ad as truly their own. Ads, then, unlike either speech or literature, do not draw attention to their sender. They do, however, by associating writing with pictures, anchor their communication firmly to a specific non-linguistic situation, simulating the paralanguage of face-to-face interaction. Consider, for example, how essential facial expression and gesture are to the television ads analysed in Chapter 3. The situation of the picture is not the situation of the ad's creation, however, but fictional. In this respect, such ads are like plays which are known only in one production, and not at all as a text.

4.4.1 The double channel in literature: use of graphology

Ads and literature thus have a much closer relation to orality than many other kinds of written text, but the nature of this closeness in the two discourses is rather different. They also differ in the degree to which they exploit the potential for paralinguistic meaning in sounds and letters.

Literature makes such little use of the paralinguistic potential of writing that exceptions are both striking and well known. George Herbert arranged the lines of his poem 'Easter Wings' to look like wings (when viewed on their side) and the lines of his poem 'The Altar' to look like an altar. Lewis Carroll wrote 'The Mouse's Tale' in *Alice's Adventures in Wonderland* in the shape of a tail. Guillaume Apollinaire wrote 'Calligrammes' in which words are arranged to form pictures of falling rain, the Eiffel Tower, a train or a starry sky. **Concrete poetry** has produced many examples of such attempts to evoke both the arbitrary semiotic meaning of words and their potential to form pictures. The signification of these poems is both iconic, because the words look like their subjects, and conventional, because the words create linguistic meaning through an arbitrary code. This technique is also used in acts (Figure 4.7).

Another well-known literary use of paralanguage is found in the eighteenth-century novel *Tristram Shandy* in which Laurence Sterne uses blank and black pages, squiggles (Figure 4.8), pointing hands (☞) and paragraphs of dashes. These are neither iconic nor conventional signs, and convey nothing very precise, though they are indices of narrative stance. In harmony with this is the book's unconventional simulation of

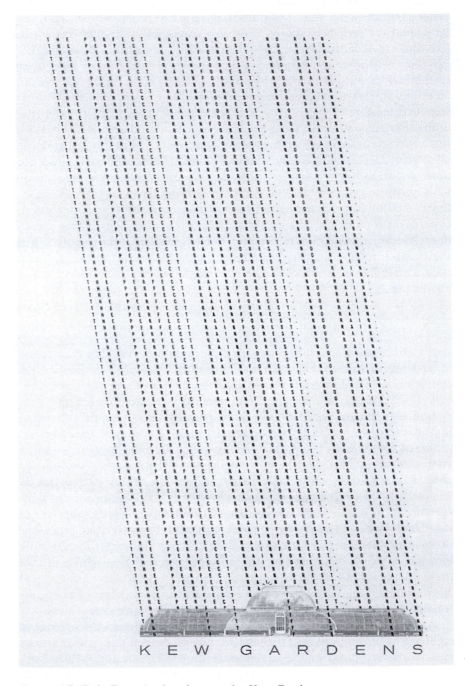

Figure 4.7 'Rain Forest': advertisement for Kew Gardens.

These were the four lines I moved in through my first, second, third, and fourth volumes.—In the fifth volume I have been very good,—the precise line I have described in it being this:

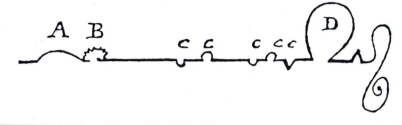

Figure 4.8 Squiggles in *Tristram Shandy*.

face-to-face interaction. The author addresses the reader as though he or she were present before him:

> How could Madam be so inattentive in reading the last chapter? I told you in it that my Mother was a papist. – Papist! You told me no such thing, Sir. Madam I beg leave to repeat it over again.

and as though the reader's immediate situation, including its time, were the same as the plot:

> It is about an hour and a half's tolerable good reading since my Uncle Toby rung the bell ... and nobody can say, with reason, that I have not allowed Obadiah time enough, poetically speaking, and considering the emergency too, both to come and go.

The immediate and personal nature of the paralinguistic and the visual, also a feature of face-to-face communication, fits well with such apparently interactive and dialogic discourse, though both are at odds with the distant, non-reciprocal nature of communication through print, and it is from the tension between the two sub-modes of writing and speech that the book gains its energy.

Yet it is indicative of the attitude of a literate culture to the paralinguistic that poetry or prose which exploits the paralanguage of writing is usually relegated to the status of whimsy, or regarded as childish. In cultures closer to orality, arrangements of words in patterns are often of intense ritual significance, or convey more serious meanings. In an analysis of Psalm 137, Halle (1989) shows how the Hebrew words of the original are written to form a picture of the temple in Jerusalem. As this psalm describes the agonies of exile, slavery and defeat, beginning 'By the rivers of Babylon, there we sat down, yea, we wept . . .' and ending

> Happy shall he be that rewardeth thee as thou has served us.
> Happy shall he be that taketh and dasheth thy little ones against the rocks.

it could hardly be described as light or children's verse.

4.5 The double channel in advertising: use of graphology

In a hierarchical, bottom-up model of discourse (see Figure 1.6), advertising is distinguished by its extraordinary innovative profusion in the lower levels. We should remember, however, that the notion of higher and lower levels in discourse is a metaphor, and like most metaphors it is loaded. What is 'higher' is also considered to be 'better', just as what is lower is considered to be 'worse' (as in the phrases 'high ideals' and 'low standards'). It is worth considering whether the hierarchy could not be reversed.

The number of ways in which advertising exploits the paralanguage of writing is staggeringly large. No catalogue could be complete, for original uses of lettering are constantly appearing. (A spectacles ad uses blurred print; the words in an ad for tourism to Australia are upside down; a cat tip-toes along the top of three-dimensional letters spelling 'Kattomeat' (Figure 4.9).) This section gives examples of technique, and also looks at some individual ads.

4.5.1 Iconicity with words

This common technique can be exemplified by an ad for Maxwell House coffee. The TV version showed a suburban family drinking coffee in the

Figure 4.9 Advertisement for Kattomeat.

Figure 4.10 From an advertisement for Maxwell House instant coffee.

garden of a semi-detached house. This house – a Maxwell House – is secure, friendly and homely. The photographic image merges into a stylized drawing, in which the angle of the roof is represented by two lines, one saying 'Is yours a Max', the other '-well House' (Figure 4.10). The imitation of the roof by the letters is iconic. The name 'Maxwell House' now seems to be both the name of the coffee and to refer to the house in the picture. The signification is not only arbitrary (naming the coffee) and iconic (picturing the roof) however. Through association, the coffee gains some of the attributes of the house. It too is 'secure', 'reliable', 'homely' and 'restful'. It is also linked to the visual image of the roof. As a roof protects and warms and is part of a house, it signifies the qualities of warmth and protection symbolically and metonymically too. Thus 'Maxwell House' comes to mean protection and warmth too.

Another example of iconicity can be found in the ad for the perfume Elizabeth Taylor's Passion. A slight displacement of the second line

be touched
by the fragrance
that touches
the woman

Figure 4.11 Elizabeth Taylor's Passion perfume ad.

Figure 4.12 'Fire Bucket': an advertisement for Guinness.

leftwards makes the outline of the block of words hexagonal, like the bottle. (A distinctive bottle shape is important in perfume branding, and invariably features in perfume ads.) The shape of the copy thus signifies the bottle iconically, because it imitates its shape. There is (as always) a further complication: the bottle and the words are also shaped like a heart.[7] The heart is a symbol of passion (arguably partly **metonymic**, because a thumping heart accompanies passion, but now largely conventional). 'Passion' is also the name of the perfume, so it refers back to the bottle. There is thus a circularity of signification leading from 'passion' in its usual sense, via two icons and one symbol, to 'Passion' as a name which leads us back to 'passion' in its usual sense again. There are other iconic echoes too. In the photograph the sparkle of the eyes resembles the sparkle of the diamonds.[8]

4.5.2 Iconicity by letter shape

Some logos and ads exploit or slightly alter conventional letter shapes, to create an iconic representation of the product or of something associated with it. The initial 'A' of Alitalia is written in the shape of an aeroplane tail; the 'G' of Guinness is sometimes a picture of an Irish harp; the elongated upstrokes of the Dunhill logo when it appears on cigarette packets look like the long cigarettes inside.

4.5.3 Mixed icons and arbitrary signs

The Lypsyl ad in Figure 4.6 employs both language ('sealed with a') and a further arbitrary sign (X = kiss), but also iconicity as the cross-strokes of the X are pictures of tubes of Lypsyl. It thus mixes iconic with arbitrary signification. A well-known example of such a mixture is found in stickers saying such things as 'I ♡ PARIS' in which the iconic shape signifies a heart which is the symbol of love. An ad for Black Heart rum extends this.

Figure 4.13 'I love Black Heart': an advertisement for Black Heart Rum.

4.5.4 Writing which provokes iconic behaviour

A double-page magazine ad for Philips colour TV displays its copy over a TV picture of a professional tennis match, as follows:

you	haven't
seen	tennis
on	television
until	you've
seen	it
on	a
Philips 41"	screen

thus causing its reader to move his or her eyes from side to side, as though at a tennis match.

Curiously, the same device had been used in a poem by Roger McGough, entitled '40–0'. We have already encountered this predilection of advertising copywriters to borrow from literature and art without acknowledgement. The Silk Cut ad showing an iron with spikes used an idea of Man Ray's; the Kew Gardens ad 'Rain Forest' (Figure 4.7) uses the same idea as a Calligramme by Guillaume Apollinaire.

4.5.5 Writing used iconically: Dubo Dubon Dubonnet

In a version of this ad from 1932 (Figure 4.14), the hollow letters of the product's name are increasingly shaded, thus iconically representing the filling of a container with liquid; the body of the man beside them is increasingly shaded in the same way, as though he too were filling up. As the filling also turns the man red, and a flushed complexion can be an index of drunkenness, it also signifies increasing intoxication. The darkening tone is also a metaphor of inebriation. (Only the last drawing is shown in Figure 4.14.)

4.5.6 Indexical graphology

Indexical scripts and typefaces are frequent in junk mail. Addresses are printed to look handwritten, thus signifying an individual rather than an official addresser. The AA Insurance ad in Figure 4.15, for example (which arrived by post) signifies a child indexically by using a child's handwriting. As the punctuation and spelling are by contrast not childlike, the child's presence is almost entirely graphological.

4.5.7 Writing imitating another writing system, creating an index of another culture

On 'TE TAO' Chinese Herbal Therapy hair conditioner, the brand name is written in the Roman alphabet, but the stylized strokes of the letters are

Figure 4.14 'Dubo Dubon Dubonnet': an advertisement for Dubonnet aperitif from 1932.

reminiscent of the calligraphy used for Chinese characters. Thus, although the words use the Roman alphabet, their form is indexical of the Far East, even to someone who does not know Chinese.

A similar technique is used in many products associated with Russia. A letter from the Cyrillic alphabet is used, although it is read as the letter from the Roman alphabet whose shape it most resembles. I used to live near a restaurant called Rasputin's, whose name was written

ЯASPUTINS

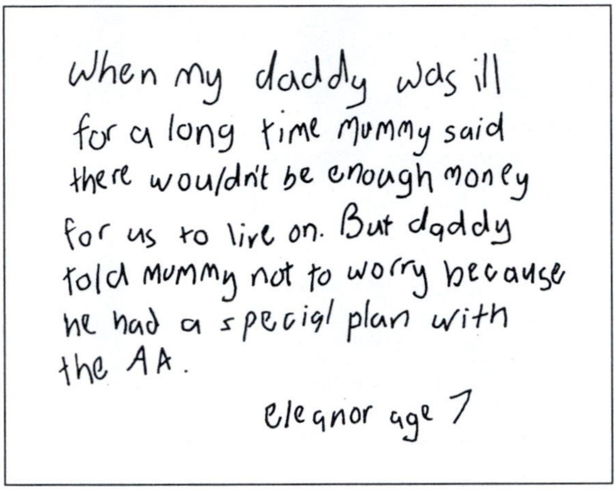

When my daddy was ill
for a long time mummy said
there wouldn't be enough money
for us to live on. But daddy
told mummy not to worry because
he had a special plan with
the AA.
eleanor age 7

Figure 4.15 Direct mail advertisement for AA Insurance.

The Cyrillic equivalent of the Roman R is not Я, but P; in Russian the letter Я is read as 'Ya'. The letter is thus not only an arbitrary sign forming part of the word as read in English, but also an index of the Russian language, and therefore of Russia, because, even when its arbitrary connection with the sound 'Ya' is unknown, it is known to be a Cyrillic letter. This technique should not be confused with that used in ads which do actually use a different writing system, such as an ad for *The Economist* which appears in shorthand, or for Tiger Beer which uses Chinese characters (Figure 4.17).

TÊ TAO
CHINESE HERBAL THERAPY

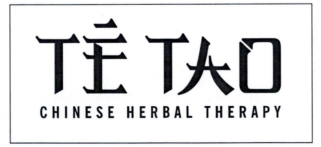

Figure 4.16 TE TAO hair products logo.

Figure 4.17 Advertisement for Tiger Beer.

4.5.8 *Mood evocation through typeface*

Many successful brand names are inextricably connected with the typeface in which they are written. So strong can this association be that some ads can refer to their product, not by naming it, but by using this typeface. The British newspaper *The Independent*, for example, ran an ad which said only

> It is. Are you?

Reference to the product was achieved not only because the word 'independent' completes the elliptical first sentence – *It is (Ø independent)* – but also because the typeface used was the same as that of the publication's title. A Guinness ad whose copy was only 'Pure Genius' relied on the same association, as did a Benson & Hedges cigarette ad showing an unmarked cigarette packet next to a safety razor covered in shaving cream, in which, like shaved stubble, could be seen the jumbled letters of the product's name.

In all these instances, a typeface is used to signify the product, in addition to, or sometimes instead of, the word or words which signify it arbitrarily in the code. It is difficult to categorize this kind of signification using the semiotic terms employed so far. In part, the connection is indexical: we associate a particular kind of print with a particular product. But there is also an element of mood evocation, of 'brand personality', which is hard to define. The signification is both indeterminate and powerful. Advertising therefore adores it.

4.6 Writing and speech

Even when destined to be spoken on television or radio, the words of an ad are almost always written down at some stage in its creation. By freeing language from time and projecting it into space, writing enables more concise and less redundant expression, and creates time to choose words carefully for maximum effect. Yet it also entails a divorce of text from a particular situation, person and voice, depriving it of the emotive richness of paralanguage, which may be so useful to the advertiser. Writing also (as discussed in Section 4.3) focuses the receiver's attention upon the words themselves, and on what is perceived to be the objective meaning or content of what is said; it enables the receiver to go back and contemplate the text more carefully – perhaps finding inconsistencies and untruths – making it less likely that he or she will be swept along by the tide of what is being said without time for reflection. In short, though writing may be to an advertiser's advantage in composition, it is not always so in reception, as it may both deprive the message of some of its power and also enable criticism and contestation. This ambivalent relation of ads to writing is perhaps the cause of the intense exploitation of written paralanguage, as illustrated in the last sections. Writing is used both to create text and simultaneously to distract attention from it by using letter shapes and patterns to create parallel iconic and indexical meanings quite separate from the linguistic ones. This reveals, perhaps, a certain lack of confidence in the text itself.

The losses of written text can in part be compensated by reading aloud, and by pictures. The contemporary world is full of such discourse, which seeks the advantages of both channels. In a literate culture, where the fundamental advantage of writing over speech is the opportunity it brings for the displacement of a message from its point of origin, and its distribution to a wider audience in time and space, the loss of speaker and situation are felt to be the lesser of two evils. The technology of mass communication partly redresses this necessary loss. Radio, telephones and tape recorders enable the displacement of language, while preserving the sound of an individual voice. In television and film, the reading aloud of written texts allows the sender some of the advantages of writing, while also reinstating or creating an image of both a speaker and a situation. Yet the speaker on TV is not always the sender, and what is happening is not truly on-line like face-to-face interaction. Broadcasting, moreover, from the receiver's point of view, despite its achievement of displacement and wide dissemination, lacks other attributes of writing; it does not enable the receiver to process a message at any pace and in any order, to glance backwards and forwards, to juxtapose linearly separate segments, and to obtain an overall impression of structure. Broadcasting, in short, gives the sender an edge over the receiver.

More recent media, particularly the World Wide Web and digital television, are commonly referred to as 'interactive', and do indeed seem to have achieved both the displaced and disseminated communication of print and broadcasting, and the capacity to respond to the individual receivers as in face-to-face interaction. (Indeed one might say that any use of a software programme – whether with a word processing programme or a bank cash machine – is interactive in this sense.) Clearly this 'perfect combination' (to use the advertisers' jargon) offers advantages and opportunities – and is already widely used by them in advertisements both on the Internet and interactive television. (For example, an interactive television ad for Persil Non-Bio on the digital channel Open engages viewers in a virtual quiz, with prizes including a trip to a health spa, a selection of Elizabeth Arden products, and a year's supply of Persil Non-bio.[9]) Yet the term 'interaction' here refers to something quite different from the interaction which takes place with a human interlocutor, in say an email exchange or a face-to-face interview. The responses of the Web page or TV screen reflect a human designer's predictions as to how the receiver may respond and make appropriate responses in return, but they can not adjust to the unpredicted. When we interact with such programmes, of course, we know that this is the case, and tailor our own questions accordingly (there is no point asking a Web page with airline information whether it is happy). It is another case of vocabulary not having kept change with technological change, and a need for more subtle distinctions. 'Interactive' advertisements do respond in ways which the older one-way media such as traditional television do not; on the other hand they certainly do not adjust intelligently to their receiver as actual human beings do. To equate our use of a pre-programmed Web page or TV screen with actual interaction with another person seriously denigrates the importance of human contact. Perhaps even more disturbing than this common confusion is the fact that, even where the interactive advertisement does put us in contact with a 'real person' by giving us a telephone number, the person who answers the call is not able to speak freely, but must follow a 'pre-programmed' script, and is in danger of being fired for any departure from it (Cameron 2000: 91–125). This is the opposite case from a computer being treated as a person: a person being treated as a computer!

Literary discourse in novels, by remaining content with writing, in general eschews the paralanguage made possible by broadcasting and the Internet. Yet it does not follow from this that it cannot, and does not, exploit paralanguage at all. It can describe, through the conventional signification of written words, such paralinguistic behaviour as tones of voice, facial expressions and gestures, though their audialization or visualization, if it takes place at all, will vary considerably from reader to reader. Consider for example the following description in *The Rainbow* by D.H. Lawrence:

> Again she turned her face to him and her clear, bright eyes, bright like shallow water, filled with light, frightened, yet involuntarily lighting and shaking with response. 'Oh isn't it! I wasn't able to come last week.' He noted the common accent.

How you and I see this face, and hear this 'common accent' are unlikely to be the same. (We might also argue about whether the snobbery is Lawrence's or the character's, or whether it exists at all.)

So literary discourse in novels does not exploit the capacity of mass communication or live performance to reinstate both speaker and situation to its texts. (When we treat plays and poems as written texts – as most educational institutions do – then this is true of these literary genres too.) Though novels may appear to set great store by the 'voice' of an author, narrator or character, or upon fictional situations, their abstinence from pictures and sound ensures that the receiver's representation of these voices and settings will be far more heterogeneous, far more dependent upon the reader, than that imparted by the pictures or the recorded voice. (I do not claim by this that everyone's perception of a recording or picture is the same, but only that they are closer than perceptions of verbal descriptions of sounds and pictures. It is in the nature of pictures and recording to constrain interpretation.)

As already discussed in Chapter 3, pictures and sound create both their own meanings and meanings resulting from their interplay with each other and with text. It is not only that sound recording makes it possible to use music. Sound also enables language to maintain, regain or have added to it the paralanguage of an individual or choral voice. (Choral singing – so common in ads – carries with it a message of solidarity, of social harmony, and of friendship.) Voice quality serves as an index of such passing emotional states as happiness, sensuality, optimism. The advantage of such associations for the advertiser is that they are both powerful and elusive. Though everyone may experience the optimism in a voice, it is difficult either to prove or measure the existence of this graded quality.

There is likely to be far more agreement about the more permanent characteristics of the speaker conveyed by the voice. These include age, class, sex and individual identity, all of which are carefully selected in ads, and are strong clues to the ideology which advertisers attribute to their target audiences. The voices of celebrities (or mimics of celebrities) bestow upon a product all the values signified by that individual: the strength of the athlete, the glamour of the star or the authority of the politician. (Here, again, the fact that celebrities whose voices are imitated without their permission are unlikely to prove deception illustrates the simultaneous power and elusiveness of paralinguistic signification.) Perhaps the most telling evidence of sexism in advertising is not to be found in 'what happens', but in the ubiquity of the male in the final voice-over, even in ads portraying or aimed at women, or which pay lip-service to the 'modern liberated woman'. An example is an ad for New Actimel Yogurt Drink from Danone. Though this begins with a woman's voice observing that 'Being a model and a Mum can be difficult to juggle' against images suggesting that, despite the difficulty, she very successfully does achieve this balance, it is an interposed male voice which sums up the product's virtues and provides us with the quasi-scientific information that it contains 'a unique culture L. Casei Imunitass'. Although women's voices are used for tampons; foreign accents for exotic food, alcoholic drinks or perfume; regional or working-class accents for humorous effect in the advertising of cheaper necessities; the most authoritative summarizing voices are almost always those of indigenous educated middle-class males, especially in safety campaigns and ads for expensive durables and financial services.

4.7 Prosody

The fact that writing is in part a representation of speech which, even when not actually read aloud, may form a 'sound image' in the mind gives rise to another paralinguistic phenomenon, which is prevalent in both advertising and literary discourse. This is **prosody,** the patterning of sound most commonly associated with verse and poetry, but also present in prose and in spoken discourse, especially conversation or polemic (Tannen 1989). It includes such phenomena as rhyme, rhythm, assonance, consonance and alliteration, and can be found both in speech, and in writing perceived as speech. It is discussed in Chapter 6.

Exercises

1   Visualize the McDonalds logo. What makes it so memorable? Why was it chosen, and what kind of meanings does it carry?
2   What is suggested by the lettering in the following logos?

Figure 4.18   Kodak, Ford and Kellogg's logos.

3   What are the effects of handwriting in the following?

In Man's fragrance
lies his Culture.
Love and Passion,
The Theatre of life,
The sense of one's origins and family.
The signs of Man That
linger in The Memory.

Gianni Versace
Profumi

Figure 4.19   From an ad for Gianni Versace perfume.

4a An ad for The Science Museum consisted of the following paragraph, in small type, repeated over and over again. What type of signification is this?

> Cloning. How is it done? What are
> the implications? And is it right?
> Cloning. How is it done? What are
> the implications? And is it right?

b Consider the emblem of The Natural History museum in London in Figure 4.20. How many different things does it signify, and how? (Name at least six.)

THE
NATURAL
HISTORY
MUSEUM

Figure 4.20 Emblem of The Natural History Museum.

5 Look back at the ads illustrated in this chapter. To what extent do you find their exploitation of graphology
   • original
   • artistic
   • effective in selling the product?
   How do these criteria relate to each other?
6 Watch, and if possible record, an advertising break and a news bulletin. Analyse and compare the uses of paralanguage in each.

Further reading

Semiotics

The theories of Saussure are easily accessible and readable in the *Course in General Linguistics*. Wade Baskin's translation is good, and the most relevant parts are the Introduction III–VI; Part 1 I–III; Part 2 I–V.

Bakhtin's critique of Saussure can be found in Volosinov (1988) *Marxism and the Philosophy of Language*, pp. 45–61.

Peirce's own writings are both more voluminous and more obscure (though see Peirce in the Bibliography). A good introduction to his ideas, together with an analysis of semiotics in general, can be found in Chapter 4 of Lyons (1977) *Semantics*.

An excellent introduction to semiotics is Daniel Chandler's *Semiotics: The Basics*.

The paralanguage of writing and design

An overview, discussion, and theoretical framework for the analysis of visual design and its relation to writing can be found in Gunther Kress and Theo van Leeuwen (1996). *Reading Images: the Grammar of Visual Design*. Particularly relevant to the issues dealt with here are Chapter 1, 'The Semiotic Landscape', and Chapter 6, 'The Meaning of Composition'.

Analysis and description of the paralanguage of writing itself can be found in Susan Walker (2001) *Typography and Language: Prescriptions and Practices*. A further useful source is James Hartley (1994) *Designing Instructional Text*.

Part II
Text

5　Words and phrases

People don't want a mortgage, they want a home.

(Leeds Building Society)

5.1 Meaning and genre

Part I has examined the many ways in which advertising exploits both what is around the language of ads (situation, accompanying discourse, music and pictures) and what is, as it were, 'inside' that language, created by the imaginative use of graphic and phonic paralanguage. Those exploitations change the linguistic message, making it more personal and more immediate, more dependent upon particular people and situations, more emotive, and less determinate. Working against this kind of communication is a literate culture's belief and ideal that a written text – and thus by extension language itself – can, and should, free communication of such qualities, creating meanings which are unambiguous and determinate, no longer dependent on individuals or situation, shared and objective rather than personal and subjective. This perceived potential of text to embody impersonal facts is commonly striven for in scientific prose, news reporting and legal documents, where reference to both sender and situation are avoided by such linguistic strategies as the use of the passive ('It was placed' rather than 'I put it'), impersonal constructions ('There are growing fears that' rather than 'We are worried that') and nominal constructions ('Non-payment of the tax will result in prosecution' rather than 'If you don't pay, we shall fine you'). Ironically, in view of their pretensions to objectivity, these habits imply a belief more in keeping with magic than with science: that a particular form of words somehow alters what happened, deleting the real agent as well as the grammatical one.

Yet even if there is a potential in language – and in particular in writing – to eliminate the personal and emotional, it is not the case that text, when insulated from its substance and situation, carries only shared, precise and unambiguous meanings. While the lawyer and the scientist may strive – albeit without hope of total success – to rid words of a subjectivity which they deem undesirable, other writers may seek to maximize it. These

	Discourse	Function	Use	Trichotomy
1	Scientific	Descriptive	Informative	Cognitive
2	Poetic	Appraisive	Valuative	Affective
3	Religious	Prescriptive	Incitive	Conative

Figure 5.1 Three types of discourse (adapted from Holbrook 1987).

opposite tendencies have often been used to distinguish two major categories of discourse: the scientific and the poetic. A third tendency is to
use words to prescribe the behaviour of others, as in moral and religious
treatises. This tripartite division of discourse, as observed by Holbrook
(1987), has ancient roots – it echoes Plato's **trichotomy** of rhetoric as cognitive, affective or conative – but it is also relevant to the identification of
contemporary genres such as advertising.

Different suppositions about the intentions of a writer and purposes of
discourse will yield quite different value judgements about the same text.
Expressions which might be perceived as lies, or as too personal and vague
in a scientific treatise, yield positive reactions when presented as a work of
fiction or as a poem.

> As Gregor Samsa awoke one morning from uneasy dreams he found
> himself transformed in his bed into a gigantic insect

is, for example, the opening of *Metamorphosis*, a novel by Franz Kafka. It
would have struck the reader in a quite different way as the opening of a
biography.

> I have been one acquainted with the night.

is the opening line of a poem by Robert Frost. It would have had a quite different effect had he used it to open a conversation. The lesson of such comparisons is that the 'truth' of a sentence cannot be assessed in isolation from
its discoursal context, as logicians have rashly supposed. There are many
types of utterance, including metaphorical ones, to which the issue of truth or
falsehood is of no relevance. They can, as E.H. Gombrich wrote of pictures

> No more be true or false than a statement can be blue or green.
>
> (Gombrich 1977: 68)

A major problem in the evaluation of advertising arises from the difficulty
of assigning it neatly to any one of the three macro categories of discourse in
Figure 5.1, leading to dispute over its moral and aesthetic status. It is
unusual in being balanced between all of these categories. In the eyes of
both manufacturer and consumers, its major function is conative (if most
frequently in soft-sell ads by implication), aiming to persuade people to do

something or to buy something, yet it is often judged as though it were descriptive, and criticised for misrepresenting or distracting from the facts. Yet its use of language and other modes is often closer to the poetic, tending towards the personal, the specific, the ambiguous and the indeterminate.

5.2 Determinate and indeterminate meanings

Chapter 1 discussed descriptions of meaning which break words down into components, and then use these components to establish sense relations between words (Section 1.5). Like scientific discourse, such descriptions of the denotation of words dwell upon, and elevate, the degree to which meanings are both fixed and shared by all speakers. They derive from Saussurean semiology: the denotation of a word is an analysis of its signified; its sense is its relation to other signs. Even prototype theory, though it moves some way towards accommodating individual variation, seeks to find out, in laboratory experiments, what is held in common by speakers and to relate words to each other through these common context-free meanings. It is often assumed, usually without much question, that semantic representations of meaning also have psychological reality: that they are not, in other words, just conveniences for linguists, or the fruits of controlled experiments, but are used in the processing of language and the understanding of what words refer to in actual communication.

In addition to these supposedly shared and stable semantic meanings, there is also **pragmatic** meaning – what a word or utterance means and does in a particular context. Pragmatic meaning is not usually conceived as an alternative to semantic meaning, however, but as dependent upon it, deriving from the interaction of semantic meaning with context. Yet a word has many aspects for its user other than its denotation, which supposedly persists across different contexts, and its pragmatic function, which supposedly varies systematically across contexts. These aspects of a word are so many and so vast that knowledge of them will vary considerably from user to user. A word has an etymology, a diachronic history, connotations, **collocations**,[1] translation equivalents, personal associations, metonymic and metaphorical uses (both standard and original), **homonyms**,[2] associations with certain genres, with images, with encyclopedic knowledge, and meanings which derive from the patterns it forms with the words around it (see Chapter 6).

Both semantics and pragmatics assume that meaning is arrived at by the application of rules: componential analysis, sense relations, logic from semantics; conversational principles (see Section 7.3) and speech acts theory from pragmatics. But neither fully describes what meaning is to participants in discourse. As attempts to theorise and describe the ways in which linguistic communication works, they reflect an understandable desire to have some reasonably solid ground to stand on, in an otherwise treacherous landscape. If your job is to describe language, it is quite sensible to tackle meaning through semantics and pragmatics, because they do provide reasonably clear-cut procedures for formulating meaning. These kinds of meaning are important to participants in certain spheres – of law, commerce, science – where people attach particular importance to the social or practical consequences of exact wording, or feel responsible for outcomes which they judge important, and where they seek to maximize, through precision, the degree to which meaning is shared. Such discourse is often confrontational, and the relationships they embody are competitive, making people actually seek to misunderstand, to catch each other out! This is not to say, however, that this is always or entirely how participants in discourse make their own meanings or perceive those of other people, especially in secure situations.

It is quite possible that, while an observer of human behaviour may formulate clear-cut rules to describe what is happening, the people he or she is observing may be using experience, rules of thumb, and guesswork (Dreyfus 1987). This is an argument advanced by Searle (ironically a leading formulator of rules for pragmatics: Searle 1975a, b). In a television debate,[3] he argued fervently against attempts to explain all behaviour in terms of rules and procedures which can be modelled on computer. He pointed out that there are complex mathematical formulae for calculating the trajectory of a ball bounced off a wall relative to the position of a person and a dog running alongside that wall. His own dog, he tells us, is an expert at catching such a ball in its mouth – but it is unlikely that it does this by using the formulae, either consciously or subconsciously. As Searle said, very excitedly: 'THE DOG JUST KNOWS!' In many situations the relationship of words to participants is rather like the relationship of Searle's dog to the ball. Both language and bouncing balls may move too fast for calculation, and are better handled by experienced guesswork.

It is the less determinate, less rule-bound types of meaning which are most frequently exploited in advertising, and on which analysis of advertising must therefore concentrate. For advertising, unlike semantics and pragmatics, does not seek to steady the ground of meaning beneath our feet, but to make it sway. Nor does it share much in common with the logical public debate of law and science; it rather adopts the features of personal interaction. Coming at its addressee when he or she is at home (relaxing with family or friends in front of the television) or alone (reading a magazine, listening to a car radio, logged on to the Internet) it talks to him or her as 'you', in the most colloquial language, about the most personal subjects (health, sex, ageing, sanitation, food, relationships) in settings which assume access to the most private – if most common – fantasies, fears and aspirations. Nor is the communication between advertiser and consumer always discussed among people who have seen the ad; the experience often remains private even if it may take place in company. In such circumstances, to focus on logical and literal meanings is to miss the point. A discourse analysis for advertising – and many other genres –

must be one which can consider the indeterminate and emotive. This second part of the book attempts to consider some of these types of meaning: first in individual words, and then in longer linguistic units.

5.3 Indeterminate meanings in ads: connotations

Advertisers have a predilection for strategies which distract from or add to the literal meaning of language. This may be effected at the graphic level through deviant spellings (Theakston's Old Peculier Ale; Beanz Meanz Heinz; Neauvember (an Eau Perrier ad)) or by fusing two words (Generationext (Pepsi); Dunlopillo). A popular use of both of these techniques is found in ads referring obliquely to the World Wide Web:

Slowwwenia   (a tourist office ad);
www.e'll help you catch more customers   (G&S net)
get around the www.orld for a quid   (Easy Jet)
Three.internetaccessdealstochoosefrom.com   (clara.net)
Don't search, just yell.com   (Yellow Pages)

At syllable level, ads sometimes exploit a resemblance between a product name and one or more syllables of another word, as in an ad for the Linn Motor Group:

Linndividual Linngineering Linntelligent Linnviromental Linntensive care AdrenaLinn Linnvestment Linn Motor Group

At word level, literal meaning can be undermined in many ways, most obviously by puns:

'Secs Machine' (for an Accurist watch); 'Get Rich Quick' (for Kenco Instant Coffee)

5.3.1 Perfume and cars

Paramount among the techniques for extending denotational meanings is the exploitation of **connotation** – the vague association which a word may have for a whole speech community or for groups or individuals within it. Connotations are both variable and imprecise. The connotations of 'dog' might include such different qualities as loyalty, dirtiness, inferiority, sexual promiscuity, friendliness; of 'stallion' such qualities as sexual potency, freedom, nobility.

I shall examine connotations in ads by looking at the presentation of two very different products: perfume and cars. Both are advertised extensively on TV and in magazines; cars are also often advertised – appropriately – on roadside hoardings. As products they are in some ways polar opposites, in others very similar. Cars are perceived as an expensive necessity, while perfume is a luxury (priced perhaps just high enough to be perceived by many people as indulgently extravagant for oneself, or lovingly generous as a gift). More than other products, they are both marketed and perceived as expressions of the self and of sexuality: a woman is her perfume, a man is his car.[4]

Traditionally, perfume advertising has been aimed at women. (Prejudice against homosexuality led male perfumes to be described euphemistically and with a false functionalism as 'after-shave' and 'anti-perspirant'.) Car ads, on the other hand were traditionally aimed primarily at men. Although the general bias still persists, the traditional target markets of both products now include both sexes. There are now many car ads – albeit often for smaller cars – aimed at women, or acknowledging the woman's interest in a couple's purchase. To some extent this reflects changed social attitudes to the roles of men and women; but, while the target markets may be merging, the roles ascribed to users are not. While perfume ads appeal to both men and women almost exclusively as lovers, there is a difference in the presentation of the two sexes in car ads. Men are not only lovers but also husbands, fathers, loners, technical experts, general status-seekers and responsible guardians of the planet's ecology (!); women are almost always only partners of men. A further complication to this association of product with one sex is that perfume – by virtue of its price, size, luxury and sensuality – is very frequently a gift of one partner to another, and as such is likely to be purchased by someone of the opposite sex from its consumer (though 'unromantic' partners may say which perfume they want beforehand, or take their gift back afterwards). Like other products playing a role in sexual relationships, both car and perfume ads tend to assume a heterosexual market – notwithstanding some breaks with this tradition in recent perfume ads.

The differences between the products lead to different techniques. Perfume ads are ticklers with very short copy (typically under ten words, sometimes with no more than the brand name itself). Car ads, on the other hand, though also 'ticklers', mix in reasons and are thus typically long-copy ads. (This distinction is complicated by the fact that some 'reasons' in car ads are so abstruse that they become ticklers. The Toyota Celica for example has 'VVVT-I engine technology' – but how many readers of the ad actually know what that is?) In keeping with their status as necessities purchased by the user rather than as gifts, campaigns for cars are typically slow-drip, while perfume, a luxurious gift, is intensely sudden-burst, especially before Christmas. The two products thus provide many contrasts.

5.3.2 Perfume names and ads

As a product, perfume not only contrasts with 'big-buy' durables like cars, but also is very different from many other luxuries. It is not an item brought into existence by marketing – like 'panty shields' (worn between periods), or 'shake and vac' (a powder first sold in the 1960s to be sprinkled on the carpet and then hoovered up!). Its history is ancient, its cultural importance universal. (Gell (1977), for example, describes its importance in the hunting, magic and dream augury of the Umeda of Papua New Guinea – a society as different from contemporary urban capitalist society as it is possible to imagine.) Yet, though it predates advertising, perfume also suits it – as an archetypical luxury. Unless it has exactly the smell of something widely known, it is also, of its nature, indescribable in words. Descriptions of a smell are necessarily indirect: synaesthetic, referring to one sense in terms of another ('sharp', 'sour', 'gentle' 'dark'), metonymic ('high society'), metaphorical ('poisonous'). A perfume may be described in terms of its effect ('seductive', 'overpowering'), the kind of person who might use it ('manly'), the place where one might find it ('oriental'), or by reference to its availability ('exclusive', 'rare'). All such descriptions may serve as indices of a particular smell, but depend very much upon that individual knowledge and association. It is impossible to describe the smell – which is apparently what matters – with any precision. (Arguably, this applies to all descriptions but, in degree, perfume is an extreme case.) A smell has no denotation, no component which distinguishes it from another!

Paradoxically, this resistance to description increases rather than decreases the verbal freedom of the advertiser. A new perfume can be called virtually anything. The naming of cars, by contrast, is more circumscribed. The name 'Jaguar' could not easily be given to a small, slow, two-door, two-cylinder hatchback. The peculiar relation of perfume to language allows the naming and description of perfumes to illuminate a process which is more limited and disguised in the naming and description of products whose features are more amenable to precise description. The Jaguar car, for example, shares certain (but not all) denotational components with the animal. Though it may not have hair or suckle live-born young as the animal does, it is streamlined and accelerates faster than others of its kind. This degree of equivalence between signifieds justifies the metaphor. But the name also invokes the connotations of the word 'jaguar' – which might include – always allowing for imprecision and personal variation – such associations as rarity, beauty, superiority, aggression, violence, sexuality, devouring of smaller creatures, and so on. (Unfortunately for the advertiser a successful naming contains its own destruction, for a well-established trade name like Jaguar soon comes to signify the product directly, rather than via another signified. In Britain, Ajax is primarily the name of a cleaning powder, not a Greek warrior.) In the naming of a perfume, a metaphor must be created, often invoking a comparison between effects. Take for example the name 'Poison'. Poison is a liquid which kills (literally); Poison perfume is a liquid which kills (metaphorically), and both are used by a *femme fatale*. Even when a perfume is given a simple manufacturer's name (Chanel, Armani) this carries connotations of its country of origin or other products of the same manufacturer. All descriptions create qualities for the perfume by fusing it with something else, and with the (variable) connotations of that something else. To call a perfume 'Jaguar' would not be to *point out* that it is fast and streamlined (as in the case of the car) but to *create* an association with such qualities.

It is sometimes claimed that advertising proliferates where there is little difference between one product and another (Williamson 1978: 25; Hoshino 1987). One bar of soap washes your hands very much like the next. Yet even where there are differences between products they are often quite obvious, and can be easily stated, without elaborate or figurative explanation. This car costs x; its maximum speed is x; it uses x litres per mile; it has a luggage capacity of x cubic feet, etc. Though mention of such facts is occasionally adopted as a gimmick – attracting attention by its break from advertising tradition (see Chapter 10) – the contemporary ad does not dwell upon such qualities but links the product to some other entity, effect or person (all or any of which I shall refer to as **sphere),** creating a **fusion** which will imbue the characterless product with desirable qualities. Fusion is a major aim of contemporary advertising. It is for this reason that puns, metaphors, symbolism and celebrity endorsements are its stocks in trade, rather than direct appeals such as 'Lovely bananas, 50 pence a pound!'. In the naming and description of luxuries like perfumes (cigarettes, alcohol, etc.) the process of fusion does not need to plead any literal or logical equivalence between the spheres. The only relevant 'fact' is whether the perfume is liked by 'you', or by the people 'you' want to like it. As Thompson (1990) puts it:

> The rational consumer chooses at the point of purchase by comparing smells. So the rational core of a perfume ad can only really consist of a sort of nudge: 'Remember, when you *are* comparing perfumes, you might want to give X a try'. The situation would be very different if you were about to purchase a computer.
>
> (Thompson 1990: 211)

Consider the perfume name 'Opium'. Semantically the word denotes a narcotic obtained from the juice of a poppy, and this primary meaning is a well-known one (unlike Ajax). Closely related to opium are the words 'morphine' (which denotes a stronger narcotic refined from opium), and 'heroin' (which denotes an even stronger narcotic refined from morphine). There is thus little semantic difference between the terms, other than the strength and addictiveness of the drugs to which they refer, and a difference between their effects (which, like the smell of a perfume, are beyond description). That it is the connotation and not the denotation of opium which is evoked as a metaphor of the perfume is strongly suggested by the unsuitability of either 'morphine' or 'heroin' as perfume names: for whereas the connotations of opium may include the Orient, dreams, Romantic poetry, and bohemian illegality, morphine is more likely to be associated with painful diseases, hospitals and accidents, while heroin has connotations of organized crime, premature death, HIV infection, unwilling prostitution and urban poverty.

The perfume name Opium thus relies on connotation. Yet it is not necessarily the case, as many analysts assume without evidence, that denotational meaning must precede connotational meaning in language processing. Bonney and Wilson (1990), for example, discussing an ad for Fidji perfume, which shows the naked shoulders of a woman with a snake entwined round her neck like a necklace, write:

> But the picture is to be read not simply as a woman holding a bottle of perfume with a serpent round her neck. The point of the serpent is to signify temptation, which it does by virtue of it place in the story of the Fall in 'Genesis'. Thus it is the connotation of that element, not its denotation, which is of prime importance. However the denotation is not irrelevant. Indeed, it is a condition of the connotation. For if the coloured shape round the woman's neck were not read first as a serpent, it could not also be read as signifying temptation.
>
> (Bonney and Wilson 1990: 192)

Yet it is possible that the image is perceived firstly as a signifier of *temptation* (which may be attractive) and only optionally as a snake (which may well be repulsive). (In a similar way, the processing of a dead metaphor – 'he hit the roof' – may not involve its literal meaning.) Thus Opium may be interpreted only connotationally. If it is interpreted in both ways, its connotations hover between the repugnant and the attractively illegal: a border area which exerts a compelling fascination. Many other names select such daring choices, often elevating attitudes – especially sexual attitudes – in a way which seems to defy both traditional patriarchal morality, and feminism. The name 'Tramp', for example, is a term of sexist abuse for a woman who 'sleeps around', and as such would not be welcomed by a woman who accepts traditional values. Yet the word, and the attitude to women it encapsulates, would be rejected – or need to be appropriated in a different sense – by many feminists. Nevertheless, the name is presumably assumed to appeal to women.

Perhaps the most effective names are those which arouse many different connotations simultaneously, allowing the product to appeal to incompatible desires within one person, or to different types of people. When I asked a group of students about the connotations of the perfume name 'White Linen' I received contradictory answers. Associations included 'purity', 'a freshly made bed (ready for sex)', 'a holiday in a good hotel', 'cleanliness', 'first communion' and 'a rite of passage from girlhood to womanhood'. (Of course the pictures in the ads for this perfume restricted such connotations. One, for example, showed a modestly dressed woman pacing pensively on a sunny Mediterranean balcony.)

The effect of names is often modified by their preservation, untranslated, for a foreign market. Many French and Italian perfumes are marketed with their original names to English-speaking consumers. Where the meaning is widely known (*Illicite, Il Bacio, Eau Sauvage*) they may preserve their original connotations, simply attracting the extra connotations of the culture of which they are an index. Where the word is unlikely to be known, the situation is different. The French word *griffe* for example can mean either 'claw mark' or 'designer label'. In a French-speaking market, therefore, the perfume name *Ma Griffe* unites elements of meaning as follows:

FRENCH Denotation:	*Meaning 1* my designer label	*Meaning 2* my claw mark	*Meaning 3* the perfume
Possible connotations:	good taste, wealth	passion, wildness	(gained from 1 and 2)

Figure 5.2 Meanings of *Ma Griffe* in French.

(In addition it is neatly ambiguous as to the owner of the mark or label: a claw mark on the skin belongs both to the animal which made it, and to the person who received it; a designer label belongs both to the designer and to the person who wears the clothes.)

In English, where the meaning of this word is unlikely to be known to most purchasers, a quite different fusion is effected, which may be represented as follows:

ENGLISH Denotation:	*Meaning 1* (unknown)	*Meaning 2* the perfume
Indexical of:	Frenchness	
Connotations:	romance, sophistication, etc.	romance, etc. (gained from 1)

Figure 5.3 Meanings of *Ma Griffe* in English.

Even where naming is motivated by some sharing of components, it is the connotations which follow from the comparison which matter. This broad difference exists in literary metaphor too. In Ezra Pound's poem *In a Station of the Metro*

The apparition of these faces in the crowd;
  Petals on a wet, black bough.

the comparison is justified by a degree of equivalence – both metro and bough are cylindrical and dark, both passengers and petals are paler and smaller than this background. Yet it is the variable and indeterminate con-notations of the 'petals' and 'bough' (of fragility, transience, etc.) which give the equivalence its power (for some people). In other metaphors, the nature of an abstract topic can be understood only by attracting to itself the qualities of a physical correlate (what T.S. Eliot termed an 'objective correlative') for the ineffable (Myers and Simms 1989: 211). Such metaphors are common – perhaps essential – to the description of the abstract and spiritual (freedom, peace, the love of god, poetic genius) and also the most physical (smells, pain, sexual pleasure). Indeed, the abstract entity or the sensation may only be able to exist conceptually through the metaphor (Lakoff and Johnson 1980: 110). In perfume ads the vehicle creates features for both the physical and abstract nature of the perfume:

Valentino. Not just a perfume. A rite of passage.

5.4 Car names and ads

Where a product is both unnamed and indescribable the options for the advertiser are immense. The wide connotative power of the names of new perfumes is a testimony to the seizure of this opportunity. (In literature the naming of characters offers similar potential, though options are limited by temporal and historical setting.) Not all products offer such freedoms. They may inherit a mundane name from a less publicity-con-scious age or be constrained by obvious facts. In either case the nature of the imposition may be neutral, positive (by happy chance) or in the worst cases negative (Milka Lila Pause chocolate, Shmuckers mustard, Pre-Gestive Tea). This is complicated by the positive connotations which a firm or brand name attracts to itself as years pass (Heinz, Kelloggs, Ford – or PG Tips, as Pre-Gestive Tea was renamed in 1955). One way for the advertiser to escape a negative connotation is to confront it with humour:

Milka Lila Pause – hate the name, love the chocolate.

or

Shmuckers – with a name like that, it's gotta be good.

Cars, more than perfumes, typically belong to this category of products which inherit a neutral name. They may make use of metonymy (a Fiesta car goes to a fiesta; a Skylark is to be found in the open country) but such names combine with trade names,[5] the alliterative Ford Fiesta or the rhyth-mic Buick Skylark, and these names are often followed by a figure indicat-ing cylinder number or engine capacity. This restricted potential of cars to effect fusion with another sphere through names, combined with the tendency of car ads to use longer copy, means that the fusion more often takes place, not at word level, but in longer stretches of text. Yet it still happens. Despite a sprinkling of technical data in the long copy of car ads, 'you' are rarely sold a car alone. Just as much as with perfumes, though more verbosely, 'you' are also sold yourself in an attractive persona, role or environment. Thus in an ad for the BMW5 each part of the car was equated to a feature of a fit and healthy human body: the seats are its flexible spine, the warning devices its alert ears, the dials its eyes. An ad for the Volvo 740 Turbo left 'you' embracing a lightly clad woman on an empty beach after a happy day's surfing. A Toyota moved with the elegance of a thoroughbred racehorse. A Saab driver was as alert as a fighter pilot and supported by the same computer technology. Et cetera, et cetera. There are perhaps as many examples as there are makes and marks of cars.

5.4.1 Long-copy car ads: an example

In illustration of how fusion is created in text, and of how words and phrases take on extra dimensions of meaning from context, as discourse, let us consider in detail a magazine car ad for the Subaru estate 1.8 and Justy 1.2 (Figure 5.4). The text is as follows:

> The Subaru of his and hers
>
> The Subaru of his and hers. Or how to keep your marriage on the road. Faithfully through the rough and the smooth. Through stormy weather and the big freeze. Gripping stuff, Subaru four-wheel drive. The world and his wife's favourite in fact. With $1\frac{1}{2}$ million four-wheel drives to prove it. Mind you, it only takes two to make a perfect marriage. The Justy for one. The world's first 1.2 4WD supermini. A poetic little mover. 3 valves per cylinder. 5–speed box. 3 or 5 doors. From only £6,198 what's more. The other partner? A Subaru estate, of course. Marries all the practical virtues to sheer desirability. With seven models to choose from. Starting at just £8,599. Which means you can both be in Subaru four-wheel drive for less than £15,000. A small price to pay for lasting harmony, don't you think?

Of the twenty-two **orthographic sentences** (groups of words bounded by a capital and a full stop) only one contains a main verb ('marries'). The text is presented alongside a picture, in which the two cars are shown parked outside a house beside the sea with roses growing around the doorway. Two Labrador dogs are beside the upper car. The dogs and the cars face in opposite directions. What is not clear from the black-and-white reproduction is that the picture is in two colours only: the cars and the roses are red, everything else is blue. The picture presents a number of pairs, pairs of pairs, and pairs within pairs: picture/text; blue/red; pets/cars; dog/bitch; house/car; car/car; land/sea; front wheels/back wheels.

Figure 5.4 'The Subaru of his and hers': advertisement for the Subaru Estate 1.8 and Justy 1.2.

The text imposed on the picture, 'The Subaru of his and hers', which is also the first line of the copy, contains a verbal pairing: 'his'/'hers'. It is also linguistically odd. A more usual way of expressing the same meaning, in narrow semantic terms, might be: 'His Subaru and her Subaru' or 'A man's and a woman's Subaru'. The oddness attracts attention (it may even be intended to evoke Japanese English) but, more importantly, it fuses genres. Its grammatical structure – a definite noun phrase post-modified by a prepositional phrase with 'of'

> (The NP (of NP))

is typical of story titles: *The Wizard of Oz, The Master of Ballantrae, The Lord of the Rings, The Tale of Jemima Puddleduck.* The next unit further encourages this impression; the word *or* after such a construction often introduces a subtitle, and a non-finite noun clause with the structure

>   VP   NP   PP
> [how (to x) (your x)   (x)]

is typical of subtitles of advisory or cautionary tales with a humorous bent ('How to make friends' or 'How to get ahead in business'). Interpreted as the title of a story, the product name, by virtue of its position in the opening unit, fuses with words which might occupy the same slot:

>   tale
> the   story   of his and hers.
>   Subaru

With only the slightest alteration (the replacement of 'the' with a demonstrative 'this' or 'that') the phrase becomes one typical of casual conversation.

> (DEMONSTRATIVE   NOUN   (of (POSSESSIVE PRONOUN)))
> (These   scissors   (of (mine)))
> (That   dog   (of (yours)))
> (That   friend   (of (his)))

I am omitting the words 'and hers' because, though they *can* be included in the grammatical analysis

> (The Subaru (of (<his and hers>)))

discoursally they do not belong. They are like an afterthought:

> The Subaru of his and – oh, I almost forgot and it's not so important anyway – of hers.

If the speaker or story-teller had had this phrase in mind from the beginning he (not she) would have said

> The Subaru of theirs.

As it stands, the construction not only presents 'of hers' as an afterthought, but also iconically represents in its grammatical form a separation
between 'him' and 'her'. The addressees are not 'they' but 'he – and she': a
man and a wife who go their separate ways. To make a parallel with a
similar use in literature, this same odd separated pronominal is used to
similar effect by James Joyce at the end of his short story *The Dead* when
describing a couple who are alienated from each other:

> He watched her while she slept, as though he and she had never lived
> together as man and wife.

> (Joyce, *The Dead*: 219)

Semantically, the signified of 'his and hers' is the same as that of 'theirs',
but the effect is quite different (Cook 1986).

This initial relegation of the woman to a secondary place by means of
grammar rather than meaning may explain a rather unusual but unani-
mous interpretation of this text, by people asked to recall it after one
reading. The ad creates the impression that it is addressed to the man of
the couple rather than the woman, and secondly that it is the larger of the
two cars which is for the man. Yet neither of these ideas is expressed
directly – they are only insinuated. Certainly, they are partly activated by
cultural schemata which the ad does nothing to contradict, but they are
also immediately reinforced by the secondary position of 'and hers'.

From its outset, the copy evokes the genres of story and casual conversation. The ad's 'own' style is difficult to identify; it exists parasitically by
attaching itself to these hosts. The verbless orthographic sentences use both
the elliptical utterances of conversation and the verbless phrases and
clauses of titles and headlines. Story-telling, already suggested by the title,
is again evoked by the phrase 'gripping stuff' (punningly referring both to
the story and the car's four-wheel drive), though as a comment *on* the story
rather than part *of* it, it also belongs to casual conversation. From this
phrase onward story-telling gives way to a conversational style which persists to the very end, evoked by fillers typical of conversational discourse
('in fact', 'mind you', 'of course'), interrogatives which imply the presence
of an interlocutor ('The other partner?', 'Don't you think?') and ellipses
which appear to complete and support utterances of that interlocutor:

> Ø Which means you can both be ...
> Ø Marries all the practical virtues to sheer desirability.

These last sentences both presuppose a grammatical head recoverable
from a previous sentence – respectively a noun phrase which the relative

clause can post-modify, and a noun phrase to act as subject for the verb. Although these can be found, they lend the whole text an air of being one half of a conversation, the answers to questions supplied by 'you'. Alternatively one may read the whole as a dialogue between two speakers with breaks in text corresponding to a change of voice, or as two voices both addressed to 'you'. In all these readings, the form of the text – whether as a story or as conversation – is interactive. It is not disembodied information, but a personal communication. The discourse types imply this presence: a story needs an audience as well as a teller, a conversation involves at least two people. Who are these two participants? Two men talking about cars in the absence of women? The probability of this impression cannot be ignored simply because it cannot be proved by semantic or logical analysis. Elusiveness and resistance to proof are the strength of such insinuation. It is equivalent at discourse level to the connotation of a word: personal, variable and more powerful than literal meanings.

The skilful avoidance of explicit reference to the male point of view under cover of addressing two partners is rather undermined at the end of the ad, where the coupon to cut out says:

Please send **me** details of the Subaru range

not 'Please send **us** ...'. Could there have been a lack of communication between skilful copy-writer and clumsy coupon designer? We know, I think, which partner 'me' refers to.

Within the general frame of these two dialogic genres (story and conversation), the sphere with which the product fuses is marriage. The cars are *like* a husband and wife, *for* a husband and wife, and create marital harmony. Like the picture, the text is full of verbal pairs, noun phrases coordinated by a conjunction: 'his and hers', 'the rough and the smooth', 'stormy weather and the big freeze', 'The world and his wife'. Semantically, there are many words which refer to dualities: 'marriage', 'two', 'partner', 'marries', 'both', 'harmony', 'other'. In addition there are many words and phrases which collocate equally with cars, with marriage, or one or other of the sexes. The metaphorical clause

how to keep your marriage on the road

takes a dead and clichéd metaphor in which marriage is compared to driving, and revivifies it by reversing it – it is driving which is compared to a marriage rather than vice versa. Once this fusion is established, every subsequent description can apply to either the marriage, or one of the partners, or one of the cars: 'Faithfully through the rough and the smooth', 'stormy weather and the big freeze', 'it only takes two to make a perfect marriage', 'lasting harmony'. The phrase 'a poetic little mover' can be both a male-to-male description of an attractive woman or of a car; while 'marries all the practical virtues to sheer desirability' sounds like a traditional description of the perfect husband. (These are perhaps the clearest indications in the text as to which car is for which partner.)

In this ad, aimed at the man of a middle-aged couple, the couple is presented as a solution to marital tension. The disjunction of the opening 'his and hers' becomes the 'lasting marital harmony' of the end. As with the single-word or short-phrase names of perfumes, it is not the literal denotational meaning which matters – that the car has four-wheel drive, grips the road, or is reliable – but, rather, the indeterminate and unprovable implications. This is not only the case with those shorter phrases, such as the 'rough and the smooth' or 'gripping stuff', which are ready-made chunks and can be treated as though they are single lexical items; it is also true of longer units, like 'marries all the practical virtues to sheer desirability'. Unlike word connotation, which a word may activate on its own, these extra dimensions of meaning are dependent on the pictorial and discoursal context.

In this ad, the marriage metaphor (itself a marriage) is multidimensional, for there are many interlocking figurative and literal marriages in both picture and text: between man and woman, car and car, two people and the two cars, car and road, practical virtues and sheer desirability, big car and man, little car and woman, purchase and marital harmony, funds and expenditure, front-wheel drive and back-wheel drive (a pair of pairs), as well as the additional pairs I have already listed for the picture. What these pairings effect is an image of a harmony in which everything in the human, natural and social world fits complacently together (as in the Wrigley's ad in Section 3.5). Sexual stereotypes are reinforced without being explicitly stated, and nothing, not even the sea and the land, is allowed to exist outside this binary universe. The abstract qualities of the relationship between the sexes are expressed by concrete metaphorical vehicles. If we split each pair and arrange them so that each component relates not only syntagmatically to its partner but also paradigmatically to the other pairs, then the world of this ad becomes much clearer:

Male	Female
driver	car
rough	smooth
Estate	Justy
£8,599	£6,198
1.8	1.2
road	home
world	wife
cars	pets
red	blue
practical	poetic
dog	bitch
car	house

In semiotic terms, the ad not only uses existing denotations and sense relations, but also creates new ones: two composite and parallel lexical sets signifying 'maleness' and 'femaleness'.

5.4.2 A literary comparison

Lest one suppose that it is only in the trivial discourse of advertising that such a seamless mythology of the masculine and feminine could exist, it may be instructive to compare the binary oppositions established in this ad with those in a literary text on a similar theme: the speeches at the opening of the third act of *Romeo and Juliet*. Here Romeo, after a single night with Juliet, is anxious to depart for fear of discovery by her family. Initial discord has yielded briefly to harmony, though one which is soon to be broken. The text is as follows:

Juliet:	Wilt thou be gone? It is not yet near day:
	It was the nightingale, and not the lark,
	That pierc'd the fearful hollow of thine ear;
	Nightly she sings on yon pomegranate tree;
	Believe me, love, it was the nightingale.
Romeo:	It was the lark, the herald of the morn,
	No nightingale: look, love, what envious streaks
	Do lace the severing clouds in yonder east;
	Night's candles are burnt out, and jocund day
	Stands tiptoe on the misty mountain tops:
	I must be gone and live or stay and die.

(*Romeo and Juliet* III: v: 1–11)

Though comparison of so respected a passage with one so lightly dismissed may seem far-fetched, artificial or pretentious, it has more in its favour than might at first appear, and rejection of the comparison may need arguing quite as much as acceptance. Both the Subaru ad and the parting speeches create an image of masculinity and femininity through a series of binary opposition. Those in the Subaru ad have been listed above; those in the speeches are as follows:

Female	Male
Juliet	Romeo
question	answer
stays	goes
night	day
garden	mountain tops
nightingale	lark
death	life
sleeping	waking
hollow	candles

In the ad, as we have seen, there are parallels between pairs both within the picture, between picture and text and within the text. In the speeches, when considered as written text, such interconnections are inevitably linguistic only (although on stage or film, there may be visual parallels too). Thus many utterances of Romeo's repeat the grammatical structures of Juliet's while substituting new lexis which reverses or changes the meaning:

	S/NP	P/VP	C/NP
Juliet:	(it)	(was)	(the nightingale)
Romeo:	(it)	(was)	(the lark)

			C/NP
Juliet:	and	(not)	(the lark)
Romeo:		(no	nightingale)

	P/IMPERATIVE VP	Od/NP	VOC NP
Juliet:	(Believe)	(me)	(love)
Romeo:	(Look),		(love)

	P/VP	Od/NP	PP	o/NP
Juliet:	(pierced)	(the fearful hollow	(of	(thine ear)))
Romeo:	(do lace)	(the severing clouds	(in	(yonder east)))

Other lines maintain the semantic content of the other lover's words while transforming the syntactic structure, as in Romeo's declarative echo of Juliet's interrogative:

Juliet:	Wilt thou be gone?
Romeo:	I must be gone.

The last line sums up the tension between parallel structure and divergent meaning in

(go)	and	(live)
(stay)	and	(die)

This counterpoint of repetition and alteration represents the conflicting motivations of the two speakers: repetition reflecting convergence and the desire to stay; changes reflecting divergence and the need to go. Perhaps the most obvious pairing – and one so obvious that it is easily overlooked – is that of the two speeches themselves. They are almost equal in length, although Romeo's, with significant asymmetry, has an extra, summary line. They have a number of lexical items in common (five content words and numerous pronouns and functors) and also an unusual rhythm, in which the ten-syllable line is divided, by reason of grammatical boundaries, either into four and six syllables, or seven and three, thus potentially lending to these words, when spoken, a certain breathless and passionate irregularity.

To some extent such comparisons of literature and ads are mere provocations – though with a serious point. It is true of course that the speeches in *Romeo and Juliet* are only an extract from a much longer text within which they establish many more echoes and parallels than those I have ascribed to them here. Their sentimental and romantic view of love is but one voice within the play, balanced with others and undermined by them (the wisdom of the Nurse and the cynicism of Mercutio). It is also true that this moment of harmony is broken by subsequent disaster, and, viewed retrospectively, has a quite different meaning. Rarely are the harmonious myths of the advertising world ever set up to be shattered in this way. Yet so strong is the reverence for Shakespeare and other literary 'giants' that speeches such as these are often artificially isolated both from their co-text and from performance, and approached as if, even in isolation, they were works of art of intrinsic and autonomous merit. In one view, the comparability of these lines with an ad may be viewed as a condemnation of this isolating, extract-worshipping approach.

Whatever one's final judgement of the relevant merits of these speeches and the Subaru ad, they are similar in their formal complexity and compression, and in their ideology. Both are formally highly complex; both express very traditional images of sexual roles. In this light, though the superior acclaim accorded to Shakespeare may indeed be justified, it may also need arguing.

Exercises

1   Consider the following names of literary characters. What connotations do they have and how do they influence expectations? How have names been chosen or formed? What limitations are there on naming?

Jay Gatsby	Mrs Rouncewell	Mercutio
Mr Allworthy	Constance Chatterley	Mr Knightley
Mr Murdstone	Maurice Zapp	Sergeant Troy

What could be done to maintain the connotations of names in translation? (The name Raskolnikov in *Crime and Punishment*, for example, derives from the Russian for 'dissent', but this is lost in English.)

2   What are the connotations of the following perfume names? Can they be sorted into groups? Which are for men, which for women, and which for either? What strategies could be adopted when translating these names into another language?

Allure	Guess	America	Boss	Egoiste
Envy	Rush	Brut	Indecence	Oui
Romance	Yvresse	XS	Tabu	Versus
L'Insolent	le Baiser	Joy	Ambush	Desirade
Desire	Dune	Contradication	Cruiser	Curve
Babylone	Animale	Sport	Samsara	Hot

What would you call a new perfume?

3 Make a list of car names and consider their connotations.

4 In your opinion, is the comparison between the Subaru advertisement and the passage from *Romeo and Juliet* in this chapter a valid one? If not, what are you objections to it?

5 Consider the copy of the following car advertisements. Three are from magazines for men; one is from a magazine for women; one is from a Sunday newspaper. Can you tell which is which? How do those for aimed at men differ from those aimed at women, and how are these differences captured in the one for both?

a The Volvo C70

> SAFE SEX
> Pleasure seekers take note. The Volvo C70 was recently voted one of the world's sexiest cars*. And it comes with WHIPS as standard. (Calm down. It stands for Whiplash Protection System.) Also with SIPS (including side airbags) and driver's airbag. The Volvo C70 Coupe. From £25,665. Car featured Volvo C70 with black paint £25,870. Call 0800 070 070 for more details. www.volvo.co.uk *THE MIRROR 5/10/98

b The new Almera

> YOU TOO COULD HAVE A BODY JUST LIKE THIS.... THE CURVY BODY WE'LL BE USING TO DRAW ATTENTION TO THE NEW ALMERA WON'T BE SITTING PROVOCATIVELY ON THE CAR. IT IS THE CAR.
> Feast your eyes on this luscious young model. The new Almera. Pert, seductive and untouched by Rod Stewart. Wouldn't you love to run your hands along its distinctive surftail roofline? To caress that dramatic bonnet, airdam and the integrated headlamps? To gently stroke those 15" wheels? To let its interior softly wrap itself around you? Okay, that's enough of all that. The new Almera. Is that the deposit for one in your pocket or are you just looking? www.nissan.co.uk 0345 66 99 66

c The Jaguar S-type

VOLUPTUOUS
IS BACK
Think 'ideal weight distribution',
'curves in all the right places'.
And the vital statistics?
3.0 litre V6
240 bhp
£28,300*
For information call 0800 708060
www.jaguar.com

d The Toyota Celica

The mood this season is cool and confident, sleek and streamlined,
on the road as well as the catwalk. For a car that looks as good as
you do, choose the new Toyota Celica. It puts superbly clean
styling, smooth performance and great handling at your fingertips.
With the Celica, you're in control.
Toyota Celica – quick to respond when the heat's on.
THE CELICA GIVES YOU
• VVT-i engine technology that delivers power with economy, at
  36.7 mpg
• Class-leading power-to weight ratio to ensure perfectly bal-
  anced control
• Long wheelbase and short overhangs for good handling
• Plenty of boot space for luggage and shopping
• Excellent value at £19,255

e Volkswagen Seat

WHAT'S MINE IS MINE
'Wow,' he said, 'a System-Porsche engine. That's high-
performance.' 'I think I was supposed to be impressed or some-
thing. Frankly, all I ask from my car is that it'll get me from A to B.'
Reliably, of course. And safely.
Rather like the car in question – a Seat Ibiza. It did look stylish.
And it drove like a dream – light, precise steering that made it
incredibly easy both to turn and park.
While he was raving about the meticulous German engineering
and quality control, I was rather more impressed with interior
design: controls closer to hand, instruments easier to read.
WHAT'S HIS IS OURS
Happily we both agreed that the price (from £5,099) and running

Figure 5.5 Car marketing in 1971. 'Nudity Sells Cars. Models Helen Jones and Sue Shaw lying on a car without clothes on at the Motor Show Earls Court, which attracts a large crowd of spectators.' Courtesy of the Hulton Getty Picture Collection.

costs (ridiculously low) were absolutely ideal. (Although we bick-ered a bit about whether to go for three or five doors.)

I won, on condition that the boy-racer got to drive it home.

He thought I was joking when I told him: 'Just this once.'

6   Look at the picture in Figure 5.5, taken in 1971, and reconsider the texts in Exercise 5 (a–d of which are from the year 2000, and e from 1990). Has car marketing changed?

Further reading

On metaphor

George Lakoff and Mark Johnson (1980) *Metaphors We Live By.*
Ray Gibbs (1994) *The Poetics of Mind.*
Charles Forceville (1996) *Pictorial Metaphors in Advertising.*

On word meaning

Ronald Carter (1998) *Vocabulary.*
Jean Aitchison (1994) *Words in the Mind.*

On brand and product names

Insights into the importance and effects of naming – from very different points of view – can be found in
Paul Stobart (1994) *Brand Power.*
Nicholas Ind (1997) *The Corporate Brand.*
Naomi Klein (2000) *No Logo.*

6   Prosody, parallelism, poetry

6.1 Prosody in discourse

Prosody, the patterning of sound, lends a text an extra dimension which can reinforce, contradict or add to its meaning. Like music and paralanguage, its communicative effect is impossible to define or relate to precise referents; the attempts of literary critics to do this only emphasize its impossibility. Universal, and highly valued in all societies, prosody can be described, but the reasons for its powerful attraction remain mysterious. A number have been suggested. Rhythm mimics the vital processes of the body and recalls the regular sound of the mother's heartbeat in the womb (Langer 1967: 324). It may stimulate neuronal circuits in the brain (Turner 1992), or, by altering the patterning of our breathing, induce both emotion and alteration of consciousness, as it does in ritual magic (Glucklich 1997: 108). By drawing attention to chance connections between linguistic structures, it may stimulate creative thought (Cook 2000). Undoubtedly, rhythmic language has a powerful emotional and mnemonic effect, yet descriptions of this power are commoner than explanations, and explanations all remain highly speculative.

All discourse uses prosody to some extent, though with differing degrees of prominence. In genres where prosody is less prominent, both words and syntactic structures are selected more by semantic and pragmatic than by prosodic criteria. To put it more plainly: in such genres, we choose our words for their meaning, or to have a desired effect, rather than for sound. If patterns of sound occur, they generally do so accidentally. Highly prosodic discourse, such as poetry, prayer and incantation, on the other hand, chooses words to create sound patterns, as well as for their meanings and functions. On occasion phonetic and phonological criteria may dominate, and a word or other linguistic unit be chosen primarily for its rhyme, rhythm or syllabic structure, and in spite of its meaning.

The dichotomy between non-prosodic and prosodic discourse is, like most dichotomies, a descriptive convenience only. Actual discourse occurs on a continuum between these two theoretical poles. Though poetry is exceptional in the degree to which it exploits prosody, and bureaucratic prose is exceptional in the degree to which it does not, most genres make more use of it than is generally supposed (Tannen 1989). The two motives behind linguistic choice (meaning and pattern) are not thus mutually exclusive. A given word or grammatical construction may be doubly determined, by sound and by meaning – and doubly apposite – for though it may be the quest for prosodic patterning which brings a particular wording to mind it may still have semantic and pragmatic appropriateness.

6.2 Prosody in ads

In advertising, prosody is extensive. I shall approach it under five headings: ad-poems, borrowed poems, jingles, borrowed songs and prosodic ads.

6.2.1 Ad-poems

Pleasure in Everything

The day begins
warm tones of light
surround me
an island of delight
washing the night
from sleepy limbs
to greet the day
re-born.

In languages using alphabetic writing, a feature of written poetry is that its lines end before the margin, motivated by some other criterion than a simple lack of space. Line-breaks and gaps between stanzas enable us to identify writing visually as likely to be poetry, even when it is out of focus or written in another language. This visual unit of the line has a conventional connection to a unit of sound, a spoken 'line' composed of one or more metrical units **(feet).** The fact that sophisticated poetry may depart from this convention, interrupting metrical units with line breaks, pausing where there is no line-break, or writing in lines which do not correspond to any metrical unit, does not invalidate this characterization. Such innovation can be defined only by reference to the norm it abandons.

Yet, although both written and spoken lineation are common in poetry, they are not commonly perceived as either sufficient or essential to it. The appellation 'poetry' has become a value judgement. To present writing in lines in the main body of a book can be a bid for this accolade, indicating that one wishes the text to be read as poetry. The layout makes a claim that the reader will find a particular kind of interest and value, and that the sound patterns contribute to this.

There are also genres and parts of genres, however, where writing in lines does not signal that a text should be read as a poem. Title pages,

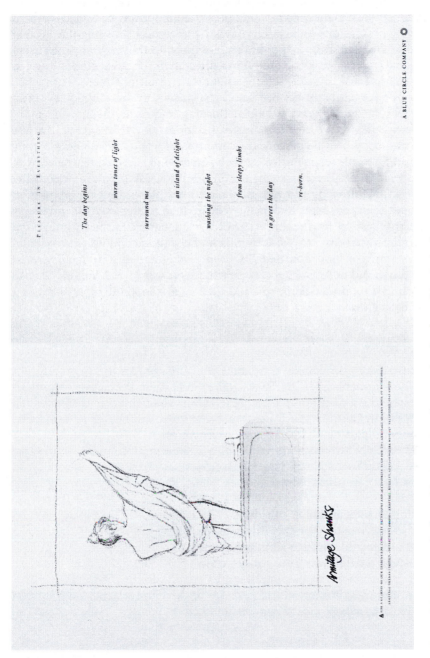

Figure 6.1 'Pleasure in Everything': an advertisement for Armitage Shanks bathrooms.

notices, labels, tickets and menus, for example, all employ lineation without making any such claim, and it would be quite inappropriate to accuse them of having pretensions to be poetry! What I have said above applies to text placed in the main body of books or magazines. In this respect, advertising is anomalous. It is very common for short copy to be presented in broken lines, or – on TV or radio – to be spoken rhythmically. Yet this practice need not necessarily attract the reading strategies evoked by poetry, even when it is accompanied by sound patterning, metre or rhyme. The more prominent the picture, and the greater its connection to the copy, the less likely that copy is to be perceived as an attempt at poetry. While the copy of the ad for Cointreau (Figure 6.2) is written on to the picture, the copy in the ad for Armitage Shanks (Figure 6.1), by its clear separation from the picture (a line drawing of a naked woman towelling herself in the bath on the opposite page) seems to demand a more independent status, and therefore consideration as a poem. The former encourages a more integrated perception of words and pictures which (despite exceptions like William Blake's *Songs of Innocence and Experience* where poems are incorporated into a picture) is unusual in poetry. For these reasons, the Armitage Shanks ad is categorised as an 'ad-poem'; the Cointreau ad, on the other hand, is a 'prosodic ad' (see 6.2.3 below).

6.2.2 Jingles

Although they also employ prosodic patterning, jingles are very different from the ad-poem. They are heard rather than read; they have no pretensions to be poetry; and they are sung to music which alters and dictates the rhythms of the written word. Yet they often make interesting and effective use of sound patterning in language.

The jingle of two consecutive Wrigley's Spearmint Gum ads in the late 1980s, 'Poster' and 'Neon' (the predecessors of 'Last Stick' described in section 3.4.2), were as follows:

Wrigley's spearmint, it's the one.
Cool fresh taste, share it with someone.
So minty cool, through and through, it
Tastes so great, you'll just love to chew it.

In one of the two TV ads which used this jingle ('Poster'), the sung rhythm was a clear four-beat line, as represented below

	1		2		3		4
	WRI	gley's	SPEAR	Mint	IT'S	the	ONE
	COOL	fresh	TASTE	share it	WITH	some	ONE
So	MINT	y	COOL		THROUGH	and	THROUGH it
	TASTES	so	GREAT	you'll	JUST LOVE	to	CHEW it

Figure 6.2 'Glow with Cointreau'.

As with most songs, the music dictates the rhythm, and stresses may fall on syllables which would be unstressed in speech (for example 'WITH'). Unstressed syllables between the major beats are pushed up together when they are numerous, or drawn out when they are few. Thus, in the sung rhythm represented above, the words slow down and gather force in the third line with a marked pause between 'COOL' and 'THROUGH'. The resulting climax is reinforced by a tension between the units of rhyme and the units of grammar. Grammatically 'through and through' belongs to cool, while 'it' belongs to 'tastes'. (The analysis here assumes that there is an ellipsis of 'being' from an opening clause: 'Being so minty cool through and through'.)

[[Ø (so minty cool <through and through>)] (it) (tastes) (so great [(you) ('ll (just) love) [(to chew) (it)]]]

While this grammatical structure encourages a pause between 'through' and 'it', the rhyming of 'through it' and 'chew it' forces the two words together. As each line in the music is followed by a pause, the subject of the sentence 'it' is left doubly suspended, held back from its predicator by both rhythm and rhyme. The fourth line thus effects a sudden and swift loosening of tension, creating an effect of 'arrest' and 'release' used in poetry (Sinclair 1966). In this case the hold is not only grammatical, but also musical and phonological, for the music and rhyme delay the completion of the grammatical unit, which, when it comes, is accentuated by the resumption of the rhythm, leading to the acceleration of the double beat on 'JUST LOVE'. The effect was also pictorial – and this again illustrates the dangers of analysing the words of ads without their images – for the scene changed smartly at line endings. Both versions used a succession of incidents involving young men and women sharing sticks of gum (and perhaps by implication each other). Relationships appeared ambiguous, as a member of one couple smiled at, kissed, or offered gum to a member of another couple, or a single young woman was seen with a group of young men, bestowing a kiss on the one who gave her a stick of gum. In both ads using this jingle, the transition from line 3 to line 4 was matched by a camera shift, so that the last 'releasing' line was accompanied by an image a young woman flirtatiously folding and inserting a stick of gum slowly into her mouth. The result was a unity in which music, images, prosody, grammar and acting came together to produce a powerful ad whose success – even fifteen years later – is often referred to in the advertising press.

The effect of a jingle is achieved through a combination of words, images and music, rather than, as in written poetry, through the interplay of the lineation, implied pronunciation, and linguistic structure. The jingle is a genre in its own right, rather than one which attempts to emulate another, like ad-poems. For this reason perhaps it lacks the pretentiousness of such attempts at poetry as the Armitage Shanks ad.

6.2.3 The prosodic ad

We have examined two opposite cases. One is the unpretentious jingle, relying heavily on music and pictures, whose words are heard but not seen, but which can nevertheless make skilful use of the sound patterning of words. The other is the ad whose words attempt to stand on their own unaided by music or image, inviting comparison with poetry by linear layout. Between these two poles is a third category I shall refer to as **prosodic ads.** These are magazine or poster ads which superimpose short copy onto or next to an image, arranging it, like poetry, in lines which suggest some correspondence between these graphological units and spoken units when the ad is read aloud, or pronounced as internal 'sound-images'.

An advertisement for L'Oréal beauty products which ran over a number of pages, included the following words.

> At the dawn
> of the year 2000
> L'Oréal
> sees
> the world
> in beauty

The words of this part of the ad follow a regular rhythm, dividing into feet as follows:

> At the <u>DAWN</u>   / of the <u>YEAR</u>   / two <u>THOU</u> sand
> l'Oré <u>AL</u>   / sees the <u>WORLD</u>   / in <u>BEAU</u>   ty

In the Cointreau ad (Figure 6.2), in addition to the obvious rhyme of 'glow' with 'Cointreau', there is also rhythmic patterning, as follows:

> <u>GLOW</u> with / Coin <u>TREAU</u> / the <u>SPI</u> rit / of <u>O</u> range / in <u>SIDE</u>

In the copy of the ad for the perfume Elizabeth Taylor's Passion (whose iconic shape has already been discussed in Section 4.5.1) there is also rhythmic patterning. When spoken it forms four **amphibrachs** (a metrical unit consisting of one stressed syllable with an unstressed syllable on either side) as follows:

> be   <u>TOUCHED</u>   by
> the   <u>FRA</u>   grance
> that   <u>TOUCH</u>   es
> the   <u>WO</u>   man

This rhythm moreover mimes that of the product name, which is also amphibrachic

e	<u>LIZ</u>	a
beth	<u>TAY</u>	lor

Nor is this patterning unconnected to the meaning. The parallel rhythms of name and copy echo the theme of reflection and contemplation of the self in this (and many other) perfume ads. The succession of amphibrachs creates a further icon of reflection, for they are the same backwards and forwards, and rhythmically the second half of the copy is a mirror image of the first. In a similar way, grammatically the relative clause in the second half mirrors the main clause.

[(ØYou)	(be touched)	(by the fragrance)
[(that)	(touches)	(the woman)]]

If we take into account the ellipted pronoun 'you' in the main clause, and consider that the relative pronoun 'that' stands for 'the fragrance', then the main clause and relative clause have simply the same meaning ('the fragrance touches the woman'): the former in the active, and the latter in the passive.

The identification of such prosody, and its interaction with graphology, music, images, grammar and meaning, raises the issue of the degree to which such devices are used consciously and intentionally by the advertiser. A common reaction to analyses such as those above is to say that they 'read too much into it', or that 'the advertiser could not possibly have done this deliberately'. Yet there is no reason why such formal patterning should be any more conscious or intentional in poetry than in advertising. There need be no claim in the analysis of formal patterns that these were either fully recognized or intended by the creator. In discussion of poetry, the literary theorist Stanley Fish (1980) has argued that such patterns as alliteration are not features of the text, but features of the reading; they come into existence only through such analyses. This argument leaves two important issues out of account. One is the degree to which such patterns can be perceived at some tacit or subconscious level; the other is the degree to which all members of a speech community read in a similar and predictable manner. Whatever differences may exist between members of an English-speaking community in ideology and experience, there is considerable homogeneity in word stress (despite well-documented differences). Most English speakers would stress the texts analysed above in the same way (saying 'WOman' and not 'woMAN' for example). The rhythm suggested by a written text is thus far more predictable, and far less individually variable, than such aspects of language as connotation or pragmatic function. Prosody has an objective quality; it is a feature of text as well as of reading. Though the appreciation of some prosodic techniques may be enhanced by education in poetic appreciation, to claim that the perception of verse rhythm in general is limited to some groups of speakers seems quite contrary to experience. Not everyone may know a means of formal description, but the perception and enjoyment of prosody is an aspect of competence in any language.

6.2.4 Borrowed poems and songs

In addition to ad-poems, jingles and prosodic ads, there is also frequent use of existing poems and songs. This might more appropriately be described as carrion than parasitic (see Section 2.4). When advertisers cannot write their own words, they appropriate others people's. An interesting and unusual relationship between ads and poetry is illustrated by 'The Night Mail', a poem commissioned from W.H. Auden for an ad for the Royal Mail. In a later version of the ad, the poem (not all by Auden) goes as follows:

> This is the night mail crossing the border,
> Bringing the cheque and the postal order,
> Letters for the rich, letters for the poor,
> The shop at the corner, and the girl next door.
> Pulling up Beattock a steady climb,
> The gradient's against her, but she is on time.
> Passing the shunter intent on its toil,
> Moving the coke, and the coal, and the oil,
> Girders for bridges, plastic for fridges,
> Bricks for the site, are required for tonight.
> Grimy and grey is the engine's reflection,
> Down to the docks for the metal collection.
> The passenger train is full of commuters,
> Bound for the office to work in computers:
> The teacher, the doctor, the actor in farce,
> The typist, the banker, the judge in first class,
> Reading *The Times* with a crossword to do
> Returning at night on the 6.42.

The borrowing of songs is far more common than the borrowing of poems. Choices are generally in the interest of mood, though there may also be a link between the words and the events or meaning of the ad ('Let Me Wrap You in My Warm and Tender Love' was used, for example, in a wool ad).

Often the songs used are from an earlier decade than the advertisement itself. Following the legendary success[1] of an advertising campaign for Levi jeans in the mid-1980s which used 1950s pop songs, this trend has continued and grown, through the 1990s and into the 2000s. The distance in time between songs and ad tends has a certain consistency. So while songs from the 1950s (Sam Cooke etc.) were favoured in the 1980s, songs from the 1960s (Jimi Hendrix, etc.) were favoured in the 1990s ads. 1970s songs (The Stranglers, etc.) are now appearing in the 2000s. Economically, the relationship between product and song is symbiotic, for the song is often re-released, and sells successfully once again. In one case, a hit was even created posthumously. A VW ad released in 2000 uses the song 'Pink Moon' by Nick Drake. It shows a couple, driving to a party, listening to the song on the car stereo. On reaching the party, instead of staying, they drive off again – the implication being that they prefer both car and song. Nick Drake was never successful during his lifetime. He suffered from depression, shunned publicity, and died of a drug overdose in 1974.[2] The ad has brought both him and his song a success they never had on its original release.

6.3 Roman Jakobson's poetics

Why is such patterning of language, beyond semantic and pragmatic demands, so prominent and valued a feature of genres such as poetry, prayer, song, political rhetoric – and advertising? Some help in answering this question may be provided by a brief excursion into literary and linguistic theory. At a conference in Indiana in 1958, the linguist Roman Jakobson (1896–1982) summed up a view of such language use which – whether accepted or rejected – has exerted a profound influence ever since. He proposed that language has a number of **macrofunctions**, each with a 'set' towards one element of communication as follows[3]

Element	Function	
addresser	emotive	(expressing feelings and states)
addressee	conative	(influencing behaviour of addressee)
world	referential	(imparting information)
channel	phatic	(checking or establishing contact)
code	metalingual	(negotiating or checking the language)
form	poetic	(foregrounding linguistic structures)

The poetic function, which Jakobson regarded as of particular importance for the linguistic study of literature, is also relevant to the study of ads. When this function is dominant, each linguistic unit is effective not only for its semantic and pragmatic meaning but also for the patterns it makes – or breaks – in its formal relationships (of grammar and sound) to other units.

The poetic function projects the principle of equivalence from the axis of selection into the axis of combination.

(Jakobson 1960)

Thus the arbitrariness of the sign is partially suspended; each signifier is important not only for its relation to its signified, but also for the relation of its form to that of other signifiers. This may depend on quite specific and superficial features: whether two signifiers rhyme, for example, or whether two sentence structures are the same.

If meaning is equivalence, then this concentration on linguistic form for its own sake, rather than as a vehicle for something else, creates a new layer and kind of 'meaning'. It follows that the 'full meaning' of a poetic message is never wholly embraced by paraphrases and translations which are semantically equivalent. The 'full meaning' is inseparable from the message's unique graphological, phonological, grammatical and lexical structure. 'Meaning' is not to be found somewhere else at all – which is the usual idea of theories of meaning – but in, and only in, the message itself.

6.3.1 Parallelism

In illustration, let us look at an extract from a literary text with particularly salient parallel grammatical structures: a stanza of Oscar Wilde's *The Ballad of Reading Gaol*.

> Yet each man kills the thing he loves
> By all let this be heard
> Some do it with a bitter look
> Some with a flattering word
> The coward does it with a kiss
> The brave man with a sword

To a degree the 'meaning' is shared by a paraphrase such as

> I'd like everyone to know that in a manner of speaking everybody destroys the object of their affection, either openly with violence, or in an underhand way with flattery and hypocrisy.

Although a paraphrase or translation may set up new formal relationships of its own (which may also be deemed poetic), none maintains the unique relationships of the signs within the original: the graphological layout in lines as a stanza; the iambic rhythm of the alternating eight and six syllable lines (x / x / x /); the rhyming of 'heard', 'word' and their **eye rhyme** with 'sword'; the alliteration of 'coward' and 'kiss'; the grammatical parallels of the lines

S/NP	VP	Od/NP	A/PP	o/NP
(Some)	(do)	(it)	(with	(a bitter look))
(Some)	Ø	Ø	(with	(a flattering word))
(The coward)	(does)	(it)	(with	(a kiss))
(The brave man)	Ø	Ø	(with	(a sword))

All these formal parallels emphasize semantic parallels and antitheses. The equivalent phonological and grammatical positions of

bitter look
flattering word
a kiss
a sword

emphasize their shared semantic role: that they are all instruments of destruction.

6.3.2 *Deviation, foregrounding, compression, representation*

In Jakobson's view such parallels are the hallmark of the poetic message. They entail four further characteristics: deviation from normal usage, foregrounding, compression of meaning, and representation. (I shall return critically to the notions of deviation and normality at a later point, but accept them as unproblematic for the moment.) If we take non-prosodic text as the norm, then the syntactic reorderings and unusual paradigmatic choices needed to create the rhythms and rhymes of verse are also likely to create deviant grammatical structures and lexical combinations. In non-prosodic English speech, though the beat falls regularly, the number of unstressed syllables between stresses is irregular; in most English verse, however, they are patterned. Thus from the perspective of non-prosodic text, verse itself is deviant.

Parallelism and deviation cause the **foregrounding** of linguistic units, 'throwing them into relief' against either the background of the norms of the language of the whole or those established internally by the parallelisms within the text. The idea of foregrounding was first suggested by the Russian Formalist literary theorists in the 1910s and 1920s, and further developed by the Prague School linguists in the 1920s and 1930s (see Cook 1994: 129–40). (Jakobson, who left Moscow for Prague in 1920, was a leading figure in both groups.) The Russian formalists had claimed that the distinctive feature of literature is its ability to **defamiliarize,** to make the reader see afresh experience which has become automatized. In the view of the Prague School, the function of foregrounding is to effect such defamiliarization. Deviant forms create compressed meanings, for they evoke both the form from which they deviate – present, as it were, as a ghost – and themselves. A sonnet by Gerard Manley Hopkins, for example, begins with the line:

I wake and feel the fell of night not day

The odd and ambiguous choice of 'fell' evokes more 'usual' variations on the phrase structure

```
(NP    (PP   (NP)))
the x   of    night
```

such as 'the black of night' or 'the dead of night', thus attracting their meanings to itself. But 'fell' also means 'a blow', 'an animal pelt', 'a moor' and 'cruel'. Phonologically, it parallels the verb 'feel'. The Hopkins line is deviant in two senses: it departs from set patterns, and it tolerates ambiguity.

The following poem by Malcolm Williams illustrates a different kind of defamiliarisation. Here the departures from expectation are syntagmatic rather than paradigmatic.

Pipe Song

Plant, Spirit,
    In me your power.
I suck burning
    From the bowl of a pipe,
And blow clouds of smoke
    From my mouth,
And see with the eye of
    Leaf buds, grass shoots.

I enter your world.
    Enter mine.

In any poem, each line is both an autonomous unit, and also part of a longer grammatical unit which may continue into the next line. Each line is thus complete and incomplete simultaneously, and this often creates conflicting interpretations. In the opening line of this poem, 'Plant' and 'Spirit' can each be read as noun or verb, depending on how one reads on into the next line. There are four possible readings, equivalent to

1 VOC NP   Imperative VP   PP
   (Oh Plant)   (spirit)   (in me)...

2 Imperative VP VOC NP   PP
   (Plant)   (Oh spirit)   (in me)...

3 VOC NP   VOC NP   PP   VP   NP
   (Oh Plant)   (Oh Spirit)   (in me) (Ø is) (your power)

4 VOC NP   Imperative VP   PP   NP
   (Ø Oh you)   (<Plant and spirit>) (in me) (your power)

In the third line, 'burning' can be interpreted as either the direct object of the verb, or the complement.

S/NP	VP	Od/NP
(I)	(suck)	(burning)

or as

S/NP	VP	C/NP
(I)	(suck)	(burning)

In other words as 'I suck something which is burning' or 'I suck and I am burning'. Similarly,

SNP	VP	Od or C/NP
(I)	(blow)	(clouds of smoke)

can be interpreted as in

S/NP	VP	Od/NP
(I)	(blow)	(bubbles)

in which case the blower stays still and the clouds move, or as in

S/NP	VP	C/AjP
(the wind)	(blows)	(cold)

in which case the speaker has become or feels himself or herself to have become part of these clouds. The words 'buds' and 'shoots' may be read as either nouns (when taken with the line before) or verbs (when the line is read in isolation).

These formal ambiguities multiply and compress the possible textual meanings of the poem. They may affect any literate speaker of English – even if he or she cannot describe them grammatically. Interpretations, varying from one speaker to another, will multiply these meanings considerably. For this reason any paraphrase must be both longer than the original and incomplete. If we assume 'Pipe Song' to be about the smoking of marijuana (rather than just tobacco), the ambivalence of the word classes and functions contributes to the communication of this. Clumsily paraphrasing, the speaker is also in a state of flux and loss of identity. Subject and object, process and entity, doer and done to, all fuse.

Somewhat similar effects are created by the ambiguities in the Cointreau ad (Figure 6.2) – also, interestingly, concerned with the pleasant effects of a drug. In the opening lines:

VP or NP	PP
(Glow)	(with Cointreau)

the first word 'Glow' can be read either as a noun or verb. In addition the prepositional phrase 'with Cointreau' is multiply ambiguous. The proposition might mean 'in the company of Cointreau' as in 'I went with Charles' or 'using Cointreau as an instrument' as in 'I wrote with a pencil' or refer to a feature of Cointreau as in 'the park with statues'. The following lines have further ambiguities. Spirit can mean either 'distilled alcoholic drink', or 'soul'. As Cointreau is a drink made from oranges, then the phrase 'orange inside' can be interpreted to refer to the insides of oranges. An analogous phrase would be 'the palace interior'.

NP	PP
(the spirit	(of (orange inside))

Alternatively the lines may refer to the spirit being 'inside you'. An analogous use would be 'these gloves have fur inside'.

NP	PP
(the spirit (of (orange)))	(inside (Ø you))

As in 'Pipe Song', the fusion between the smoker/drinker and what they are smoking/drinking are represented by the fusion of different possible interpretations. This **representation** through linguistic patterning and ambiguity is a kind of iconicity (Widdowson 1984b). The form of the signs resembles their conventional meaning. The poem does what it means. In a simple form, this kind of iconicity is often found in graffiti: 'I can't spel' or 'I used to be able to finish things but now I'.

There remains, however, an important issue of evaluation, which no merely formal analysis can address. Can an ad such as the one for Cointreau – however clever in its use of language – say anything as important as a poem like 'Pipe Song'? The former is commissioned for a single purpose – to sell; the latter is created freely, for whatever purposes the writer wants. Formalist and stylistic criticism often assume without much debate that compression of meaning through parallelism, deviation, foregrounding and representation is a virtue in itself. Yet there is no necessary correlation between devices creating density of meaning in a text and a positive evaluation of that text. This is the major, if often unaddressed, problem for **literary stylistics** (the discipline which has developed Jakobson's work on the relation between linguistic choices and meaning in literature). In poetry, quite as much as in music, value and formal complexity have no necessary connection. While the exegesis of formal complexity seems to explain the power of a poem, and thus satisfies the critic who cannot tolerate the unexplained, there are many poems whose power does not yield in this way.

Advertising further disrupts this approach, in that it often has the same formal complexity as lyric poetry, but its evaluation by the critical establishment is quite different. We shall return to this issue in Chapter 10.

6.4 Parallelism in ads: an example

Parallelism may be found at all levels: graphology or phonology, lexis and grammar, semantics and discourse. These different levels of parallelism may coexist in a single text. An American magazine ad for the children's drink Sunny Delight, for example, shows a mother pouring Sunny Delight into glasses held out to her by four children's hands. Underneath is the following text:

> 'I FOUND A WAY TO BE A GOOD MOTHER AND STILL BE A GREAT MOM.'
> Every time you buy Sunny Delight, you win two ways. You're still a good mother because you're giving your kids something healthy. Plus, they'll think you're great because they're getting something delicious. Kids love the refreshing taste of orange, tangerine and lime. You'll love the vitamins they get in every glass.

Here, there is graphological parallelism between the phrases 'Good Mother' and 'Great Mom' because both use the same word-initial capitals (a repetition which could be perceived even by someone who knew neither the English language nor the Roman alphabet). There is also phonological parallelism because, when spoken, both phrases repeat sounds in the same sequence: /g/ /m/ /g/ /m/. There is lexical parallelism: 'great' is a synonym of 'good' and 'mother' of 'mom'. (Denotationally equivalent, the phrases 'Good Mother' and 'Great Mom' have very different connotations and can be distinguished discoursally, in terms of who would use them to whom in what situation.)

There are five parallel grammatical constructions. (In the following analysis only elements in parallel are labelled grammatically.)

1.	S/NP	VP	Od/NP	RCl	VP	C/NP
	(I)	(found)	(a way	[	(to be)	(a Good Mother)])
and	Ø	Ø	Ø Ø	[(still)	(Ø be)	(a Great Mom)])
2.	S/NP	VP		Od/NP		
Every time	(you)	(buy)		(Sunny Delight)		
	(you)	(win)		(two ways)		
3.	S/NP	VP				
	(you)	('re)	(still)	(a good mother)		
because	(you)	('re giving)	(your kids)	(something healthy)		

4.

	S/NP	VP	Od
Plus,	[(they)	('ll think)	[(you) ('re) (great)]]
because	[(they)	('re getting)	(something delicious)]

5.

	S/NP	VP	Od/NP
	(Kids)	(love)	(the refreshing taste (of (<orange, tangerine and lime>))
	(You)	('ll love)	(the vitamins [(they) (get) (in (every glass))])])

These grammatical equivalences are reinforced by lexical repetitions, for the second of each pair of structures repeats, in the same grammatical slots, some of the words of the first: 'be' in 1, 'you' in 2, 'you' in 3, 'they' in 4, 'love' in 5. The effect, as in *The Ballad of Reading Gaol,* is to create equivalence of meaning between those units which are lexically different, but occur in the same grammatical positions:

to be a Good Mother	=	to be a Great Mom
buy Sunny Delight	=	win two ways
being a good mother	=	giving your kids something healthy
they think you're great	=	they're getting something delicious
the refreshing taste	=	the vitamins they get in every glass
of orange, tangerine and lime		

There are also two discoursal parallels. The first is between the mother in the picture and '*you*' the reader. She is for this reason black in a magazine whose readership is black *(Ebony),* and she looks directly out of the page. A second parallel is between two ways of perceiving a relationship: with regard to people outside it, or with regard to people inside it. In the first perspective, being a mother is a position in society in the second, it is a relationship with one's children.

6.5 The product as a fusion of public and private

The product as a mediator between public and private is common in ads targeted at women, for it promises reconciliation between the apparently rival claims of femininity and feminism. The Actimel ad beginning 'Being a model and a Mum can be difficult to juggle' (see Section 4.6) is a good case in point. The very name 'Actimel' seems to be created through a fusion of opposites: action and mellowness. Like many ads it seems to offer a message of reconciliation – via use of the product – between impossible competing demands.

The fusion of public and private can also be expressed more directly. An outrageously illogical – and for that reason amusing and memorable – example occurs in an ad for Charnos lingerie. A sophisticated young woman is seen in a café in France, a moment after confidently sending back her order – the waiter can be seen departing in the background. The copy reads:

> What gave her the nerve to send back her espresso? Was it her underwear?

and underneath

> Be bold in Fever. A sultry range of lingerie. Try it on. With Charnos.

Inset in the corner is a photograph of the same woman reclining with a self-contemplative air in black lace underwear. In this ad, what is traditionally important in the sexual sphere suddenly becomes important in a public service encounter, though it remains unseen and irrelevant. The punning 'try it on' enables the copy to refer to both spheres at once.

6.6 Deviation in ads

Like literature, advertising frequently uses language in ways which depart from convention. It produces stretches of language 'which cannot be generated by an English grammar but are nevertheless interpretable' (Widdowson 1972). At the lexical level, for example, there is frequent word coinage ('provodkative', 'cookability'). At the grammatical level it includes such techniques as **functional conversion** in which a word of one class behaves as though it were in another. Widdowson (1975: 15) illustrates this with reference to a line from Shakespeare's *Antony and Cleopatra* in which the word 'boy' is used as a verb. The despairing Cleopatra, contemplating suicide, imagines how in future dramatisations of her life, her part will be played – as it was on the Elizabethan stage – by a boy actor:

> And I shall see some squeaking Cleopatra boy my greatness.

Advertising also freely turns nouns to verbs ('B&Q it'; 'RAC to it'). In stylistics, as mentioned already, such usages have sometimes been referred to as **deviation** (Leech 1966, 1969).

However, the notion of deviation assumes a norm – in language as anywhere else – and consensus about linguistic norms is as problematic as consensus about norms of behaviour. Is the standard against which deviation is measured that of some institutional but arbitrary authority? Or is it just the majority view? Neither possibility is straightforward. The acceptance of an arbitrary authority is susceptible to changes in political power, and assumes that there will be no conflicts between rival authorities. The argument that normal usage is that of the majority of speakers, however, soon becomes circular, for speakers of a language are defined as people who use the language in the 'normal' way. There are also the dimensions of historical change, group and individual variations, and differences between genres. 'Normality' exists in the context of specific participants, a time, a place and a purpose. What is normal in one context may seem quite deviant in another. Yet, despite the absence of any rigorous definition of norm and deviation, or any indisputable method for identifying instances of them, it remains true that there is substantial agreement among speakers of a language about instances of both. This misfit between theory and practice is no cause for alarm. It throws more doubt upon the validity of a descriptive method which insists on rigorous proof than it does upon the validity of the terms 'deviant' and 'normal', and it provides further evidence that what is most powerful and effective in language is also what is most indeterminate, variable and indefinable. The idea of linguistic deviation is still valid – despite the fact that all judgements are relative and open to challenge.

Deviation in advertising, as in any discourse, may involve deviation from an external norm – however elusive – or from a pattern established within the text: **external deviation** and **internal deviation** respectively.[4] An instance of internal deviation in a text may conform to an external norm, and conversely an instance of external deviation may conform to an internal norm. In a text where every sentence is verbless the sentence with a verb stands out; in a similar way, there is nothing odd about one misspelt word in a text which is all misspelt.

Yet all kinds of departure from the norm, if over-used, soon become coated with what the Russian formalist Viktor Shklovsky described as 'the glass armour of the familiar' (Shklovsky 1974: 68). This phenomenon is especially pertinent to advertising, a genre where such external deviations as graphological innovation, misspelling, puns, ungrammaticality, sustained ambiguity and so on have become so expected that in a sense the most truly deviant ad is that which has no external deviation at all.

6.6.1 Foregrounding in ads: an example

The words of a television ad for P&O Scottish ferries are:

> Lorries go
> Drills go
> Lambs go
> Caterpillars go
> Cargo
> P&O

On television, each of the first four lines is accompanied by an appropriate noise and a picture (Figure 6.3) in which letters are used – as in concrete poetry – to create a picture (see Section 4.4.1). This ad sets up a number of

Figure 6.3 From an advertisement for P&O Scottish ferries.

grammatical and semantic parallels which are broken in the last two lines. The first four lines all have the grammatical structure

NP + VP

the VP being the same verb ('go') in all cases. 'Go' is a pun meaning both 'make a noise' and 'travel/are transported'. The first meaning is suggested by the sounds which accompany each shot. It is a meaning restricted to the discourse of, or for, small children[5] – 'Cows go moo', etc. The second comes into being retrospectively when the receiver realizes that this is an ad for a ferry company – and this double meaning will then operate on subsequent viewings. The nouns all refer to entities which make noises, and which also might be transported by a Scottish ferry service. They also fall into two broad semantic categories: the inanimate and mechanical ('lorries', 'drills') or animate ('lambs'). 'Caterpillar' (itself a dead metaphor when applied to a vehicle) can be either. This ad is parasitic on the genre of the children's rhyme, in which the reactivation of the literal meaning of 'caterpillar' is quite appropriate. In this context, the fifth line 'cargo' lends itself to an initial and disturbing interpretation as a deviant (or child's) version of a sentence on the same pattern as the first four:

    NP   VP
    (Car)   (go)

before being reinterpreted as

    NP
    (Cargo)

A further step away from the pattern is

    P&O

which, though it rhymes and has the same rhythm as 'Lorries go', cannot be interpreted as NP + VP. The name of the firm is thus not only foregrounded by its difference from, but also made equivalent to, the movement of lorries, cars, animals and machines.

6.7 Jakobson's poetics in perspective

Parallelism and deviation are widely spread across genres, and by no means peculiar to literature. Werth (1976) found parallelisms in a newspaper article on pest control, while Tannen (1989) observes that they are a recurring feature of conversation, political oratory and storytelling. Carter and McCarthy (1995) demonstrate that wordplay and parallelism are central and frequent features in casual talk, and Cook (1996) analyses their occurrence in graffiti, tabloid journalism, pop songs and jokes. Conversely, there are many texts regarded as literary classics which manifest neither deviance nor patterning. In some quarters it has become fashionable to cite such evidence to criticize and even ridicule the Jakobsonian approach. Such criticism may accept the general idea of deviant and patterned language, while not accepting the claim that it is unique to literary discourse. A more radical attack denies that there are linguistic norms so independent of differences between speakers or situations that they can be treated as features of text at all. In this view, such features as alliteration are not *in* the text but *read into* it, only becoming important if importance is attributed to them (Fish 1980). A further problem for the Jakobsonian approach is the dimension of historical change. What can be said, in Jakobsonian terms, of the literariness of seventeenth-century verse, when it is encountered – as it often is – away from the context of the non-literary language of its period? Culler (1975: 113–30) argues that even in contemporary texts the perception of patterns and deviations may not be part of the linguistic competence of a native speaker, but a 'literary competence' dependent on education. As deviation often depends upon knowledge of different genres, it will vary with the reader's experience. Science fiction, for example, often plays off the 'plain' language of the scientific account against fantastic facts, in much the same way as some ads invoke the language of empirical science.

Leaving these reservations aside, however, it seems fair to say that advertising, like literature, intensively foregrounds the poetic function of language. This is far more the case at the beginning of the new century than it was in 1958 (the date of Jakobson's presentation), when advertising was in many ways still in its infancy. (Television advertising, for example, had only begun in Britain in 1956.) Yet the problems which advertising poses for the Jakobsonian approach, though formidable, are by no means catastrophic. Jakobson had never regarded the poetic function as exclusively literary:

> Any attempt to reduce the sphere of the poetic function to poetry or to confine poetry to the poetic function would be delusive oversimplification. The poetic function is not the sole function of verbal art but only its dominant, determining function, whereas in all other verbal activities it acts as a subsidiary, accessory constituent.
>
> (Jakobson 1960)

Indeed, he introduces his discussion of this function of language with reference not to a work of literature, but to a political slogan of the time: 'I like Ike' (used in the campaign to elect Dwight Eisenhower – whose nickname was 'Ike' – as US president). To identify the poetic function in such instances, however, is not to say that it is the 'dominant' function. That might reasonably be said, in the case of this slogan – and of advertisements in general – to be 'conative' (i.e. persuasive). In other words, though advertising may share literature's preoccupation with the poetic function, this is by no means its only, or even its main, characteristic. Similarly, in the case of a literary text, the formal characteristics need not be regarded as the determining and dominant function. For many people they would seem to be – as they are in advertising – only devices in the service of other aims. What those aims may be, is in the case of literature, far harder to identify – but it is safe to say that they are not primarily to get the reader to do something or to buy something.

One way out of these definitional problems would be to drop the claim that literature is characterized by formal features. Another would be to admit certain ads – or even advertising in its entirety – to the status of literature. But this is playing with definitions in a way which departs radically and unusually from normal usage. Whatever may be understood by the term 'literature', ads are not included in it, and though they may tickle they do not attract the same acclaim. Ads are a parasite discourse which has attached itself to literary discourse (among other types) as a host. The indefinable function of literature, its adaptability and range (as well perhaps as the presence of literature graduates and aspiring writers in creative departments of advertising agencies) all make this inevitable. But the reasons for the continuing exclusion of advertising from literature lie more in the reader than in the text. However 'poetic' advertising language may be, this does not bestow upon it the status of poetry.

Exercises

1   Part of the poem in Section 6.2.4 is by W.H. Auden, another part was written by the advertising agency. Is it possible to tell which part is which? If so, how?
2   Identify and evaluate the parallelism, deviation, and representation in the following:
    1 Beanz Meanz Heinz.

    2 Father Phil's
    Fat Face Filled
    Full of Freezing
    Phish Food
    Felt Flaming Fab

    3 Savour the sensual pleasure of pure Arabica coffee captured in the 'arôme absolu' of Carte Noire. Surrender yourself to the ultimate sensual coffee experience. Sample the deeply satisfying aroma as our exquisite French blend caresses your palate with its uniquely rich and velvety flavour. Carte Noire – un café nommé désir. Prepare to be seduced.
3   Compare the following poem and advertisement:
    a A poem by William Carlos Williams

    This is just to say

    I have eaten
    the plums
    that were in
    the icebox

and which
you were probably
saving
for breakfast

Forgive me
they were delicious
so sweet
so cold

b An advertisement for Marks & Spencer (the picture shows three
   peaches)

You, you and you

All our peaches are individually chosen.
They're handpicked from the sunniest outside branches.
So they're plumper, sweeter and juicier.
For the freshest fruit, pick Sunburst at Marks & Spencer.

Could (a) be used as an ad in place of (b)? Would it be diminished or
spoiled in any way?

Further reading

Jakobson's theory can be found in his (1960) 'Concluding statement: linguistics and poetics'.

Excellent introductions to stylistics are Henry Widdowson's books
(1975) *Stylistics and the Teaching of Literature*, and (1992) *Practical Stylistics*. A representative selection of writings on stylistics is brought together
in Jean-Jacques Weber (1996) *The Stylistics Reader*.

I have written extensively elsewhere on the issues discussed in this
chapter. More detailed discussion and description of the formalist and
Jakobsonian approach to literature can be found in my book *Discourse
and Literature* (Cook 1994a). The universal human liking for patterned
and rhythmic language is discussed in my book *Language Play, Language
Learning* (Cook 2000).

7 Connected text

7.1 Connectivity in discourse

Some linguists confine their studies to the formulation of rules for the selection and combination of units in sentences. They regard the sentence as the upper limit of linguistic enquiry on the assumption that rules governing the combination of sentences – if they exist at all – must make appeal to areas other than the linguistic: the shared situational, cultural and world knowledge of the participants. When these factors are taken into account, the perception of connections between sentences varies from participant to participant – what appears connected to one speaker may not appear so to another – so *both* language and participants must be described. The resultant proliferation of variables has led some linguists to the hasty conclusion that there are no rules above the sentence, while others have attempted to extend to discourse the kind of rules which apply within sentences, but are quite alien to the open, context-dependent and indeterminate nature of discourse. The idea that discourse may be governed by factors which vary between people and places is quite alien to 'scientific' linguistics. Ironically, the 'harder' natural sciences, from which it derived its approach, have more easily accepted relativity.

The most productive view is one which steers between the extremes of abandoning discourse as a realm of impenetrable anarchy, and one which tries to colonize it with sentence grammar. The 'rules *v.* no rules' debate is unhelpful. In discourse analysis, the notion of 'rules', in the sense of dictates and restrictions on choices and combinations which constitute a language, is best replaced by that of 'regularities': probable choices and combinations which can be related to specified participants and genres, but are always prone to innovation and extension. The distinction between rules and regularities, however, is a fuzzy one. It is not that there are regularities above sentence level and rules below it; rather, that this point in the linguistic hierarchy marks a radical change in the degree of flexibility.

The phonological and syntactic parallelism described in Chapter 6 provide one kind of connection between sentences which can be described in purely formal terms, without appeal to semantic reference or pragmatic context. For this reason it is often overlooked in descriptions of **cohesion** (formal connections between sentences in a text) which appeal to semantics. The fact that the connection through parallelism is one of surface form rather than of logic or underlying meaning, dependent on coincidences between signifiers rather than between signifieds, does not endear it to the 'scientific' approach (for which 'cat' and 'bat' are alike because they are mammals rather than because they rhyme, and certainly have nothing to do with 'hat'). Parallelism retains a child's inability to separate signifier from signified (Vygotsky 1962: 223) or the approach to language of a pre-literate pre-scientific culture, where it is often used (and presumably needed) as a mnemonic[1] (Turner 1992). While in some cultures the signifier is held in greater esteem (the name of a god, the words of a spell), in the modern world (with the exception of taboos on certain words in particular spheres such as sex, excretion and death) the signifier is often regarded as mere packaging for a 'fact', which can be disposed of once opened. Consequently, though parallelism continues to exert its power in poetry and song, it is often disdained, and associated with 'lower' discourse types. Even in literary discourse, it is regarded as insufficient to warrant acclaim for itself – hence the distinction between 'verse' and 'poetry'.

Though tolerated in fiction and poetry, parallelism is often regarded as deceptive in the treatment of 'facts', where it is perceived as a substitute for logic and reference to the world. In the popular view of a science-dominated culture, political discourse and advertising (two common non-literary sources of parallelism) are blamed for replacing facts with rhetoric (in the pejorative sense). Poetry has no facts to hide, and is forgiven. Yet the discourse of advertising and politics often has scant referential function. It is largely emotive, conative and phatic, using language to establish identity and differentiate that identity from others. It may be reduced to a single message endlessly elaborated: 'Here I come' (Halliday 1975: 37).[2]

It is, as Goffman observes, equivalent to **display** in the animal kingdom:

> the capacity and inclination of individuals to portray a version of themselves and their relationships at strategic moments – a working agreement to present each other with, and facilitate the other's presentation of, gestural pictures of the claimed reality of their relationship and the claimed character of human nature.
>
> (Goffman 1979: 7)

Like spells and prayers, display elevates a signifier – the name of a product, a team or a political party – above what it signifies. Though similar to the phatic function of language, it is nevertheless distinct from it; for, while phatic communication establishes and maintains relationships, the main purpose of display is to establish and maintain identity. Our harsh judgements of display might soften if we regarded it as akin to the ritual boasting of warriors – a genre which survives in the modern world in the pre-fight hype of boxing. If we despise such talk, we do so because we share the assumptions of our age and the elevation of fact and logic over other forms of truth. Incantation, bragging, name-calling, and the repeated patterns they engender, may have functions other than the communication of facts. The persistence of poetry and the burgeoning use of parallelism in ads – quite out of proportion to its conative or referential function – both testify to this possibility. They seem to answer a universal need for display. Yet we should also notice that in the contemporary world participation in display is often passive and vicarious. We express our identity by accepting somebody else's product, political programme, sporting prowess, or art, rather than by making our own.

7.2 Cohesive devices

Cohesion is the term used in discourse analysis to refer to linguistic devices which create links between sentences and clauses. A number of cohesive devices, for example, are present in the words of a television ad for Pretty Polly tights (set out here with each sentence numbered for ease of reference).

> In the 1930s one man touched the lives of millions of women. (1) He wasn't a film star or a singer but a scientist. (2) He invented nylon. (3) Yet two years later, beset with doubt, he took his own life. (4) Wallace Carothers dedicated his life to women. (5) Nylon by Wallace Carothers. (6) Nylons by Pretty Polly. (7)

- **Repetition** of lexical items. For example, 'women' is repeated in 1 and 5, 'life' in 4 and 5, 'Wallace Carothers' 'in 5 and 6.
- **Sense relations** between lexical items or phrases. For example, 'man' in 1, and 'film star', 'singer', 'scientist' in 2, are all related semantically by a single component of meaning: 'human'.
- **Referring expressions** which refer to a unit in another sentence. For example, the noun phrase 'one man' in 1 has the same reference as the chain of referring expressions ('he ... he ... he') in 2, 3 and 4. These pronouns refer back **(anaphorically)** to 'one man', and forward **(cataphorically)** to 'Wallace Carothers', and are continued by 'his' in 5.
- **Ellipsis**, in which an omitted unit is recoverable from a previous sentence. There are two instances in this text: 'but ØHE ØWAS a scientist' in 2, and 'two years later ØTHAN ØTHE ØTIME ØHE ØINVENTED ØNYLON'in 3.
- **Conjunctions** (words and phrases which indicate a logical, temporal, causal or exemplifying relationship). The examples in this text – 'but' and 'yet' – are both conjunctions.[3]

All these devices, which can be described without reference to non-linguistic context, give this text cohesion, and help to link the sentences within it together. Yet they do not account entirely for the perception of these sentences as coherent discourse, with meaning and purpose. This can be illustrated, by maintaining the cohesion, but making some other changes.

> In the 1870s one man touched the lives of sixty women. He wasn't a greengrocer or an astronaut but a stationer. He invented the paper clip. Yet two years later, tormented by mosquitoes, he took his own life. Harold Digby dedicated his life to women. The paper clip by Harold Digby. Paper clips by . . .

This passage does not make sense. Only lunatics and linguists invent such texts. But it does reveal a number of factors which establish coherence. So strong is our desire to *make sense* that, if it were encountered outside a book such as this one, the reaction would be to try to do so. As Leech (1981: 7) puts it: 'a speaker of English faced with absurd sentences will strain his interpretative faculty to the utmost to read them meaningfully.' When such attempts fail, and a text remains incoherent (even though the failure may be that of the receiver) its sender, as a last resort, is likely to be described as 'mad'.

What is it then which makes the ad for nylons make sense, while the derived version about the paper clip does not? Firstly, the ad assumes a great deal of cultural knowledge in the receiver. We know that stockings and tights are made of nylon, and that their use is widespread. We know that famous and successful male film stars and singers have female fans; that scientists can be successful too, but are considered less glamorous. We also know that scientists invent things; that the inventor of a successful product, because of patent laws, could become very wealthy; that wealth is desirable. Following from all this, it is surprising and unexplained (hence 'yet') that such a man should commit suicide. This factual gap, which maintains the interest of the text, may also activate a stereotype: the pauper inventor who foolishly sells a patent; the wealthy and successful person who is nevertheless miserable. The quantity of knowledge needed for interpretation is vast, and its boundaries indeterminate. This summary only skims its surface. Each assumption makes further assumptions, and depends on further shared knowledge for interpretation, thus revealing a paradox in the notion of communication as transfer of knowledge: communication can only take place where there is some knowledge in common in the first place. It is impossible to say everything.

The text also establishes connections through surface form. 'Star', 'singer' and 'scientist' alliterate. There are lexical and grammatical parallels

S/NP	VP	Od/NP	
(one man)	(touched)	(the lives (of (millions (of (women)))))	
(he)	(took)	(his own life)	A/PP
(he)	(dedicated)	(his life)	(to women)

suggesting, illogically, that these actions are in some way equivalent. 'Touched' – meaning both to move and to come into physical contact – is a pun. The second sense suggests the contact between nylon and skin. In the last two sentences, which adopt the verbless grammar of a title, parallelism is the ascendent means of connection, for the equivalent position of 'Wallace Carothers' and 'Pretty Polly' suggests that the latter has all the scientific genius, sensitivity, altruism and tragic glamour of the former.

7.3 Pragmatic principles and coherence

Coherence is the overall quality of unity and meaning perceived in discourse. Although aided by cohesion, and almost always accompanied by it, it is not created by it (as the incoherent version of the Pretty Polly ad illustrates) but depends upon other pragmatic factors. Before proceeding with a discussion of cohesion, let us consider some of these pragmatic factors, and how they influence the type and density of cohesive ties.

One of the standard explanations of how addressers organize text and how addressees perceive it as coherent – how in other words a text becomes discourse – is an appeal to theories of **conversational principles**. According to Grice (1975) discourse is interpreted as though the speaker were following four maxims of a **co-operative principle**: to be true, clear, relevant, and as brief or as long as necessary. At times these demands pull in opposite directions, and one may oust another. They may also be flouted to produce a particular effect (irony, for example, flouts the truth maxim). Lakoff (1973) suggests a further **politeness principle**. Speakers follow three further maxims: to avoid imposing, to make their hearer feel good, to give him or her options.

The balance between the two principles changes with the purpose of the communication and the relationship between the participants. In interaction whose function is primarily phatic – to establish or maintain social relationships – the politeness principle may be uppermost. The desire to make someone feel good may win out over truth or brevity. (Consider how you would answer a host's question about a tasteless dish prepared in your honour.) The reverse holds where the communicative purpose is collaboration to effect some change in the social or physical environment. (Consider the same question when two chefs are making a joint entry to a competition, and trying to decide which dish to submit.)

Participant relationships also affect the balance between the two principles. (How well do you know your host? How touchy is the other competitor?) Where the relation is already established and secure, there may be less need for politeness strategies. This accounts for a similarity in behaviour in relationships of marked power difference on the one hand (say, police officer and suspect) and of equality and intimacy on the other (say, close friends or partners) (Wolfson 1988, 1989). Both generate bald statements and commands, physical proximity without apology, the broaching of intimate subject matter, interruption and abrupt topic switch.

Though the co-operative and politeness principles may be a cultural universal, there is considerable cultural variation in their manifestations, or the balance between their demands. Tannen (1984), for example, suggests that some cultures favour a 'high involvement' politeness, making the hearer feel good by taking interest in personal affairs, while others favour a strategy of non-imposition, making the former seem intrusive and the latter unfriendly when the two come into contact. Brown and Levinson (1987) suggest that while every culture recognizes territory on to which the polite person should not trespass without reason or redressive action, the nature of that territory may vary considerably from culture to culture. In different cultures, different emphasis is given to different types of territory: time, property, friendships, bodily functions, expertise, etc. These differences are a further source of cultural misunderstanding.

While the two conversational principles may well be culturally universal, they are not equally applicable to all genres. They belong very much to spoken phatic discourse in which relationships are neither of unequal power nor of great intimacy. Such civil relationships are of a kind so common in modern urban industrial democracies that Wolfson (1988) has termed them the **bulge**. Yet, while such relationships may be numerous, they do not account for all interactions, nor for those which the participants themselves deem most important. A brief consultation with a doctor or a short exchange with a partner may well outweigh hours of civil intercourse in service encounters or the workplace. For discourse analysis, the easiest data to collect are from the bulge or from public interactions of differentiated power, such as legal proceedings, but a comprehensive approach to discourse, which is qualitative as well as quantitative, needs to consider intimate discourse too (Cook 1994b).

Neither advertising nor literature can be easily accounted for in terms of conversational principles. The relationship of addresser to addressee, and the purpose of the discourse are far removed from the phatic communication of the bulge. What is the truth, relevance, clarity, brevity or politeness of a novel or poem? The standards against which these questions can be answered are internal rather than external (in *Othello* Iago was lying, yet within a fiction in which all events were untrue) and judgements by external measures can seem quite beside the point. Literature is both true and untrue, relevant and irrelevant, often economic in expression but also, by utilitarian yardsticks, superfluous. The relationship of addresser to addressee is simultaneously one of extreme distance – the author has not met the readers – yet one of extreme intimacy. Like the voice of a friend, the literary voice addresses us, not for some practical or social purpose, but sometimes to understand itself, or for the pleasure of talking. Both the subject matter and the language of literature are often those reserved for intimate relationships, and many people experience a sense of companionship and intimacy with their favourite authors.

Advertising shares – or attempts to share – many of these qualities. Admittedly, it usually has a clearer purpose than literature – to sell – and the information which it gives in pursuit of this aim may be judged by the standards of the co-operative principle for its truth, clarity, brevity and relevance. Yet factual claims and direct persuasion take up less and less space in contemporary ads. Attention is focused away from them to a world where questions of truth, relevance and politeness seem as beside the point as they do in literature. As advertising has matured, formidable restrictions have grown up alongside it, imposed by publishers, broadcasters, the law or advertisers' own organizations. If factual claims are untrue, the advertiser is held responsible. Ads are withdrawn, goods are returned; and, because literal untruth is also bad advertising, it is now shunned by advertisers quite as much as by their moralistic critics. Of course, advertisers continue to use deceptive strategies for disguising or avoiding unattractive facts, for presenting descriptions in such a way that the inattentive may miss the bad aspects or imagine good aspects of a product. But these tactics are well known, over-analysed, and distract attention away from more powerful strategies. In many ads (perfume, chewing gum) there is no truth value to assess (Thompson 1990). In ads where there are 'facts' (about cars, insurance, orange juice) they are often far from the focus of attention.

7.4 Economic extravagance: cohesion in ads

Cohesive devices all serve the co-operative principle and vary with the emphasis on its four maxims. Repetition makes co-reference in text clear, though it may be at the expense of brevity; lexical cohesion may add new information economically while also aiding clarity; referring expressions are brief, though they may sacrifice clarity; conjunctions make connections clear, though they also increase length. Broadly speaking, where there is mistrust and/or an accompanying desire to minimize ambiguity, the truth maxim will be elevated over the clarity maxim. (Instruction manuals and legal documents favour repetition over referring expressions, in the belief that the latter, being more ambiguous, are conducive to misunderstandings and the construction of loopholes.) Where there is trust, where connections can be inferred or clarification obtained, brevity may be ascendant. Narrative thus often lacks the repetition, explicit connectives and density of conjunctions of legal and technical prose. Casual conversation is full of ellipsis – although this is balanced by conversation's own peculiar prolixity: apparently meaningless phrases designed to gain or hold turns, signal

turn type or topic change, or simply gain the time necessary for the production and processing of speech (Levinson 1983: 284–370). Where there
is repetition or lexical cohesion which cannot be accounted for by the co-
operative principle, it is often motivated by the politeness principle. An
excess of language often indicates a sense of occasion, ceremony, respect
or intimacy.

In referring to the product, or spheres it wishes to associate with it,
advertising favours repetition over referring expressions. (Its idiosyncratic
use of the latter is discussed in the next section.) One obvious function of
repetition is to fix the name of the product in the mind, so that it will come
to the lips of the purchaser lost for a name. But repetition of a name is also
an index of rank, esteem, intimacy or self confidence. Consider the repetition of names in ceremonies, prayers, by lovers, or by arrogant individuals
who just 'like the sound of their own name'.

Conjunctions are notoriously absurd in ads, and an easy target for analysts obsessed with demonstrating ads' verbal trickery. Their illogicality
can pass unnoticed by its sheer blatancy and nerve, as in this US magazine
ad. (The picture shows a little girl sitting on a clean carpet. She is feeding
her dolly red fruit juice and spilling it.)

> *Got a life? Gotta ask for Scotchguard.*
> Her dolly's thirsty and only juice will do. So don't leave the store
> without buying a carpet with genuine Scotchguard protection. Nothing
> protects better or lasts longer. No wonder Scotchguard products are
> used to take care of more carpet than any other brand. So whether
> you walk on it, sit on it or wear it, make sure to ask for Scotchguard
> protection.
> There's protection. Then there's Scotchguard protection.

This use of 'so', however, exploits the ambiguity of the word; for, while, in
written discourse, 'so' is often a synonym for 'therefore', in conversation –
and the style of ads is conversational – it is only a filler, which holds or
gains the turn for the speaker.

Many ads even start with a conjunction, elliptically referring to an
inferred utterance such as 'Buy our product' or 'Use this'. An early 1990s
ad encouraging people to use seat belts said simply:

> Because you know it makes sense.

Conjunctions, then, are used deftly, to jump over illogicalities. The important and foregrounded fusion of product with user, situation or effect is
more usually achieved through pun, connotation or metaphor, rather than
through any logical or sequential connection in the world.

Lexical cohesion is used to allow fusion between the product name and
other phrases, by treating them as though they were semantically related

to it. ('There's protection. Then there's Scotchguard protection.') It is a process which generates verbosity. Although ads pay for space and thus endure a discipline which can lead to economic and condensed expression, the lexical and phrasal chains in ads often appear extravagant and unnecessary:

Galaxy Minstrels chocolate
Silk with a polish. The rounded silk of smooth, creamy Galaxy's chocolate dressed in layer upon layer of chocolate shell. Coat after coat. Creating the softness of silk against the gentle crispness of chocolate shell. A delicate study in contradictions, Galaxy Minstrels.

Here there is nothing but the cohesive chain of noun phrases:[4] a seductively indulgent over-description whose excess iconically represents the luxury of eating the product, and successfully presents the nouns in each phrase ('silk', 'Galaxy', 'coat') as equivalents, accruing the qualities of each other.

7.5 Pronouns in ads

A particular genre may have strong association with a particular type or density of cohesive ties. This does not mean, however, that they are definitive of that type, but only that they have an affinity with it.

One of the most distinctive features of advertising is its use of pronouns. In discourse in general, the third person pronouns may be either **endophoric**, referring to a noun phrase within the text – as 'he', for example, refers to Carothers in the Pretty Polly ad – or **exophoric**, referring to someone or something manifest to the participants from the situation or from their mutual knowledge ('Here he is', for example, on seeing someone who both sender and receiver are expecting). The first and second person pronouns are, other than in quoted speech, most usually exophoric. Their reference is apparently straightforward: 'I' means the addresser; 'you' the addressee.

Certain genres favour certain pronouns: diaries, for example, favour the first person; written narratives the first or third; prayers the second; scientific discourse the third – and so on. Ads use all three persons, but in peculiar ways. 'We' is the manufacturer; 'I' is often the adviser, the expert, the relator of experiences and motives leading to purchase of the product; 'he/she' is very often the person who did not use the product, distanced by this pronoun, and observed conspiratorially by 'you' and 'I'; but most striking and most frequent, even in narrative, and also most divergent from the uses of other genres, is the ubiquitous use of 'you'.

In face-to-face communication, 'you' assumes knowledge of the individual addressee. In printed and broadcast discourse, however, there are too many addressees for the pronoun, when it is used, to be so personal and particular. Before such use is condemned as false and hypocritical, however, it should be remembered that advertising shares this use of 'you' in displaced and disseminated communication with religious evangelism, official documents, political rhetoric, recipes, lyric poetry and songs. This similarity to the use of 'you' in other genres, however, may blind us to the particularity of 'you' in advertising.

The difference may be brought out by comparison with another genre. In songs, 'you' functions in a number of ways simultaneously. It may refer to many people in the actual and fictional situation. Take, for example,

> Well in my heart you are my darling,
> At my gate you're welcome in,
> At my gate I'll meet you darling,
> If your love I could only win.
>
> (Traditional folk song: *East Virginia*)

This is the plea of one lover to another. 'I' is the addresser (in this song a woman), and 'you' the addressee (in this song a man). But there are at least four ways of achieving specific reference for these pronouns. The receiver of the song may treat the song as half of an overheard dialogue between two other people. 'I' is the singer and 'you' is her lover. Alternatively, a female listener may project herself into the persona of the addresser and hear the song as though it is her own words to her own lover. Alternatively, a male listener may project himself into the persona of the singer's lover and hear the singer addressing him. (I am assuming that listeners are most likely to identify with singers of their own gender.) Lastly, the pronouns of the song can be interpreted as they would be in conversational face-to-face discourse: 'I' = the singer; 'you' = the addressee. The listener, in other words, imagines that the song is addressed to them. (This perhaps is how besotted pop fans like to hear the love songs of their idols!)

In another kind of song, still involving projection into the singer, the words are perceived as an externalization of an internal dialogue in which 'you' refers to the self:

> You load fifteen tons, what do you get?
> Another day older and deeper in debt.
>
> (The blues song: *Fifteen Tons*)

The 'you' of ads, though also departing from conversational use, functions differently from either of these types of song. The tendency to project the self into the 'I' and address somebody else as 'you' is hampered by the frequent absence of 'I' and the clear address to the receiver. The 'you' of ads has a kind of **double exophora** involving reference to someone in the picture (salient because pictures dominate words) and to the receiver's

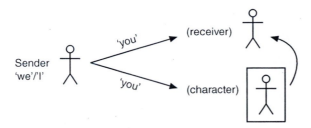

Figure 7.1 Double exophora of 'you'.

own self (salient because everyone is interested in themselves). The characters of ads sometimes look out of the picture (as in Figures 7.2 and 7.3) and directly at the receiver, allowing them to take on the role of either addressee or addresser. This double reference, originating in the text, encourages a completion of the triangle which effects a co-reference between the receiver and one of the people in the picture (Figure 7.1).

This dual identity of 'you' is matched by the mysterious identity of the sender, which is not revealed, though sometimes referred to as 'we'. The visual presence of another person (the character) distracts from this absence, creating an illusion that the dialogue is between character and addressee.

Characters in ads are also sometimes referred to in the third person, which – though more distant that 'you' – by no mean precludes the receiver identifying with them. In literary narrative, the reader may make a similar projection of the self into the pronouns 'he' or 'she' referring to one of the characters. The device of opening a narrative with a third person pronoun whose reference is unclear encourages such projection, for the character appears as a man or a woman rather than any specific person.

> He was working on the edge of the common.
> > (D.H. Lawrence, *England, My England* opening sentence.)

> Now she sits alone and remembers.
> > (Carlos Fuentes, *The Old Gringo* first sentence.)

In lyric poetry third person pronouns can remain unspecified throughout (as in the poem by Byron which begins 'She walks in beauty like the night') while the use of 'you' invites the same variety of interpretation as in pop songs. But these literary uses offer the reader both the option of involvement, projecting the self into characters, senders and receivers, and the option of detachment, interpreting any of the pronouns as referent to somebody else. Ads are more intrusive. Their 'you' is part of a

Figure 7.2 Advertisement for Philips cordless phones.

high-involvement strategy which attempts to win us over by very direct address; they step uninvited into our world, expressing interest in our most intimate concerns.

Lastly, there are ads – as there are novels and lyric poems – in which one character speaks in the first person. The text of the Philips phone ad in Figure 7.2 for example reads as follows:

> I understand that the Philips Onis 2 range of cordless telephones, with their unique Crystal Sound System have a digital sound quality that's second to none. I understand the really simple text menu system, 40 name phonebook, caller display and handsfree speaker phone. I understand everything. Except how they fit so many features into one little telephone. I've got to admit it's getting better.

Here again, the receiver may either identify with the character, making the 'I' their own, or treat the character as someone speaking to them.

7.5.1 Pronouns in ads: two examples

The Clearasil Facewash ad (Figure 7.3) is based upon one, perhaps two metaphors. Firstly there is the comparison of the facewash to an ideal man who is both gentle and powerful. Secondly (perhaps) the combination of these qualities in the facewash is compared to the perfect couple which will be formed when the reader of the ad has managed to form a relationship with him (probably with the help of the facewash). There is a good deal of fusion and confusion here.

The metaphors are aided by the symmetry and parallelism of both the language and the layout. 'Your ideal man' above the picture balances with 'your ideal facewash' below, and the two phrases are linguistically parallel with only the head noun changed. Similarly the words on the right are balanced visually with those on the left. Their typography is identical (both use two different fonts and black and white letters in exactly the same way). And they are linguistically parallel

Gentle soft	on the skin,	tender like his kiss.
Power tough	on spots,	strong like his arms.

Everything then – or almost everything – is symmetrical, top to bottom and side to side. All that is needed to complete the harmony is the reader, facing the ad, to balance the handsome young man looking out of it!

Repetition and parallelism also characterise the text below the picture , which reads

> Gentle yet powerful. The perfect combination with gentle Power from Clearasil. It's powerful enough to help beat spots, but kind enough to

Figure 7.3 'Thomas': advertisement for Clearasil Facewash.

use every day. Our unique microbeads will gently exfoliate your skin, while you'll be left feeling fresh and clean. So, with both power and gentleness, opposites really do attract. New gentle Power from Clearasil.

The lexeme *power/powerful* occurs four times and *gentle/gently* five times. The rhetorical balance of parallel grammatical constructions is very similar to that in the Sunny Delight ad (Section 6.4.) which is also about uniting opposites. Here we have

	S/NP	VP	C/AjP	NCl
	(It)	('s)	(powerful enough	[to help beat spots])
but	Ø	Ø	(kind enough	[to use every day])

	S/NP	VP	
	(Our unique microbeads)	(will gently exfoliate)	(your skin)
while	(you)	('ll be left)	[(feeling)
			(<fresh and
			clean>)]

In addition if we juxtapose the opening two sentences with the two closing sentences – the frame around the central part analysed above – we find substantial lexical parallelism and repetition

Gentle yet powerful. The perfect combination with gentle Power from Clearasil.

So, with both

power and gentleness, opposites really do attract. New gentle Power from Clearasil.

As this ad appeared in magazines for teenage girls we can assume that the addressee will not identify herself with the character, but see him as someone who is looking at her. Yet it is not he who addresses the words to her (he would not be so vain to describe himself as 'the ideal man' surely) but someone else. One advantage of the second person 'you' in ads is that it enables the advertiser to avoid identifying their own voice. In this ad it appears only towards the end, when the wording slips into a quasi scientific description of the product 'our unique microbeads will gently exfoliate your skin'. Here however, as so often in ads, words which seem to be precise and technical, are used rather for their connotation of expertise than for their denotation, presumably on the assumption that they are not actually known to the average reader. What 'microbeads' are we can only guess; 'exfoliate' is defined in the *Collins Concise Dictionary* as 'to peel off in layers, flakes or scales'! There is a tension then between the scientific and the poetic uses of language, and the ad, even in this intruding 'factual' sentence, clearly relies primarily upon the latter.

In the ad for Secret Weapon (Figure 7.4), though this is also for a beauty product in a magazine for teenage girls, the use of pronouns is somewhat different. Here the reader looks into the scene, in which a snap-shot of a dramatic situation is depicted. Three girls are looking in the mirrors of a washroom, presumably checking their appearance while 'out' at a party or club. The central character (both visually and dramatically) is putting on lipstick while the other two are looking at her. The one to her left (whose face is clearly visible in the mirror) is slim and conventionally attractive, but wears an expression of jealousy. Someone – perhaps this jealous companion – has attached a 'post-it' to the central character's back, bearing the words 'fat cow'. Above the picture is a parody of a statutory warning (of the kind that appears on cigarette ads) saying 'WARNING: May cause outbreaks of jealousy'. The words in small print underneath the picture read as follows;

> Get yourself noticed and add some sparkle with new Shimmer and Glitter Rollerballs, part of the new Secret weapon range of make up. Choose between six explosive colours in a fragranced body gel, all for under £3 each. Guaranteed to outshine even your most annoyingly pretty friends.

Here there is no specific reference to who is speaking these words. There must however be someone behind this voice which warns, advises, informs, guarantees, and encourages. The default assumption might be that it is the manufacturer, though the voice mixes sales language ('new range', 'all for under £3 each') with the more colloquial voice of a confidante or mentor ('get yourself noticed', 'add some sparkle', 'annoyingly pretty friends') – and the washroom is traditionally the place where young women exchange advice and information. Thus a fusion is created between the sphere of friendship and intimacy on the one hand, and the sphere of marketing and purchase on the other. This complication of the sender's identity is further aided by a touch of self-parody in the manu-facturer's voice, not only in the spoof warning, but also in the 'guarantee' ('to outshine even your most annoyingly pretty friends'). What is interest-ing here in terms of pronoun use is that while the picture is – as it were – in the third person, the text is in the second person, but the fact that the third person character (she) is using the make up which the reader (you) are also advised to use, invites identification with the central figure and her situation. The reader's anxieties about appearance and weight are played to, but also flattered, for the central character is in fact unlikely to be con-sidered either overweight or unattractive.

Figure 7.4 Advertisement for Secret Weapon lipstick. Produced by Bates UK for Superdrug.

Exercises

1   Instead of merely repeating the name of the product, many ads refer
to it in a number of different ways. What are the advantages of this for
the advertiser? In an ad for rings, the following noun phrases were all
used to refer to the product.

> The ring ... this creation ... a continuous band of 18 carat gold
> Forget-Me-Not flowers ... the perfect eternity ring ... a ring to
> treasure throughout a lifetime ... a ring which binds your love ...
> a ring to pass on to your loved ones ... your ring ... this fabulous
> piece of jewellery.

List the qualities claimed for the ring through this device.

2   Consider the use of referring expressions in the following. What is the
cause of ambiguity? And what is its effect?

> a   'My husband said Mates were for teenage sex. I said, when can
> we get some?'
> (An ad for Mates condoms)
> b   'Who are you mixing it with?' (An ad for Southern Comfort
> Bourbon)
> c   "The first time we did it was on the boss's desk ..."
>   I knew we had a meeting first thing so I got in early. I was a
> little nervous going up in the lift, but when it came to it, I was
> surprised how easy it was. Trouble was, we got carried away.
> When my boss came back we were still at it. He took it very well.
> In fact, when I told him I'd saved £100 on a £500 TV, he couldn't
> wait to have a go himself. Even highly paid bosses can see the
> sense of shopping online at intersaver.intersaver.co.uk are you
> experienced? (An ad for on-line shopping at intersaver.co.uk)

3   Consider the texts of the following ads. What uses do they make of:
  • parallelism
  • cohesive devices (especially pronouns)
  • assumed knowledge.

a   Dole Pineapple

> Getting kids to eat fruit isn't rocket science. It's astronomy.

> Some kids don't like fruit. And getting them to eat it has been
> quite a challenge. Until today. because now Dole fresh pineapple
> comes in cute, little shapes. There are stars and moons for little
> astronomers. Fish and turtles for little oceanographers. And,
> thank heaven, a little piece of mind for you.

b ThinkNatural.com

Everybody should ThinkNatural.com
Healthy bodies, relaxed bodies, invigorated bodies: there's something for everybody at ThinkNatural.com
ThinkNatural.com is the UK's definitive natural health & body-
care website. There's a huge amount of information on aro-
matherapy, vitamins, minerals, herbal supplements and much
more. Plus you can buy online whenever it suits you, choosing
from our vast range of natural healthy products.
That's why every body should ThinkNatural.com

c Wholetree.com
(The picture shows an elderly Chinese man in traditional costume
looking at a laptop computer screen.)

WHOLETREE.COM THE LANGUAGE OF E-BUSINESS
He speaks Chinese. Your web site doesn't. But your site could if
you speak to us. As the world's leading multilingual e-business
provider, we can turn any e-business into a global success simply
by having it talk to people in their native tongues. Like Zhang-
san, 80% of the world doesn't speak English. So, if that's the only
language your site is in, do you really have a worldwide Web?
Talk to us. Then you'll be able to talk to the whole world.
ZHANG-SAN IS A TECHNO GEEK. BUT HE STILL CAN'T
FIGURE OUT YOUR WEB SITE.

Further reading

Cohesion

The standard work on cohesion is Michael Halliday and Ruqaiya Hasan
(1976) *Cohesion in English;* a shorter and modified description is in
Chapter 9 of Michael Halliday (1994) *An Introduction to Functional
Grammar.* See also my own book *Discourse* (1989), Chapter 2.

Pragmatics

Good readable introductions to the theories of pragmatics referred to in
this chapter can be found in
Henry Widdowson (1979) *Explorations in Applied Linguistics*, Chapter 9.
Henry Widdowson (1984) *Explorations in Applied Linguistics 2,*
Chapter 8.
Michael McCarthy and Ronald Carter (1994) *Language as Discourse.*
Jenny Thomas (1995) *Meaning in Interaction.*

Representations of women in ads

Interesting insights from different perspectives are provided by:

Erving Goffman (1979) *Gender Advertisements*.

Keiko Tanaka's chapter 'Images of Women' in *Advertising Language* (1994).

Reina Lewis and Karina Rolley's chapter in Nava *et al.* (1997) '(Ad)dressing the dyke: lesbian looks and lesbian looking'.

Suzanne Romaine's chapter on women in ads in *Communicating Gender* (1998).

Mary Talbot's article in the *Journal of Sociolinguistics* (4/1 2000) '"It's good to talk"? The undermining of feminism in a British Telecom advertisement.'

Ann Cronin's (2000) book, *Advertising and Consumer Citizenship: Gender, Images and Rights*.

Part III
People

8 Narrative voices

My face in thine eye, thine in mine appears.

(John Donne)

8.1 Introduction

This third section moves on from the materials and texts of ads dealt with
in the first two sections to a consideration of the voices which speak to us
through ads and receivers' responses to them. It is important not to regard
the subjects of these three sections – materials, texts, people – as discrete,
for each is better understood in conjunction with the others. People are
identified by the texts and materials they use; texts depend on materials
and people; materials become significant when used by people to make
texts. There is thus no clean break between this part of the book and the
last one, but only a change of emphasis. In illustration of this, this section
begins with a re-examination of one element of cohesion – ellipsis – not
this time in formal terms, but as an entry to the kind of participant relationships created by ads.

8.2 Ellipsis in use

As we have already seen, ellipsis and other cohesive devices which serve
the brevity principle allow the advertiser to achieve two commercially
desirable effects: to save space where words cost money, and to avoid
drawing attention to features of the message which do not serve the advertiser's interest. An American ad for Cascade dishwasher detergent exem-
plifies these reasons for economy. It shows three women sitting around a
table, happily chatting, drinking white wine from spotless glasses. On the
table is a vase of tulips, a white cloth, appetizers of fruit and cheese. The
atmosphere is one of companionship, sophistication, good humour, relax-
ation, cleanliness, luxury and harmony. The text reads:

> When Lisa made a surprise visit, you didn't have time to worry about
> spotted glasses. Fortunately, you didn't have to. Cascade. Because you
> don't have time for spots.

The second sentence contains ellipsis:

> Fortunately   you   didn't   have   to Ø   worry Ø   about Ø   spotted Ø glasses.

with the ellipted elements corresponding to, and recoverable from, the preceding sentence. This is straightforward enough. Repetition of these elements would be quite superfluous; and, short of deliberate perversity, there is no room for misunderstanding what is omitted. The second instance of ellipsis, however, is complicated by unconventional punctuation. 'Cascade' (a single word) and 'Because you don't have time for spots' (a subordinate clause) are both presented as orthographic sentences. That is to say they begin with a capital letter and end with a full stop, even though they are not grammatically sentences. In the latter case, a main clause seems to have been ellipted in entirety:

> [MAIN CLAUSE   [SUBORDINATE CLAUSE]]
> [ØØØ   [because you don't have time for spots]]

But the missing elements are by no means clear. One solution is to interpret the word 'Cascade' – (despite its being marked off by a full stop) as part of that missing clause, and provide the other elements, creating perhaps

> MAIN CLAUSE   SUBORDINATE CLAUSE
> You ought to use Cascade
> You ought to buy Cascade   because you don't have ...
> We recommend Cascade

In the age of the soft sell, such bald statements of purpose are avoided.

Though made much of by critics who believe in a gullible public, the two motives for ellipsis – to save space and omit direct appeal – are likely to be obvious in a general way to all participants, even when those participants cannot describe the phenomenon formally. Ads exist to sell, and every member of contemporary societies – other than very young children – knows this. Once an ad is identified, such conative components as 'buy our product' or 'we recommend that' are understood by default, and to condemn ads for omitting them is like criticizing a novel for not beginning with the words 'I have invented a fictional world which I should like you to share with me', or the writer of a tax demand for not saying 'It is my job to tell you that ...'. We need to move beyond such criticisms, and consider the effect of such textual features as ellipsis on the relationship and identity of participants.

Besides economizing with words, ellipsis has other important effects, resulting from its association with particular genres, situations and relationships. Firstly, it frequently occurs in conversation and other face-to-face interaction, for the simple reason that failure to recover the missing elements can be remedied by a request. The following extract, from a conversation between two close friends, is typical:

> A: I think you ought to.
> B: Ought to what?
> A: Apply for the job.

Thus the frequent use of ellipsis creates a conversational tone. Secondly, it is associated with interaction in a situation which is mutually manifest to addresser and addressee, as when, for example, a surgeon utters a single word command, such as 'Scalpel!'. It therefore suggests immediacy. Thirdly, it is indicative of shared knowledge and interests (as in both the above examples). Fourthly, it suggests a trusting relationship, in which people assume a desire to understand on the part of their interlocutor, and do not feel they need to spell out every detail legalistically. So its use can imply co-operation, informality, shared knowledge and intimacy.

The corollary of this is that, as these features diminish in communication, the more words we need to communicate. Participants need to make their discourse more explicit and complete. Lack of extensive ellipsis implies formality, social distance, distrust, or a lack of shared knowledge. This also applies to the use of explicit connectives (such as 'therefore' or 'for example').

Thus ads' use of ellipsis – a formal, textual phenomenon – has a discourse function, in that it creates an atmosphere of proximity and intimacy. It enables ads to draw parasitically on the genre of 'conversation': the prototype of interactive reciprocal communication in which formalities and differences of rank are often diminished or partially suspended (Cook 1989: 51).

8.3 The dialogue of ads

8.3.1 *Given and new information*

Another formal textual device with implications of reciprocity is the ordering and selection of information within clauses. This reflects the sender's assumptions about the knowledge and interests which he or she shares with the addressee, and also the focus of attention which the sender seeks to impose.

Even in written discourse this ordering and selection is motivated by an interpersonal concern: it pairs information which is assumed to be known to the addressee with information which is assumed to be new. Known information tends to come at the beginning of the clause, new information towards the end, where it receives greater attention. English possesses a number of grammatical options which allow the order of information to be shifted around, creating different **sentence perspectives**, such as:

> Grandma adored this old country recipe.
> What grandma adored was this old country recipe.
> It was this old country recipe which grandma adored.
> This old country recipe was what grandma adored.

As with parallelism, the difference between these sentences is a surface phenomenon, and disappears in any 'deep' grammatical or semantic analysis. They have the same 'meaning', in the sense that they refer to the same state of affairs. Yet what matters interactionally is their differences. In speech, this is complicated by the use of intonation to focus upon any element, and its interplay with grammatical focus.

> GRANDma adored this old country recipe.
> grandma aDORED this old country recipe.
> grandma adored this OLD country recipe etc. etc.

In speech, there is frequent ellipsis of known information. If I ask you what grandma adored, you might well just reply: 'This old country recipe'. In written and more formal discourse, on the other hand, known information is less frequently ellipted. This both allows greater ease of processing and makes the sender's perception of the nature of information quite clear. If all information were new, in a situation where clarification cannot be sought, the message might soon become incoherent and incomprehensible. If all information were already known on the other hand, it would simply be pointless and boring. But a balance of the two allows discourse to progress step by step, relating each new item to one which is already known. The new information of one clause becomes the known of the next, establishing an **information chain**.

An ad for the web site handbag.com creates such an information chain. The picture in this ad shows a woman standing alone in misty and windswept moorland, looking around her and shading her eyes to try to make out something in the distance. The text reads as follows:

> **A woman is lost without her handbag.com**
> handbag.com is a new Internet site offering everything a woman needs. From health and career advice to house buying and cinema listings. You can access it directly on the Internet or pick up a free CD-ROM at any Boots store. Just click your handbag.com open, and you'll find just what you want inside. www.handbag.com

She is stylishly dressed, though inappropriately for this wild landscape, and she is not carrying a handbag. The picture thus supplies a piece of information as a starting point: 'A woman is lost ...' The opening of the first clause thus supplies no new information. It is given by the picture. The second half, however, does supply new information, by stating the reasons or circumstances which cause her to be lost.

GIVEN	NEW
A woman is lost	without her handbag.com

This second part in effect make the phrase 'a woman' into a kind of pun, meaning simultaneously 'this woman in the picture' and 'women in general', inviting the female reader to identify with the picture, which now becomes metaphorical. The moorland is the difficult, treacherous, stormy landscape of modern life, through which the resourceful and sophisticated individual must find her way! Just as in the past, as the cliché had it, a woman needed a handbag in a literal sense, she now needs the modern metaphorical equivalent. The second part of this first sentence however, raises a question. We now know that there exists something called 'handbag.com'. The second sentence takes what is now given information and adds to it something new.

GIVEN	NEW
handbag.com is	a new Internet site offering everything a woman needs.

But each new piece of new information, attached to a given, creates a new question. In the next sentence it becomes the Given element, onto which another new element can be hooked. However, in the next orthographic but grammatically incomplete sentence, this given element is ellipted:

GIVEN	NEW
[Ø A woman needs advice on everything]	From health and career advice to house buying and cinema listings.

Note, though, how through this device of ellipting the given element of the sentence, the priorities of the modern woman are taken for granted and stated as though there is no debate about them.

As we can infer that handbag.com must be accessible (otherwise why advertise it?) the first clause of the next sentence can be divided as follows:

GIVEN	NEW
You can access it	directly on the Internet.

But here there is an interesting implication. One would expect the reader to have already inferred, from the suffix '.com', that 'handbag.com' is a World Wide Web site, and thus by definition something which 'you' can access directly on the Internet. Behind the structure of this clause therefore is an assumption by the advertiser that the reader may be someone unfamiliar with, or without access to, the Internet. It seems even to be teaching them something about the Internet – that it is a place where you can access information 'directly'. The second clause of this sentence, also with an ellipted element, confirms this assumption by indicating an alternative:

GIVEN	NEW
[Ø alternatively you can]	pick up a free CD-ROM at any Boots store.

The next sentence however seems to assume knowledge that one opens by clicking, though here an ingenious analogy with a literal handbag, which also opens with a click.

GIVEN	NEW
Just click	your handbag.com open,

It can be taken as given that, once you open a bag or a Website, you find something. Rather vaguely, the new element of the next clause informs us what that something might be:

GIVEN	NEW
and you'll find	just what you want inside.

8.3.2 *Topics and interaction*

To organize discourse in this way the sender must predict both what the addressee does and does not know, and what he or she wants to know. Placed at the beginning of a clause, an item of known information becomes the **topic** of that clause. Topics in discourse relate to each other hierarchically, so that we may talk about **main topics** of the discourse as a whole or **sub-topics** of a section or single clause. In this discourse the main topic is the Website handbag.com, and sub-topics include what a woman needs, and how to access the site. In a sense, the topic of an ad is always the product or service, though there is usually an apparent or surrogate topic too. (In a successful ad, this surrogate topic arouses interest, as people are eager to find out 'what this ad is for'. It may appear to be about people on a tropical beach, but turn out to be about chocolate bars!) In non-reciprocal discourse (e.g. a novel or a news bulletin) the topic is imposed by the sender; in reciprocal discourse (e.g. a conversation) it may be more collaborative and influenced by the addressee.

Yet even in non-reciprocal discourse the trace of a second voice is still present. Perhaps – both in an individual child's development and historically – monologue develops out of dialogue through a gradual deletion of this second voice. For this reason perhaps, from the dialogues of Plato, through catechisms and sermons to university lectures and news broad-casts, there are many non-reciprocal genres which present themselves in the form of two voices, or as face-to-face interaction. Yet the apparently independent second participant makes little contribution, and exists only as a foil. The move towards the openly non-reciprocal discourse of extended writing[1] – from Platonic dialogue to philosophical treatise, from lecture to book – is a change of form rather than of participant power.

A way of dramatizing this trace of the second voice is to imagine non-reciprocal discourse as one half of a dialogue in which the sender pre-empts questions from the addressee (Widdowson 1979: 25–6). Each unspoken question prompts both the content and form of the next utter-ance. The dialogue imagined by the sender of the handbag.com ad may go something like this.

A. Why is a woman lost?
B. A woman is lost without her handbag.com.
A. What is handbag.com?
B. handbag.com is a new Internet site.
A. What does it offer?
B. Everything a woman needs.
A. What sort of things are they?
B. [Everything] From health and career advice to house buying and cinema listings.
A. How can I access it?
B. You can access it directly on the Internet.
A. And if I haven't got the Internet?
B. [You can] pick up a free CD-ROM at any Boots store.
A. What do I do then?
B. Just click your handbag.com open.
A. What will I find then?
B. You'll find just what you want inside.

In conversation, it is the first part of each clause which can most easily be omitted, and the following answers by B would be quite acceptable.

B. Without her handbag.com.
B. A new Internet site.
B. Everything a woman needs.
B. Everything from health and career advice to house buying and cinema listings.
B. Directly on the Internet.
B. A free CD-ROM at any Boots store.
B. Just click it open,
B. Just what you want.

Many ads manipulate this dialogic structure of discourse to their advantage. They assume shared opinions which are not shared. The Cascade ad assumes that spotted glasses cause problems with your friends. The Subaru ad (Figure 5.4) assumes that women should drive small cars, the Sunny Delight ad that it is difficult to be on good terms with your children while also giving them a healthy diet. The voice of each perspective may be associated with its own genre. In the Sunny Delight ad, for example, one genre may be intimate family banter, another a health information booklet with a title such as 'How to Be a Good Mother'.

In print, or on traditional television, this dialogic nature of the ad is either 'written into' the text – as in this instance – or dramatised, so that the various voices are separated out into those of characters. On the Internet and in other 'interactive' media, the situation is somewhat different, as the ad itself seems to interrogate and respond to the receiver. Yet as already discussed in Section 4.6 this apparent interactivity is different only in form from the encoded interactivity in a print ad like that for handbag.com. Questions from the reader have been guessed beforehand and written in, in a process which is very similar to that in written text. The main difference is that whereas print, being linear, is structured by one hypothesised line of questioning, an 'interactive' programme allows for branching in different directions, and some retracking to follow different routes, on the part of the receiver. Print too, however, can cope with new routes, though in subsequent pages, rather than by returning to earlier 'Web pages'. With regard to a preordained dialogic structure, the process remains essentially the same.

8.2.3 Unspoken and shared assumptions as an index of ideology

Both dialogue and monologue are structured by assumptions about shared information. Often, this shared information seems so obvious to participants that they are not even aware of the assumptions they are making. The handbag.com ad, for example, assumes that we know about the existence and nature of the Internet.

In fact, any text must make assumptions about the knowledge of its readers, and it is sometimes very informative to spell out exactly what this may be. Consider, for example, how much knowledge of contemporary social organisation and economic practices is assumed in following short text:

> Take out Home Insurance with Sun Alliance and you cut out all the traditional complexity and confusion. Alongside a clearly put policy you'll be given our new helpcard which bears some useful telephone numbers. By dialling one of these, you can obtain clear and straightforward advice on your policy. A second number offers free legal advice. While another provides a domestic emergency service.

- Many people own a dwelling.
- The dwelling contains property.
- The property belongs to them.
- It costs money to replace.
- Home insurance involves regular payments in return for payment when property is lost or damaged.
- Home insurance involves a legal agreement.
- Legal agreements can be complex and confusing.
- People do not like complexity and confusion.
- The terms of home insurance are described in a policy document.
- Telephone numbers are to be dialled on a telephone.
- Insurance claims involve legal knowledge which most claimants do not have.
- Home insurance is to do with accidents, losses and burglaries.
- Such events demand urgent action.
- They may happen at a time when offices are closed.

To tell a prospective purchaser these things would be both insulting and superfluous. They constitute a group of related facts, a **schema,** known to all adult members of the society. To spell out these facts initiates a process of infinite expansion, for each statement involves further assumptions: about the law, or accidents, or homes. Yet many of these assumed facts are culture specific rather than universal. Home insurance is not commonplace in all countries, and might well need to be explained to someone coming from say, rural India, to live in England.

The absence of reference to shared information has led to the observation that it is what is omitted in discourse, the gaps within it, which constitute the shared ideology of the participants (Althusser 1971: 136–69; Macherey 1978: 87; Fairclough 1989: 78–90). A parent asking for information about a particular secondary school, for example, would not expect to be told that it is a place to which a number of children come during the daytime to be instructed and cared for by a smaller number of adults, that each of those adults specializes in one or two subjects, and that groups of children have lessons from one adult at a time. All these features of schools are taken for granted, together with the cultural beliefs about upbringing from which they stem. They are assumed to be true unless there is a statement to the contrary. It is not therefore misleading to omit mentioning teachers, or that these teachers are in charge of the children. On the other hand, in contemporary Western society, a parent might feel misled if it were not mentioned that one of the aims of the school was to teach children that their monarch is divine. In other times and places, this might be an unremarkable (and therefore unmentioned) function of a school. It is what is not said in a discourse – because everyone in the society knows it – which is most important.

Ads are a case in point. Their intention to sell is often unstated; but it is as ludicrous to criticize them for this as it would be to criticize a head teacher for not mentioning that there are lessons to a prospective parent. On the other hand, when approaching advertising, as with other social phenomena such as schools, it is illuminating to imagine oneself as an outsider to whom everything must be explained, for whom all gaps must be filled. Why do the children in school sit at desks and listen to one adult at the front? Why is the city full of big pictures of happy healthy people and new objects (which we call advertisements)? Why does the sender care if your glasses have spots? And who is the sender anyway?

There is a strong assumption that people who address us are saying things which are coherent. We *make* sense even where there is none, using some unstated cultural assumptions to fill in the gaps. People are reluctant to suppose that the sender cannot see the sense of his or her own discourse and assume the fault must be their own. Discourse has to be conspicuously and extensively nonsensical before it is perceived as such. There is a simple experiment to demonstrate this, which usually works. Pick a short phrase at random out of another discourse and insert it into a conversation. Then ask the people you are talking to if they understood why you said it. They will usually find a connection! They want you to make sense.

Through ellipsis and assumptions of shared knowledge, ads create an atmosphere of intimacy and informality. It is a mood very well expressed in the picture accompanying the Cascade ad, showing three women characters in friendly interaction in one of their living rooms. This atmosphere is further reinforced by the ubiquitous use of 'you' already discussed in Chapter 7. But who is the conversation between? Often there are conversations going on between characters – sometimes we overhear them. Yet the 'you' of the ad is addressed by a voice outside these scenes. The voice simultaneously addresses one character (unheard by the others) and the potential consumer, the ad's addressee. On the Internet, the illusion of conversation is even further developed because the potential customer can apparently actually interact with this 'voice', by making choices, responding to questions, etc. Yet there is in fact little change. The sender on the Internet is no more actually 'there' and talking to 'you' (i.e. us) than is the voiceover on a TV ad or the face looking out at us from a still photograph.

8.4 The worlds of an ad and their inhabitants

Many ads exist in four participant worlds: the world of the sender (in which the products are manufactured and distributed); the fictional world of the characters; the fantasy world of the receiver; and the real world of the receiver (in which the product may be purchased). A minority of ads may dispense with the second and third of these worlds.

In product ads, the aim of the sender is to push this product, often via the worlds of fiction and fantasy, into the real world of the consumer. Movement is effected by those elements and participants which seem to belong to more than one world at once: the product itself, the actors/characters, and the addressee. The product can exist in all four worlds; real celebrities and manufacturers appear in the fictional world, as do apparently real consumers. All receivers (i.e. all of us) inhabit both real and fantasy worlds – though if it were not for ads, it would be unlikely that mundane objects such as beer cans and shampoo bottles would appear in our fantasies complete with specific brand labels! What an ad seeks to achieve is enough contact between fiction and reality, sender and receiver, characters and consumer, fantasy and fact, for the passage of the product from one world to another to be feasible.

One common connection between the fictional world and the real world of the addressee is the direct address or gaze of a character. (In this respect ads are like plays with asides directed to the audience, or novels in which a first person narrator apostrophizes the reader.) A further connection between worlds is the product itself, which may exist in all four, and whose purchase brings the receiver's world closer to that of the fiction. A third connecting force is the disembodied narrative voice which addresses both characters and receivers, with actual or ellipted 'you's', but does not name itself. (On TV or radio this may be an actual voice. In a print ad it may be a line or text in addition to anything attributed to any characters. On the Internet it may be prompts to pursue particular links.) Though in some ways like an apostrophizing narrator in literary fiction, this voice also shares features with the narrators of those novels in which authorial, narrative and characters' voices merge. The identity of the 'I' or 'we' who speaks the 'you' is unclear. Sometimes it seems to emanate from the fictional world, sometimes from the sender beyond it, sometimes from elsewhere. And we (the addressees) are distracted from this absence of identity by the compelling and attractive characters to whom the 'you' is also addressed, and into whom, if the ad is successful, we project a part of ourselves. This could also be described as a kind of ellipsis: not of words or phrases or clauses, but of the sender and addresser of the message. This omission often passes unnoticed, a gap which discloses the ideology of both manufacturer and consumer. We are not told whose voice this is, because we apparently already know.

Or do we? Ads have so many senders and addressers that it is hard to say whose voices speak in them. A TV ad such as, say, the Wrigley's ad 'Last Stick' (discussed in Section 3.5) involves at the very least a manufacturer, an agency, a copywriter, an art director, a TV producer, a director, assistants, a camera crew, musicians, actors, technicians, costume designers, a hairstylist.[2] Internet ads involve Website designers and so forth. Moreover, some of the senders described here with grammatically singular collective nouns – e.g. 'the manufacturer' – are in fact multiple. All these senders/addressees (and which is which?) are seldom mentioned – other than in trade ads for advertising agencies aimed at manufacturers, and the occasional gimmicky ad which refers to its own construction.

DISCOURSE	SENDER	ADDRESSER	ADDRESSEE/RECEIVER
Advertising	client	creative team	public
Literature	author	publisher	public

Figure 8.1 A view of equivalent participants in literature and ads.

But whose voice speaks in the ad? Arguably, the sender is not the creative team at all, but the firm; the creative team is the addresser, equivalent to the publisher in literary discourse. In this view, a simplified comparison of participants in literary and advertising discourse might be expressed as in Figure 8.1 – although in some ads, where the brief from the client is very open, the advertising agency might be justifiably identified as the sender.

In addition, there are the fictional characters (happily consuming or miserably lacking the product) and a third, most mysterious identity (the speaker of the voice-over, author of lines and links) who, like the narrator of a third person novel, both is and is not the author, and cannot be identified with any one participant. The opinions expressed by this voice are unlikely to be those of the copy writer; away from work, like most other people, he or she probably considers different brands (of washing-up liquids or whatever) much the same.

8.4.1 Who is speaking thus?

In an essay on the literary narrator called 'The death of the author', Roland Barthes quoted a passage from Balzac's *Sarrasine* describing a castrato disguised as a woman:

> This was woman herself, with her sudden fears, her irrational whims, her instinctive worries, her impetuous boldness, her fussings, and her delicious sensibility.

and asked:

> Who is speaking thus? Is it the hero of the story bent on remaining ignorant of the castrate hidden beneath the woman? Is it Balzac the individual furnished by his personal experience with a philosophy of woman? Is it Balzac the author professing 'literary' ideas on femininity? Is it universal wisdom? Romantic psychology? We shall never know, for the good reason that writing is the destruction of every voice, of every point of origin. Writing is that neutral, composite, oblique space where our subject slips away, the negative where all identity is lost, starting with the very identity of the body writing.
>
> (Barthes 1977b)

The questions are as pertinent to ads as to novels. 'Who is speaking thus?', for example, in the Cascade ad: the manufacturer, the copywriter (out of conviction or as a job), the voice of proper behaviour, a friend of the character, the inner voice of the woman?

A clue to the nature of the voice may be found in the frequent use of 'you'. This 'you' of ads expresses two types of sender/addressee relationship at once, a conflation which is possible in English but much harder in languages with a distinction between an intimate (T) and formal (V) second person pronoun (such as *tu/vous* in French). In such languages, the choice of pronoun is highly significant, and in ads will be influenced by such factors as the nature of the product or the age of the targeted addressees. Generally, the T form is both an index of intimacy and equality, and of clear superiority or subordination: used to God and parents, and to animals and servants, as well as to friends. (This dual function of the T form lends support to Wolfson's bulge theory (see Section 7.3).) The V form indicates not only service and respect, but also distance. Ads, the most public of discourses, adopt the strategies of the most private. The voice of an ad must simultaneously be one of friendship, authority and respect. Ads in languages with a T/V distinction must make a choice, or seek to avoid the second person altogether.[3]

8.5 The theories of Bakhtin

The role of language in this complex interplay of people and worlds is best understood by examining the relation between participants and their words, rather than either in isolation. This relationship is not well dealt with by Saussurean semiotics or Chomskyan linguistics, which treat all speakers as homogenous and take no account of how the meaning of words varies with participants. It is quite one thing to be told that a particular beer is 'probably the best lager in the world' by its manufacturer, another to be told this by a celebrity one likes and respects, another by a fictional character, yet another by a close friend.

The theories of the Russian linguist and literary theorist Bakhtin (1895–1975) are helpful to an understanding of how the identity of the sender is an integral part of linguistic meaning.[4] Developed through the 1920s, 1930s and 1940s, his ideas were for a long time neglected both in Russia and the West. Their late emergence on to the academic scene from the 1960s onwards – but most spectacularly in the 1980s and 1990s – has distorted their importance and originality as a contribution to linguistics and literary theory. They became known after many developments which they preceded and foreshadowed in linguistics and literary theory.[5] I shall first give a brief outline of Bakhtin's approach to communication, and in particular his theory of **voice,** then use this to compare the voices in ads with those in the novel: a genre of particular importance in Bakhtin's theory. Though this analysis may seem to

digress from our main topic, it is one which I believe is particularly relevant to it.

8.5.1 Meaning and identity

Bakhtin observed that, despite a professed belief in the primacy of speech,
semiotics and linguistics are deeply affected in their view of language by
the written word, which creates an illusion of linguistic meaning as something relatively fixed, existing separately from sender and receiver (Volosinov 1986: 73). In Bakhtin's view no meaning can be divorced from people:
the study of a text must always be of words and participants together. To
treat language as an impersonal object is to simplify and misrepresent.

This is not merely a question of a different methodology and emphasis in
linguistic description, but a challenge to a view – deeply rooted in Western
philosophy – of the nature of the self, society and the world (Cook 1994c).
In a critique of Saussure, Bakhtin disputes the view of individual identity
and thought as self-contained and separate from language (Volosinov 1986:
45–63).[6] In his view, it is not that we exist first, in isolation from each other,
and then attempt to overcome that isolation through communication; but,
rather, that we come into existence through our language and the social
relationships it creates. What we refer to as the self, or as an individual, is
not something pre-existing and independent of communication, but a projection from an intersection of discourse. Thought is internalized discourse
('I', for example, am the intersection of this book and other communications
in which I am or have been involved.) The 'self', the 'individual' and the
'participant' are to be found in discourse rather than outside it. It is in this
sense that I shall try to use these terms from now on, although the idea of
the self as separate from discourse and society is so deeply 'written into' our
way of speaking that it is very difficult not to fall back on it.

Both in Western philosophy and in our day-to-day view of the world,
the identity of the individual is frequently conceived as independent,
somehow locked away inside the head. Communication is the attempt to
transfer thoughts from one sealed mind to another. De Saussure's diagram
of two talking heads (see Figure 4.3) and his description of language as
'the social product deposited in the brain of each individual' (1974: 23)
express this idea very simply. But there is confusion in the Saussurean
view, as in Western philosophy in general, between the physical person – a
body-and-brain- and the self. Bakhtin suggests that individual identity is
not within the body-and-brain, though these are essential to it, but created
through interaction with another person through language. Our identities
are entangled together, in discourse. In this way Bakhtin frees himself
from the equally weak positions of objectivism, in which meaning is
independent of people, and subjectivism, in which it is wholly within an
isolated person. We cannot exist without discourse, but neither can discourse exist without us.[7]

Analysis of an act of communication must involve analysis of both the participants and their words, although – or because – the two cannot be disentangled. Meaning is not a product of a self-contained and impersonal code, but creative and fuzzy-edged. In Bakhtin's words:

> Meaning does not reside in the word or in the soul of the speaker or in the soul of the listener. Meaning is the *effect of interaction between speaker and listener produced via the material of a particular sound complex*. It is like an electric spark that occurs only when two different terminals are hooked together. Those who ... in attempting to define the meaning of a word, approach its lower, stable, self-identical limit, want, in effect, to turn on a light bulb after having switched off the current. Only the current of verbal intercourse endows a word with the light of meaning.
>
> (Volosinov 1986: 103, original emphasis)

Whereas the semiotic approach tends to divorce text from both senders and receivers, viewing analyst and text as quite separate from each other, in a Bakhtinian view the identity of the receiver is so bound up with the genres which dominate the society through which he or she exists that this neat and secure separation is no longer possible. This has repercussions for the study of those genres which are prominent in the society from which the analyst comes, and with which he or she is involved. If we live in a society permeated with advertising, and receive these communications every day from childhood (as I and probably you have done), then advertising is not some external curiosity which we examine, from which we are separate and superior, but something of which we are part, and which is part of us (whether we like it or not).

Bakhtin rejected dichotomies as simplifications. For this reason he attacked the Saussurean dichotomies of *langue/parole*, diachrony/synchrony (Volosinov 1986: 58–63), the Freudian dichotomy of conscious/unconscious (Volosinov 1973), and (less openly) the Marxist dichotomies of base/superstructure, oppressor/oppressed (Bakhtin 1968).[8] Semiotics views meaning as an equivalence between a signifier and something else (concept, an object in the world, another sign in the same or a different language) which can be dispassionately described by an observer whose own identity is somehow unaffected by his or her discoveries. Such equivalences may help understanding and create insights, but each one leads to another, endlessly altering their observers in the process. The tendency to 'interpret' ads in terms of something else (signifieds, unconscious desires, economic relations) and then rest satisfied with that finite equivalence contributes to understanding, but also simplifies. A rather different reason for interest in advertising is that, as one of the major genres which construct our contemporary identity, it enables us to study a part of ourselves.

8.5.2   *Voices*

A central concept in Bakhtin's theory of communication is that of **voice** and **voices**, the presence or presences evoked by an act of communication. Voices and genre are often closely bound together, and often imply each other. (A trial must have a judge, and a judge must have a trial, for example.) The voices within a text may be described as those of different people or, alternatively, as those of other genres. In the Subaru ad (see Section 5.4.1), for example, the voices are those of a bar-room conversation and a cautionary tale; in the Sunny Delight ad (see Section 6.4) an advisory booklet and family banter; in the Philips phone ad (see Section 7.5) a legal document or a confession. For Bakhtin, the concept of voice forms the basis of a typology of discourse: **monologic** (with one voice); **dialogic** (with two voices); **heteroglossic** (with many voices at once). In Bakhtin's writing, this division involves a value judgement. Monologic discourse, attempting to silence all voices but one, is the hallmark of the authoritarian individual or society, which is neither open nor tolerant.

Bakhtin developed this theory by analysing dialogic and heteroglossic discourse at both the level of the single utterance (Volosinov 1986: 109–59) and at the level of discourse (Bakhtin 1968, 1984). For the former he concentrated upon reported speech, and for the latter upon parody and the novel. Not surprisingly he did not consider advertising – there was none in the Soviet Union at the time he was writing. But it is a genre to which his theories are particularly relevant.

8.5.3   *Voice at sentence level: reported speech*

In reported speech, by definition, the voice of one speaker is contained within the voice of another. Let us consider how this might be used in the pronouncements of a political executive, or the reporting of those pronouncements as news. Suppose the president of a country said

    1   Troops will fire on rioters.

The meaning is created by the speaker's presidential power. It would have quite different meaning if uttered by a child watching TV. It will also change according to the addressee, being different when uttered in a nationwide TV presidential address, or privately to an intimate adviser. (All utterances are to somebody; even when talking to ourselves we project an imagined interlocutor.) A spokesperson for this president might then say:

    2   The president said: 'Troops will fire on rioters.'

In version (2), the two voices are clearly separate. There is a sender and an addresser. The spokesperson says: 'The president said' and the president said 'Troops will fire on the rioters'. Each voice reveals them through lexical and grammatical choice. It was the 'president', not the 'dictator'; the people are 'rioters', not 'protesters'; the simple declarative form, used by both addresser and addressee, has possible connotations of bluntness and authority. The two voices and their judgements seem quite distinct and clear. Yet as soon as one voice is relayed by another, they inevitably begin to merge in complex ways. (That is why this presidential use of spokespersons, though justified by busy schedules, is also a confusion tactic, introducing another voice, giving the sender a later option of withdrawal and dissociation.) It is possible to imagine this reporting of one voice by another moving off in different directions in which the two voices gradually entangle with each other to such an extent that it is quite unclear either what was originally said or whose judgements the utterance reflects. At each stage of remove the options multiply.

1   Troops will fire on rioters.
2   The president said: 'Troops will fire on rioters.'
3   The president said that troops would fire on rioters.
4   The president warned that troops would fire on rioters.
5   The president made it clear that troops would fire on rioters.
6   The president threatened that troops would fire on rioters.
7   The president gave a firm warning that he would reluctantly order troops to fire on rioters.
8   The president made another of his dictatorial announcements, callously ordering the use of violence against innocent people.

In the last two versions, the voice of the president is submerged in that of the second reporting voice, so that the second voice, in effect, will not allow the receiver of this message to judge the president for themselves. Where there is more than one voice, either one will submerge another, or the discourse will allow tolerance of difference.

There are thus a number of possible relationships of voices:

• One voice only.
• Two or more voices, clearly separated.
• Two or more voices, one of which dominates and distorts the others.
• Two or more voices, coexisting (and possibly contradicting) each other.

To Bakhtin, this last preferable possibility is inherent in certain genres: notably the novel (1984) and the parodies of medieval carnival (1968). These have no single voice, but are a mixture of many. Bakhtin termed this **heteroglossia.** As the voices within heteroglossic genres are often the voices of other genres, as well as of individuals, there is a connection between parasite discourse (as discussed in Section 2.4) and heteroglossia.

Ads, as already illustrated, have many voices. The key question to decide is whether the parasitism of ads is truly heteroglossic, or whether the apparent interplay of voices is illusory, masking a monologic discourse, in which many voices are dominated by one. To do this, we shall need to consider heteroglossia at discourse rather than utterance level. In longer extended discourse the options for the merging and submerging of many voices are multiplied, existing not only within sentences, but also in the interaction and contradiction of longer sections of discourse.

8.6 Voices in the novel: two examples

In the novel, one of the most heteroglossic of genres, the entanglement of voices is particularly evident. As a way of assessing the degree of heteroglossia in ads, it may be instructive to compare them with examples of novelistic discourse. This section analyses two passages which are representative of two very different narrative techniques – one from Henry Fielding's *Joseph Andrews* (1742) and one from Jane Austen's *Persuasion* (1818) – and then makes some comparisons between their narrative voices, and those of ads. Once again this will involve us in an apparent digression from our main topic, but one which will, I believe, be useful in highlighting both similarities and differences between the uses of voices in literature, on the one hand, and advertisements, on the other.

8.6.1 *From* Joseph Andrews

In this passage, the eponymous hero, a handsome but comically naïve young man, working as a servant, escapes seduction by his employer's elderly and ugly companion Mrs Slipslop, a woman whose pretensions to education lead her into frequent malapropisms. (This passage spans a transition from one chapter to another.)

> 'Madam,' says Joseph, 'I am sure I have always valued the Honour you did me by your conversation; for I know you are a woman of learning.' 'Yes but Joseph' said she, a little softened by the compliment to her learning, 'If you had a Value for me, you certainly would have found some method of shewing it me; for I am convicted you must see the Value I have for you. Yes, Joseph, my Eyes, whether I would or no, must have declared a Passion I cannot conquer, – Oh! Joseph! –'
>
> As when a hungry Tygress, who long had traversed the Woods in fruitless search, sees within the Reach of her Claws a Lamb, she prepares to leap upon her Prey; or as a voracious Pike, of immense Size, surveys through the liquid Element a Roach or Gudgeon which cannot escape her Jaws, opens them wide to swallow the little Fish; so did Mrs Slipslop prepare to lay her violent amorous Hands on the

poor Joseph, when luckily her Mistress' Bell rung, and delivered the intended Martyr from her Clutches.

She was obliged to leave him abruptly, and defer the Execution of her Purpose to some other Time. We shall therefore return to the Lady Booby, and give our reader some Account of her Behaviour, after she was left by Joseph in a Temper of Mind not greatly different from the inflamed Slipslop.

CHAPTER VII (...)

It is the Observation of some Ancient Sage whose name I have forgot, that Passions operate differently on the human mind as diseases on the body in proportion to the strength or weakness, soundness or rottenness of one or the other.

We hope therefore a judicious reader will give himself some pains to observe...

The many voices, though mixed, are yet reasonably distinct. The narrative voice speaks directly to the reader, and alternates between two communicative worlds, the second of which owes its existence to the first. The first world appears as the real world in which author addresses the reader, the second as a fictional world in which character addresses character. Movement between these two worlds is effected by such statements as:

We shall therefore return to the Lady Booby, and give our reader ...

These guide us into the fictional world, leaving us there unescorted, listening unaided to the voices of the characters (though we know in another part of ourselves that they do not speak autonomously and that their words are as much Fielding's words as any others). There are, as it were, apparently two narrative pathways from author to reader (Figure 8.2).

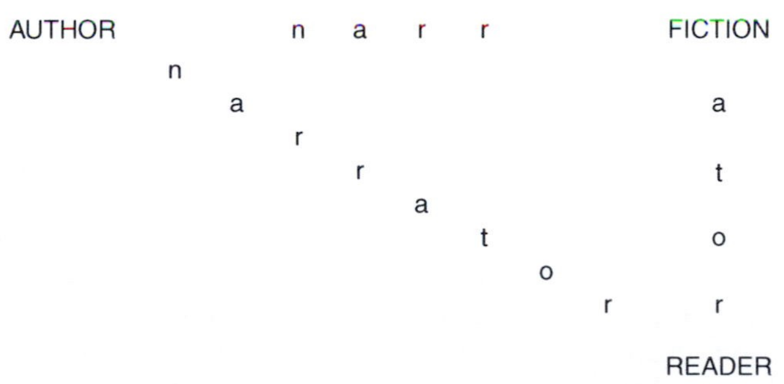

Figure 8.2 Narrative pathways from author to reader (1).

Yet there are a number of complications. The direct, self-declaring authorial voice is itself heteroglossic. It is sometimes an unobtrusive story-teller and observer ('said she, a little softened by the compliment to her learning'); sometimes the elaborate voice of classical epic ('As when a hungry Tygress …'); sometimes a polite guide to the reader ('we shall therefore return … and give our reader some Account'); sometimes the moralist ('It is the Observation of some Ancient Sage'); sometimes collo-quial and offhand ('whose name I have forgot'). Even within the fictional world, away from direct address to the reader, the authorial voice is still evident in such detail as the words 'poor … luckily … delivered', which convey and invite a judgement of the characters. The interweaving of voices and genres makes us doubt both the authenticity of the authorial voice and the autonomy of the fictional world, thus foregrounding the act of story-telling. The comment 'whose name I have forgot', for example, draws attention to the convention of suspended disbelief in the fictional world, treating names within it as though they existed independently and were not invented by the author.

A further multiplication of voices can occur if characters themselves create fictional worlds in which other characters come into being, and the characters who apparently create these other characters themselves adopt narrative positions. The overall voice of the novel is the totality of all these voices. Yet even here, we have not exhausted all the voices which might be taken into account. Like the novel itself, this view ignores the intermediate role of publishers, printers, editors, binders and distributors.

In *Joseph Andrews* worlds and voices are relatively separate. Chapters begin with direct address of author to reader, move on to report the fic-tional world, and in the heart of the chapter apparently abandon control, letting characters speak for themselves. This onion-like structure is found in many other novels, either repeated in each chapter as it is here, or – as in novels presented as journals or stories within stories – in the structure of the whole work. The bulk of such novels may be enclosed in a fictional editor's or publisher's preface explaining how the journal came to light,[9] or an outer narration recounting how the story was told.[10]

Many television ads – even within thirty or sixty seconds – manage to employ this structure too. They begin and/or end with a voice-over and/or written message in which the receiver is directly addressed, and general claims are made; in the middle, they present a fictional situation, some-times including a conversation between characters. The device of the framing journal, which gives fantastic events a setting of sober scientific authority,[11] is echoed by toothpaste and disinfectant ads which begin and end with a scientist's report. Sometimes a white-coated boffin even appears, like the good angel of medieval drama, in the kitchen or bath-room, either invisible to all the characters, or conversing with only one of them while unseen by all the others!

Yet, while the framed narratives of novels often begin with an authoritative voice, they often finish open-ended, without further editorial comment. In ads, the reverse is true, and the voice of authority occurs or recurs at the end, to leave nothing to the receiver.

8.6.2 *From* Persuasion

As the novel developed, it tended increasingly to merge voices through the development of narrative techniques which fuse first and third person narrations into one which is simultaneously neither and both. An early example is Jane Austen's *Persuasion,* a novel whose suspense and power derive from the conflicting interpretations of events which result from the fusion of authorial, narrative, societal and characters' voices. The plot centres upon Anne Elliot's continuing love for Frederick Wentworth, a man whose offer of marriage her family once persuaded her to reject as beneath her. He returns from the Napoleonic War, rich, successful and as attractive as ever, while Anne, though less subservient to her family, believes herself too old and plain to attract his interest again. Suspense hinges upon the fusion of narrative and characters' voices, and the ambiguity inherent in reported speech. Consider this central passage, which has given critics and students the material for lengthy debate:[12]

> On one other question, which perhaps her utmost wisdom might not have prevented, she was soon spared all suspense; for after the Miss Musgroves had returned and finished their visit at the Cottage, she had this spontaneous information from Mary:
> 'Captain Wentworth is not very gallant by you, Anne, though he was so attentive to me. Henrietta asked him what he thought of you, when they went away; and he said, "You were so altered he should not have known you again." '
> Mary had no feelings to make her respect her sister's in a common way; but she was perfectly unsuspicious of being inflicting any particular wound.
> 'Altered beyond his knowledge!' Anne fully submitted, in silent, deep mortification. Doubtless it was so; and she could take no revenge, for he was not altered, or not for the worse. She had already acknowledged it to herself, and she could not think differently, let him think of her as he would. No; the years which had destroyed her youth and bloom had only given him a more glowing, manly, open look, in no respect lessening his personal advantages. She had seen the same Frederick Wentworth.
> 'So altered that he should not have known her again!' These were words which could not but dwell with her. Yet she soon began to rejoice that she had heard them. They were of sobering tendency; they allayed agitation; they composed, and consequently must make her happier.

Frederick Wentworth had used such words, or something like them, but without an idea that they would be carried round to her. He had thought her wretchedly altered, and, in the first moment of appeal, had spoken as he felt. He had not forgotten Anne Elliot. She had used him ill; deserted and disappointed him; and worse, she had shewn a feebleness of character in doing so, which his own decided, confident temper could not endure. She had given him up to oblige others. It had been the effect of over-persuasion. It had been weakness and timidity.

At every level from word to discourse, meanings are multiplied by the ambiguous identity of the voice which speaks them. Thus we do not know whether the 'spontaneous information from Mary' is judged to be 'spontaneous', perhaps wrongly, by Anne, or by the narrative voice; and, if the latter, we do not know whether the word is to be taken at face value, or as an ironic indictment of Mary's cruelty (the assumption being that spontaneity is less likely to be dishonest). Crucially we do not know the extent to which Mary's rendition of Wentworth's words distorts them, and, even if these were his words, whether they were uttered in the knowledge that they would be relayed to Anne. The meaning of confidential critical remarks even when noted verbatim is distorted when they are repeated to the person criticized – a fact which the reporter very often knows and calculates (Tannen 1989: 105–10). Yet even assuming that Wentworth uttered the words exactly as reported, fully aware and perhaps intending that they should be repeated to Anne, they are still not clear: 'altered' does not necessarily mean 'altered for the worse', for example. Nor can we rely, as in Fielding, upon a clear alternation between the perceptions of the characters and a detached and reliable narrative judgement. This earlier convention is now manipulated to tease. Narrative control appears to return in

Frederick Wentworth had used such words

but this is immediately followed by

or something like them.

which abdicates responsibility and denies any privileged knowledge. The passage is full of puzzles. Who says 'the years had destroyed her youth and bloom'? Austen? General opinion'? Anne at her most objective? Anne when she is pessimistic and depressed? Who says Wentworth has a 'decided confident temper'? Perhaps only Wentworth, trying to cheer himself up. The strength of this novel lies in this plethora of possible interpretations, which resist reduction to a single uninteresting voice, and keep the reader on tenterhooks as to whether the couple will reunite. Iconically,

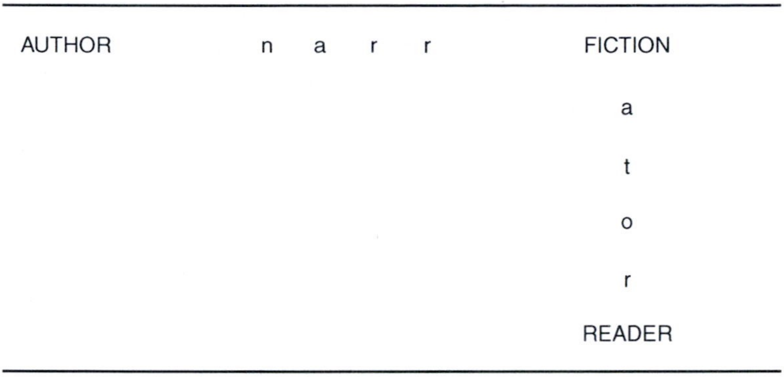

AUTHOR	n	a	r	r	FICTION
					a
					t
					o
					r
					READER

Figure 8.3 Narrative pathways from author to reader (2).

the ambiguity and open-endedness of this narrative mimics the uncertainty and intensity, the alternation between hope and fear, of the central characters. The voice of the author, accessible only through the voices of characters, is thus never clearly perceived, but remains both mysterious and intriguing (Figure 8.3).

If these two novels represent two poles of narrative technique, we might then ask which, if either, is closer to the narrative technique of ads.

There is no simple answer to this question, for ads, like novels, provide too many exceptions. Yet there is in ads a reluctance to leave matters open, which results, even in the most heteroglossic ads, in the assertion of a single monologic and authoritative voice at the end. This in turn leads to a clearer separation of voices. The reason for this is the constraint imposed by the client: the overall judgement must be final and closed. This perhaps will prevent ads ever developing more heteroglossic narrative techniques in the future, and denies them the degree of freedom available in literature.

8.7 Intertextual voices in ads

Many ads contain the voices of other ads or of other genres. The meanings deriving from these echoes are usually described as intertextual (as in Section 1.2), and this phenomenon may thus be subdivided into two types

1   **intra-generic intertextuality**: containing the voice of another example of the same genre, as when an ad assumes knowledge of another ad. (The 'Secret Weapon' ad in Figure 7.4, for example, with its 'Warning; may cause outbreaks of jealousy' alludes to the health warning on cigarette ads.)

2   **inter-generic intertextuality**: containing the voice of a different genre,
    as when an ad evokes knowledge of a film or story. (The text of the
    Philips cordless phone ad in Figure 7.2 for example echoes the
    wording of a legal statement ('I understand that...')

The passages from Fielding and Austen contain examples of both. *Joseph Andrews,* by dealing in its ribald way with the tribulations of a young person besieged by lecherous older people, almost certainly evoked, for its contemporaries, if not for us, the presence of another, more serious novel on the same theme, Richardson's *Pamela.* The convoluted clauses and elaborate similes of the paragraph beginning 'As when the hungry Tygress ...' parody classical epic (and translations of it) and use this to ridicule Mrs Slipslop. Jane Austen makes a less tangible allusion to the conventions of other novels[13] – including Fielding's – by appearing to return from characters' perceptions to authorial comment, but shying away at the last moment in mid-sentence ('or something like them'). Such voices, based on an author's prediction of a reader's likely experience of other discourse, now need pointing out and annotating – and illustrates the strange but common phenomenon of the parody proving more durable than its target.

Ads, like novels, contain both intra-generic and inter-generic voices. These have increased as ads have grown in quantity and salience, and accumulated their own history and tradition. If, as suggested in Chapter 1, advertising has changed dramatically since the mid-1950s, creating in effect a new genre, then it is not surprising that early ads are uninteresting and impoverished in terms of intra-generic echoes. (The same cannot be said of early novels – but that is what makes the early novel so remarkable.) Lacking a tradition of other ads on which to draw, early ads slavishly employed the voices of other genres to lend credence to a straightforward act of persuasion. Favourite among evoked genres were the scientific report (transmitted by a white-coated male scientist), the conversational advice of a confidante (such as a more experienced mother/housewife/woman of fashion), or the sales rap (delivered by an eloquent and enthusiastic man in a suit!). All these are gifts to ridicule. They still appear in ads, though less frequently.

As the tradition of ads has grown, the nature and number of intra-generic voices have changed. Sometimes, ads assume and exploit knowledge of another product and its ads merely to attack a competitor. In 1991 the slogan for the Peugeot 405 'Takes Your Breath Away' was parodied without direct reference in an ad for the VW Polo whose copy reads 'It doesn't take your breath away' – a device which both attracts attention and makes the claim that the Polo's catalytic converter reduces air pollution.

Such cross-references reflect serious competition between manufacturers of similar products. The long-running war between Pepsi and Coca-Cola provides many examples. In such cases, the concern is the comparison of products more than the comparison of ads. At other times, however, one ad will make use of another, not because it is purveying a competing product, but simply to attract attention, often through parody. If we extend the metaphor of ads as parasites, these ads are parasites on parasites.

Very often, the target of the parody is the kind of naïve and simplistic ad – familiar in the 1950s and 1960s – someone who knows, such as a mother or housewife, dentist, baker or farmer, endorses the product in a highly stereotypical way. This for example, was an ad on British TV in the summer of 2000.

Kingsmill Tasty Crust bread

The main character is apparently a conventional looking housewife with shoulder length hair. In the first scene she appears smiling outside a super-market with a full trolley, and is joined by a female friend.[14] She addresses the camera.

Housewife:	My many friends ask me as a busy housewife and mother how I find time to bake my own bread.
Friend:	So . . .
Housewife:	(*Aside to her friend.*) Not now! (*To the camera.*) And how do I get it so tasty and crusty.
Housewife:	(*Back home, she is carrying a plate of sandwiches from kitchen. Aside to the friend who is following her.*) Don't do this! (*To the camera.*) It certainly makes me popular with my family.
	(*She puts the plate down in front of two children and husband waiting at the dining room table.*)
Friend:	You're not a housewife. You're not a mother. And this is new Kingsmill tasty crust.
Housewife:	Try my bread. It's so tasty.
Friend:	(*pulling off the housewife's wig to reveal short cropped hair underneath*) That's not your hair.
Director of the ad:	(*Bursting into the scene*) Cut!
Voiceover:	(*Male voice*) New Tasty Crust. Fresh Thinking from Kingsmill.

Picture shows a loaf of bread unpackaged merging into a loaf in packag-ing.

Other parodies can be much more specific, and a tradition of allusion can run over decades. For example, a succession of ads have made use of the spectacularly successful Levi 501 ads which appeared in Britain in 1985–7.[15] The extraordinary popularity of these ads virtually guaranteed their exploitation by others. An ad for Carling Black Label lager released not long after the original, for example, showed the same situation, and used the same music, as one of the first Levi ads, 'Launderette' in which a young man strips down to his boxer shorts in a launderette. In the Carling ad, there are also two older, fatter men in the launderette, completely naked with their hands folded modestly across their laps. One comments: 'I bet he drinks Carling Black Label.' The other replies: 'No. He doesn't wash his underpants.' Not long afterwards, an ad for the beverage IRN BRU (= iron brew) parodied a later Levi's ad 'Parting', which showed a young GI saying goodbye to his girlfriend at the bus station. In the Irn Bru ad, the young soldier is splattered with mud as the bus departs. This ad contains a pastiche of such parodies. When a boy inserts money into a drink-dispensing machine, as in a contemporary Coca-Cola ad, the machine does not work. When he shakes it, it responds by banging him on the head. (A later ad even parodied this parody by creating expectation of this bang on the head, but instead has the boy thumped in the crutch by a can shooting out of the delivery slot at the bottom of the machine.) Such cross-references can be multi-layered, for the ad to which another ad refers is itself likely to make references to other genres. 'Parting', for example, assumes knowledge of romances in films and novels.

Ironically, Levis themselves joined in the stream of parodies, which continued throughout the 1990s, perhaps because, by 2000, a new campaign was needed to halt a fourteen-year slump in sales.[16] The ads for the 501s' successor, Twisted Originals, were as mocking of the original ads as anything for other products in the intervening years. One for example shows a romance between two inflatable sex dolls ending when they burst on barbed wire. The name 'Twisted Originals' refers as much to the ads as the jeans. (For further discussion of Levi's ads, see Myers 1999: 22–8.)

The growth of such traditions, and the accumulation of knowledge of past ads which increases the scope for intra-generic references immensely, leads to a growing complexity. Inter-generic possibilities, though they have always been available, are constantly extended and exploited.

Exercises

1   An ad for Waterman fountain pens shows a fountain pen and two cherries on a black plate. The copy reads:

> Envy. Desperately sinful. Wickedly Waterman. And absolutely forgivable. The Man. Waterman.

Is it possible to supply ellipted elements which convert these orthographic sentences into full grammatical sentences with main verbs? What cultural knowledge do you use to make sense of this ad?

2 Consider the following ads in terms of
- their assumptions of shared knowledge and value
- their narrative technique
- their use of parallelism and cohesion
- their intra- and inter-generic intertextuality
- how allusions are established and how successful they are in increasing the impact of the ad.

a Citizen Watches

> Before the night was through they would reveal a lot more to each other than just their watches.
> Copacabana danced below as he came face to face with her bewildering elegance. Her movements held him spellbound as she slipped her immaculately manicured fingers inside her leather handbag to emerge with a cigarette pack.
> It was the same American brand of Light 100's he always carried. Her pack was empty. 'Have one of mine.' Hesitating slightly, she took one and lit it herself.
> That's when he noticed her watch. Like his, it was a modern Roman face, gold cased with a stitched leather strap. 'We obviously share the same excellent taste in watches, too. What's your favourite champagne?'
> She laughed and spoke at last. 'Same as yours?'
> Citizen First Class

b Clinically proven to give you grottier looking skin. There's only one product that guarantees fast, effective results when it comes to skincare. Every cigarette contains special active ingredients called 'toxins' that constrict blood vessels, starve your skin of oxygen and remove the lingering traces of a healthy complexion. In fact, the only thing glowing about your face will be the cigarette end. (Figure 8.4)

c Royal Navy (Figure 8.5)

> 'She's still scared of the wind but loves our helicopters.'
> 'After two weeks at sea the call for help came. A typhoon had hit the mainland blocking all roads to rescuers, leaving the only route in from the sea. We flew in emergency supplies with Lynx helicopters, our Medics took care of the wounded and bad cases were flown out of the ship. We restored power, erected temporary shelters and set up teams to prevent looting. A task as tough as Disaster Relief Training back at home.'
> Royal Navy. The team works.

Figure 8.4 'Ash Tray': anti-smoking advertisement.

Figure 8.5 Recruiting advertisement for The Royal Navy.

5   Is the density of narrative voices in a story a measure of quality? If so, how do ads compare with novels and short stories?

Further reading

Bakhtin

Bakhtin's theories of language, including his critique of de Saussure, can be found in *Marxism and the Philosophy of Language* (Volosinov 1988), a book which Bakhtin published under the name of his friend Volosinov. A more easily accessible introduction to Bakhtin's theories of language and the novel are Chapters 10–11 and 13–14 of Katerina Clark and Michael Holquist's (1984) biography, *Mikhail Bakhtin*. Further comment on Bakhtin and de Saussure as representatives of two opposed philosophies of communication can be found in my own (1994) essay 'Contradictory voices: a dialogue between Russian and Western European linguistics'.

Voices in the novel

The description of narrative technique in the novel in this chapter owes a great deal to Chapters 6 and 8–10 of Leech and Short (1981) *Style in Fiction*, which provides one of the best introductions to the discourse analysis of fiction.

9 Ways of hearing

9.1 Senders, receivers, observers

Chapters 7 and 8 discussed the narrative voice of ads (the 'we') and the kind of reception it assumes and encourages in the receiver (the 'you'). It would be a mistake however to assume that the narrative voice can be treated as identical to the people who created the ad, or that the 'you' to whom it speaks is straightforwardly equivalent to the receiver. It seems more likely that creators of ads, quite as much as novelists, lawyers, newscasters or scientists, adopt a voice which is suitable to the discourse of their profession, and that receivers also, once they have identified the genre, adopt a particular stance, or stances, of interpretation. Both writers and readers play roles.

Generally, it is quite naïve for a competent member of a culture to be unable to disentangle the various roles adopted or demanded by different genres. In the public sphere, we know that the prosecution lawyer has private feelings about a case, but accept that he or she speaks as though convinced of the defendant's guilt; that a teacher admonishes a pupil for behaviour which privately he or she might find amusing; that the teller of a detective story knows who the criminal is, but withholds this information, and so on. In the private sphere, we know that people with whom we are intimate, who talk to us frankly and often emotionally in private, perhaps using 'baby talk' or taboo language to do so, do not talk like that in more public roles. Knowledge, recognition and acceptance of such conventions is part of our cultural competence. Inevitably problems arise when people interpret one genre as another: fiction as fact, a joke as a serious comment, political debate as a personal attack, an off-the-record remark as an official statement, and so on. Words must be interpreted within the genre to which they belong. 'Dear John' means one thing in conversation, something else at the beginning of a letter.

The role of the receiver in creating meaning has generally been neglected in the study of language, which usually focuses upon either the disembodied text or the sender.[1] Even Bakhtin's approach lacks this focus, stressing the voices in discourse, and ways of speaking. Yet voices exist only if they are heard. What is needed is an equivalent focus on the receiver, on the different ways of **hearing** which can co-exist, even within one person. An absence of attention to reception leads to a considerable simplification of receivers' roles and abilities, and in analyses of advertising has meant – as we shall see – that they are often simplified, patronized and misrepresented.

Because of its relative novelty, and its ambiguity and instability as a genre, advertising causes problems, and has often been read by conventions imported from other situations and genres. The voice of the advertisement is treated as the voice of the advertiser, or interpreted by the conventions of another genre. The purpose of this chapter is to examine this phenomenon and its results: attitudes towards advertising; ways of reading them; and some judgements of ads by their receivers.

Chapter 8 has provided a framework which will distinguish the **senders** of ads (the people who write, direct, photograph and act in them) from the **narrators** of ads (the personas, characters and voices which senders adopt). In considering the hearing of ads we need a parallel distinction between the **recipient** (the receiver responding to an ad by entering into its conventions) and the **observer** (the receiver adopting a more detached perspective, seeing ads in the context of other genres). Hearing as a recipient and hearing as an observer are not mutually exclusive. The borders are fuzzy, and there is an infinity of possible positions along a continuum between the two. One person may hear in both ways at once, or in different ways on different occasions.

Although the voice of the narrator is part of the wider personality of the sender, and that personality in turn expresses part of itself through the ad it creates, the senders of ads may maintain some distance from their professional role. A further complication to neat divisions is that senders are also recipients and observers (like everybody else). The people who write ads, in other words, are also consumers and purchasers, and also individuals with their own values and judgements. For everyone, observation of ads is bound to be affected by experience as a recipient and vice versa. Nor is this necessarily something detrimental to analysis. Contrary to the conventions of the scientific approach to language, the most effective observers may also be recipients or narrators.

In the creation of an ad, there are likely to be multiple senders: manufacturers, photographers, writers, models, actors, Web page designers (see Section 8.4) and so forth. As senders, these people may either dislike the product or have no experience of it. As narrators, they adopt a voice which may be interpreted as the inner voice of the character, of a confidante, of society in general, or of the addressee. Similarly, an addressee of an ad, as a recipient entering into its spirit, may find it amusing and attractive, or, conversely, silly and unconvincing; simultaneously, as an observer, he or she may stand back from it, knowing that there is no necessary connection between a good ad and a good product, and judging it according to his or her personal views on gender roles, ecology, economics, politics, aesthetics, and so on. Many analyses of ads depend upon the unproven assumption that addressees have only one impoverished way of responding to discourse, and are too stupid to distinguish fact from fantasy or fiction. It is often argued that people are tricked into believing that if they buy the product they will experience the attractive lifestyle of the characters (Berger 1972: 131). As Thompson (1990) sensibly observes (commenting on the prevalence of this view among his students):

> The problem with this is that clearly anyone who did believe any such thing as a result of exposure to the advertising message would be gullible to the point of madness, as eccentric as those often-posited, rarely-met individuals who believe in the reality of soap-opera fictions. Students themselves never own up to any such belief, and it is not likely that advertising's power can be based on any *mass* delusional system of this sort.
>
> (original emphasis, Thompson 1990: 211)

As advertising is not a remote and specialized discourse, but a prominent genre in contemporary society, of which people have vast and daily experience, reactions to it are correspondingly complex, experienced and sophisticated. They involve many ways of hearing at once.

9.2 Negative hearings

There are undoubtedly many reasons to dislike ads, whether individually or as a genre. Many people do so, either consistently, or from time to time. Let us consider here some of the arguments which can be advanced against them.

Ads are uninvited and intrusive, thrust upon the reader or viewer without consultation. It is true that print ads can be skipped, TV ads zipped or zapped, and Internet ads never clicked on. Yet it is virtually impossible to avoid ads entirely. Junk mail (both paper and electronic) is particularly persistent, and to many people very irritating. The large databases of personal information maintained by marketers, and often compiled surreptitiously (through Internet cookies, automatic supermarket checkout records and so forth) are infringements of privacy.

While some ads are witty, imaginative, poetic or well filmed, at least an equal number are trite, sentimental or unoriginal. Although creative, they usually ask only passive involvement on the part of the receiver (though so does a good deal of art). Even the cleverest and most entertaining ads (however interesting at the level of detail, form and execution) can often, in quantity, become dull and trivial – a fact which seems to be borne out by the limited success of attempts to string collections of advertisements together into films.[2]

Ads glorify widely accepted values. A positive evaluation of them may reflect the degree of the observer's belief in the status quo. To the feminist opposed to patriarchy, the gay opposed to heterosexual hegemony, the environmentalist opposed to over consumption, the socialist opposed to capitalism, ads may seem to advocate values to be lamented.

Ads promote consumption in a world which needs to save resources, and the acquisition of personal wealth in a global society which desperately needs fairer distribution. In the case of junk mail (which threatens to increase) they waste resources even more directly. In the UK between 1991 and 1996 expenditure on direct mail almost doubled in real terms to reach £1.4 billion (Wilmshurst and Mackay 1999: 131). With an estimated 200 items received per household, this amounts to something in the order of three billion items a year – the majority of which are immediately thrown away. By any standards, this is a considerable waste of energy and resources.

Such criticisms as these are relatively straightforward, and no doubt shared by many people. Against them it can be said that ads are often criticized for failing to do things they never set out to do: vying with works of art, providing sustained entertainment, making radical changes to our perception of the world. If they express objectionable social trends or states, it could be argued that they are indices of the enemy, not the enemy itself; if so, they should not perhaps be the first line of attack for those who seek change.

Do arguments about ads, then, boil down to some rather straightforward matters of opinion. Are ads trivial? Are there too many of them? Are they unwanted? Do they represent unpleasant values of consumerism and environmental damage, and, if so, are they a major force in promoting those values or only peripheral? Are ads comparable to art? These are matters which every observer must decide for themselves, and it is not my intention to argue for one side or the other. (I could not do so even if I wanted to, for like many people I hear ads in several contradictory ways at once.) It is the difficulty of finding simple answers to these questions which, in my opinion, makes ads so interesting as a genre. (This is not the same as saying that every individual ad is interesting.) Many analyses, however, do take sides, and seek to impose an unequivocal view, using ads as a starting point for pronouncements for or against them – which often say more about their authors than about the ads.

It is on a selection of such pronouncements that the following sections focus: encompassing the hearings of artists, writers and academics; of the public; and inevitably – as I also am recipient – myself. I make no claim to objectivity or inclusiveness in this survey. The theoretical view throughout this book has been that the 'meaning' of discourse is always inevitably partial and relative to particular hearers. My hearing of other people's hearings – unlike that of many other analysts – makes no pretence to be otherwise.

9.3 How ads are heard by artists and writers

In literature, song, film and painting (henceforth 'the arts' for brevity), reactions to ads, as among the general public, range from violent hostility, through indifference and amused detachment, to appreciation (see Section 1.6). Though it is impossible to survey such a field in entirety, it is worth citing some examples.

Broadly speaking, reactions follow the rise of advertising: the occasional curiosity of the 1930s and 1940s, when ads were relatively peripheral, was replaced by a more aggressive attitude during the rapid expansion and hard selling of the 1950s and 1960s. This in turn gave way to a degree of wry tolerance during the 1970s to 1990s, when ads became both more established and more sophisticated. Early criticisms are mild, very much in the spirit of Raymond Chandler's Philip Marlowe who, talking about chess, remarks that it is

> about as elaborate a waste of human intelligence as you could find anywhere outside an advertising agency.
>
> (quoted in E. Clark 1988)

(This is, however, the voice of a character, whose presupposition that chess is a waste of time may tell us more about himself than about the author.) Such mildness was not to last. In the early 1950s, the surrealist René Magritte, asked what he hated most in the world, answered unequivocally:

> advertising ... imbecilic ... mediocre stuff for the public.[3]

Allen Ginsberg in *Howl* (1953) included among the forces which destroyed 'the best minds of my generation':

> blasts of leaden verses and the tanked up clatter of the iron regiments of fashion and the nitroglycerine shrieks of the fairies of advertising and the mustard gas of sinister intelligent editors.

Perhaps more dangerous to advertising than such furious attack is indifference, appropriation or laughter. Both ads and the arts are robust, parasitic and self-confident. When there is contact, both struggle to assimilate the other: borrowing, stealing, parodying, smothering, debunking. When the arts have not ignored advertising, they have often approached it with detachment, ridicule and a sense of absurdity – confident that ads are a peripheral and inconsequential phenomenon posing no threat to its own ascendancy. Bob Dylan's 1963 song 'I Shall Be Free' provides a good example:

Oh set me down on the television floor,
I'll flip the channel to number four.
Out of the shower comes a grown-up man
With a bottle of hair oil in his hand.
(It's that greasy kids stuff.)
[...]
Well, the funniest woman I ever seen
Was the great granddaughter of Mr Clean.
She takes about fifteen baths a day,
Wants me to grow a moustache on my face.

As advertising has preyed upon the arts, stealing many of its ideas and incorporating them into its own creations, so the arts have been quite prepared to respond in kind, reincorporating ads, using them for their own purposes. In painting, ads and bits of ads have appeared in collage and background since the turn of the century. In song, two Beatles songs – 'Being for the Benefit of Mr Kite' and 'Happiness Is a Warm Gun' are based on the words of advertisements. In literature, advertising often appears as a symbol of absurdity, a realization of false values in contrast with those of the people into whose lives it intrudes, only emphasizing an absence of meaning. An early example – from 1926! – is the giant poster which broods over the 'valley of ashes' in F. Scott Fitzgerald's novel *The Great Gatsby*:

> above the grey land and the spasms of bleak dust which drift endlessly over it, you perceive, after a moment, the eyes of Doctor T.J. Eckleberg. The eyes of Doctor T.J. Eckleberg are blue and gigantic – their retinas are one yard high. They look out of no face, but, instead, from a pair of enormous yellow spectacles which pass over a nonexistent nose. Evidently some wily wag of an oculist set them there to fatten his practice in the borough of Queens, and then sank down himself into eternal blindness, or forgot them and moved away. But his eyes, dimmed a little by many pointless days, under sun and rain, brood on over the solemn dumping ground.

The climax of the novel, a car accident bringing death and separation to the protagonists, takes place near this ad, whose superficial resemblance to a divinity – though one which is uncaring, decayed and outdated – emphasizes the absurdity and hopelessness of the drama acted out beneath it. Since *The Great Gatsby*, there have been many literary contrasts between the bright optimistic images of ads and the drabber, more painful world of everyday life. Philip Larkin's poem 'Sunny Prestatyn', for example, contrasts the advertising image of a seaside resort, showing a girl

kneeling up on the sand
in tautened white satin

with the obscene graffito ('a tuberous cock and balls') drawn between her legs.

From the late 1980s, a new tone has appeared alongside attack and ridicule, which, while maintaining the stereotypes of deceiver and deceived, is marked by a willingness to perceive advertising from inside the mind of its creators as well as through the eyes of the deceived. An example is *Bliss,* a novel by Peter Carey about an ad man who moves to a commune dedicated to environmental protection, forsaking the stressful life of the city to become a tree planter. Although there are many voices in this novel, both for and against ads, and even if both writer and many readers may prefer his second life, there is also a willingness to adopt, albeit temporarily, the voice of the creator of an ad:

> Imagine this: a colour poster thirty inches long and eight inches deep. A photograph of a match, very large, occupies almost the entire length of the poster. Beneath it, in Franklin Gothic type, these words: 'All the wood you need to burn this winter', and beneath that, the logo: Mobil LP Gas.
>
> All this for stores in country areas, to stick on walls for flies to shit on, for mutants to stare at. But look at it there, lying against the pink wall with its cell overlay: a thing of beauty destined to take its place in the One Show in New York ... All the client had asked for was something cheap and nasty to shut up the country dealers who were complaining about a lack of promotional support. He had not asked for this pristine piece of art lying against the pink wall.
>
> (Peter Carey, *Bliss*, 1982: 205)

In film a similar progression to that in literature is evident in the postwar decades. Advertising appears only comic in the films of the 1940s and 1950s.[4] Directors of the 1960s and 1970s express their disdain by never – that I know of – making advertising a central topic, but using it only as a symbol of greed or superficiality. It is in films of this period that the device of ads as a symbol of absurdity – rather as in *The Great Gatsby* – becomes prominent. A typical – perhaps seminal – example occurs in Makavejev's *W.R. The Mysteries the Organism* (1971), where the comment that 'The American Dream is dead' is immediately followed, as though in illustration, by a Coca-Cola jingle. In films since then, the contrast between the jolly voices and affluent images emanating from radio and posters, and the poverty or anguish of characters, has become a cinematic cliché – though still an effective one. Such contrasts reflect constant tension between the world depicted in ads and the world in which they appear. The 1980s and 1990s, while still critical, produced films which make advertising a centre of attention and present the people who work it as complex and creative. Robinson's *How to Get Ahead in Advertising* (1989), for example, is the story of an advertising 'creative' whose agonizing over a brief for a new acne cream causes him to develop a pimple on his neck which grows into a talking head, takes over its host, and arranges for his death. In *Crazy People* (1990), the central character is a creative director who makes truthful ads for reasons of principle, only to find that this is the most successful marketing strategy of all. While still anti-advertising, to a degree, these later films – rather like the novel *Bliss* – yet present the topic from inside, with understanding of the complexity of the emotional, moral and personal issues for both the senders and the recipients of ads.

However, all of these representations – whether antagonistic, sardonic, or sympathetic – assume an established order of genres with a clear border between them. Whatever ads may be (good or bad) they are viewed as something quite separate from paintings, poems, songs, novels and films. Perhaps the real change in the artistic landscape of the 2000s is not in the attitude of art to advertising, but of some erosion of the boundary between genres. Advertising is beginning to break out of the cordon which was placed around it at its inception, so that it is harder, in some cases, to draw boundaries. Questions like that posed by the W.H. Auden poem *The Night Mail* (was it a poem or an ad?) arise ever more frequently (see Section 6.2.4). Can songs and melodies become inextricably linked with advertisements in which they play? Does sponsorship convert even the 'high arts' such as opera and classical concerts into partial advertisements?

9.4 Academic attitudes

Academic attitudes to advertising display a similar range to those in the arts, and have been through similar stages. Perhaps one of the most influential critiques of advertising was one of the earliest. Vance Packard's book *The Hidden Persuaders* (1956) drew upon the psychological theory of the time to suggest that ads, by inserting images and words at speeds which cannot be consciously perceived, could operate through **subliminal persuasion**, that is to say 'beneath our level of awareness'. Perhaps no single work has done more to fuel public fear of ads – and understandably so, for had Packard been right, public powers of discrimination and resistance would indeed be undermined. The irony is however that it was Packard who persuaded without evidence. The possibility of subliminal persuasion has never been scientifically demonstrated (Eysenck and Keane 1990: 77–84) – and in any case legislation following the scare made the techniques Packard claimed to be making use of it illegal. Yet the notion that advertisers use subliminal methods persists and – in my experience – commonly crops up early in most discussions of the morality of advertising. Yet perhaps the ultimate irony is that this book – so often drawn upon as 'evidence for the prosecution' – is far from anti-advertising. Advertisers, wrote Packard, fill an important and constructive role in our society. Advertising not only plays a vital role in promoting our economic growth but is a colourful, diverting aspect of American life...'

(Packard 1956)

Despite the alarm generated by Packard, in the 1960s and 1970s, work on ads in sociology, semiotics and linguistics (McLuhan 1964; Leech 1966; Barthes 1973; Goffman 1979; Williams 1980), though at times very critical, remained calm. With a new, uncharted and innovative genre before it, it provided equally new and suitably perceptive analyses. Work continuing this rich tradition in the 1980s and 1990s, while by no means uncritical of the values and techniques of advertising, has also not been blind to its frequent complexity, creativity and wit (Davis and Walton 1983; Vestergaard and Schrøder 1985; Umiker-Sebeok 1987; Myers 1994; Tanaka 1994; Forceville 1996; Nava *et al.* 1997; Myers 1999).

A middle period, however, with its heyday in the late 1970s and early 1980s, was one of ferocious and emotional attack. The reasons for the antagonism during this period are worth analysing in some detail, together with the effects they have had on some more recent considerations of the rights and wrongs of advertising.

The mood of the period is illustrated by the entry under 'advertising' in the 1988 edition of the *Fontana Dictionary of Modern Thought*, a scholarly, wide-ranging encyclopedia of twentieth-century ideas, whose general tone is informative, factual and non-partisan, even in entries for 'Nazism', 'Stalinism' and 'Apartheid'. In the entry for 'Advertising', however, this tone disappears:

> Creativity [in ads] means instant attention-getting, resulting in a glibness or lateral cleverness, not to be confused with creativity in, say, film, literature or art.... Concern that such creativity has hidden shallows has resulted in a plethora of self-aggrandizing award festivals, locally and internationally, at which 'creatives' award each other glittering prizes.

(The rest of the short entry is in the same vein.) Though there are valid reasons (listed in Section 9.2) why many people regret the advent and rapid growth of mass advertising, such all-out abuse in a publication with pretensions to scholarly detachment is intriguing. There may be other reasons than those advanced by the critics themselves why advertising arouses stronger feelings in this period than mass murder and oppression.

To examine this approach, and speculate on its causes, I shall look at two representative works: Judith Williamson's (1978) *Decoding Advertisements* and Michael Geis's (1982) *The Language of Television Advertising*. These are longer, more detailed works than the encyclopedia entry, but their conclusions, though extended, are as sweeping in their condemnation. As they raise important issues, and typify a species of common but self-defeating criticism, I shall deal with them at some length.

The argument, and the anger, have three bases: an emphasis on text which ignores or simplifies its relation to participants; an unquestioning acceptance of 'scientific fact', 'naturalness' and 'reality' as centres of belief; and lastly, though not explicitly, a fear of a genre which the authors cannot identify with any existing well-established categories.

In the world of Williamson and Geis, the divisions between types of participant are distinct and unproblematic. They are dealt with swiftly, allowing attention to be centred on the text. The observers regard themselves as above the process, and in no way like the recipients. This swift disposal of participant roles rests upon a gross caricature: the senders of ads are villains, intent on deception; the recipients are uneducated, vulnerable and easily deceived; the observers are superior to both, and unaffected by the text, because they can decode it. (It is a Saussurean rather than Bakhtinian model of communication, treating meaning as a feature of the code.) Geis describes receivers as 'logically and linguistically naive speakers' (1982: 70), lacking any insight into their own everyday lives; they are 'speakers untutored in logic' who 'do not control' the fine distinctions of his analysis (1982: 12). And they suffer accordingly.

> To some degree, viewers get the commercials they deserve, that is, commercials to which they respond.
>
> (Geis 1982: 110)

> if language scholars do not draw attention to linguistic abuses in public uses of language we leave the field open to various self-styled language experts whose critiques are usually shallow and misinformed.
>
> (Geis 1982: xiii)

It is unclear why Geis does not consider himself 'a viewer' along with everybody else, nor why other experts, but not he, are 'self-styled'!

9.4.1 *Logic and fact*

For Geis, decoding means transforming the text into its underlying logical and factual form. (He appeals to the formal logic of propositional calculus.) But this logical meaning is not seen as a *part* of the meaning, but its totality. This leads to consternation and outrage when language resists transformation. Of a cereal ad which begins 'Mother Nature sweetens apples for two good reasons' he writes:

> Everything claimed is false, for there is no such thing as Mother Nature.
>
> (Geis 1982: 88)

Of a margarine ad which describes its taste as 'buttery':

> if someone says something is buttery there is no objective basis for determining whether or not what is said is true.
>
> (Geis 1982: 122)

To a pet food ad with the words:

> she thinks she's still a puppy, and she looks like one too, but she's 14 years old.

he objects, firstly on the grounds that dogs can't think in this way, and secondly that the simile is not apt because, although

> The older dog does look like a puppy in that she has four legs, two ears, a tail, a dog shaped body and head etc. . . it is difficult to see how a 14 year old dog could actually look like a puppy unless it had oversize paws, much puppy fat, etc.
>
> (Geis 1982: 123)

At the centre of such an approach is the belief that the surface forms of language are mere translations of a 'deeper', hidden, but superior language – in this case a logical representation. Substance and situation (see Chapters 2–4), connotation, metonymy and metaphor (see Chapter 5), the emotive, conative, phatic and poetic function of language (see Chapter 6), the interactive potential of the text to mean different things to different people in different situations (see Chapter 7), the different stances of senders (see Chapter 8) and receivers (see this chapter) are all ignored. In many genres, however, the underlying factual or logical content is of secondary importance; yet this does not deprive them of value. If we return, for example, to the stanza of Oscar Wilde's *The Ballad of Reading Gaol*, cited in Chapter 6 as an example of parallelism, it is possible to translate this stanza into underlying logical and semantic representation. (Geis would presumably conclude that the stanza is nonsense, because one cannot kill with a 'bitter look' or 'flattering word'.) But such 'facts' are of little relevance to an analysis of the effect of this stanza on a receiver. This will owe more to surface linguistic phenomena such as prosody and parallelisms, and, on the other hand, to knowledge, recognition and judgement of facts which are not referred to in the text – about Oscar Wilde, crimes of passion, capital punishment and so on. If the aim of linguistic analysis is to account for understanding of texts, then it must take all this into account, and describe sender, text and the receiver. In certain genres, including poetry and ads, the underlying logical representation – if it exists at all – may not be particularly important.

9.4.2 'Natural' and 'real'

Closely wedded to the unquestioning belief in the logical and factual basis of the text as an evaluative measure is the insistence that it be 'natural' and 'real': terms which are bandied about in criticisms of ads quite as freely as they are in ads themselves! (This irony seems to have passed unnoticed.)

In *Decoding Advertisements*, Williamson (1978) allots to each element in a picture a single 'meaning'. These equivalences reveal that ads are both 'unreal' and 'unnatural'. They 'violate natural human needs' (1978: 110). In them

> We are placed in reconstructed and *false* relationships to *real* phenomena. We misrepresent our relation to nature, and we avoid our real situation in time.
>
> (Williamson 1978: 102, original emphasis)

> Advertisements obscure and avoid the real issues of society. . . . Real objects are lifted out of our physical reality and absorbed into a closed system of symbols, a substitute for reality and real emotions.
>
> (Williamson 1978: 47)

> this prevents us from assessing the real relationship between sign and referent, finding out ads' real process of signification.
>
> (Williamson 1978: 73)

For Williamson, it is the equivalence between the surface form of an ad and its signified or – as she is also influenced by Freud – its latent unconscious content. Like logic for Geis, this 'reality' needs to be interpreted by an authoritative figure who knows the code. All other meanings are 'unnatural' and 'unreal'.

It is not my intention, in commenting upon this confident distinction between real and unreal, to criticise any writer on advertising for their opposition to the capitalist system (now *global* capitalist system) within which advertising flourishes, on which it depends, and whose values it reflects. There are good reasons to share the view that this system is divisive and destructive, perpetuating social injustices and hastening environmental catastrophe. My argument here concerns rather the loose use of the term 'real', which I believe weakens the political argument, and has left the case against advertising both vulnerable and exposed. In what sense, precisely, is the production and reception of advertising not 'real'? Is the objection that the content of ads is often fiction? If so, is all fiction being condemned? It is not clear. It seems that the criticism for being 'unreal' applies both to the fictional world portrayed within ads and to the kind of producer–consumer relationships they create in the world outside.

In such criticisms ads, and the relations within them and around them, are contrasted with 'real emotions', 'real situations in time', 'real relationships', 'real meanings'. But why is one community, one kind of human relationship, one mode of existence more 'real' or 'natural' than another? Ads, the world they portray, and the world in which they exist, have indeed replaced other kinds of genres, situations, communities, relationships or meanings, and this is may be a cause for regret. But that is to say that the economic, political or social system of the present is undesirable – not that it is unnatural or unreal. In the new political world order of the twenty-first century, the current relationships of manufacture and consumption, and their genres, are – perhaps unfortunately – as real as those of any other period of history.

A major problem is that attacking ads for materialism, unreality, or illogicality, highlights features which are also present in many other genres, including those of art. Williamson, for example, criticizing the notion that a possession may express the personality of the owner (1978: 47), would, as well as any advertisement, damn the two paintings of Van Gogh's which contrast his own plain wicker chair with the velvet armchair used by Gauguin (at a time when the two artists were living together). Likewise the insistence on the representation of reality would condemn the whole realm of fiction, myth and symbolic meaning. Demands for logic and fact (like Geis's) exclude all phatic, emotive, connotational or metaphorical expression. If ads are to be singled out for criticism, it must be for features which they do not share with other genres. All political orders and ideologies have their myths. In that sense ads represent nothing new. It is not the ascendancy of myth and fantasy in modern life as such which should be a cause for concern, but *the kind of* myth and fantasy constituted by ads.

Perhaps one unacknowledged reason for venom against ads has been their ambiguity as a genre. Their relatively recent entry upon the scene has rebounded on other genres. Their use of literary and artistic techniques, for example, has provoked reappraisal of these techniques in art. It is claimed by Lévi-Strauss (1969) that people or entities which cannot be classified within a cultural or semantic system become taboo, and objects of hatred. In this context, the charge of 'unnaturalness', often made against ads during the 1970s and 1980s, is revealing – for it seems to assume a range of genres which predate the advent of advertising, and to view this range as in some way sacred. Geis (1982: 150–9) criticizes the dialogue of an ad for not being like that of a conversation. It is, he says, not 'natural', 'not the sort of thing one would ever say spontaneously' (1982: 159). This criticism (which applies equally to the language of Shakespeare's plays) denies advertising its own status and conventions as a genre and demands it conform to another, in comparison with which it is inevitably found lacking. Favourite genres for comparison are conversation, news, law and poetry. This point does not absolve ads from criticism; but it distinguishes two different lines of attack. One approach recognizes ads as a genre which it analyses and evaluates; the other seeks to deny them even their existence.

9.5   Critiques and public opinion

As ads have consolidated their prominent position among the contemporary range of genres, this latter line of criticism has ironically found itself increasingly out of tune with 'reality', and been by-passed by other approaches. It may even have done harm to the case against ads by providing an easy target for apologists, allowing opposition to be easily dismissed as 'academic and dated' (Wilmshurst and Mackay 1999: 20). Indeed the new pro-advertising marketing literature which has emerged during the 1990s generally pays scant attention to such critiques, preferring to jump back in time to the arguments of Packard, or to recount the history of advertising regulation, arguing with the various legal challenges made against its factual claims and tangible social effects. Meanwhile, contemporary commentary on ads in sociology and linguistics (e.g. Nava *et al.* 1997, Myers 1999) is far less concerned with the morality of ads than earlier writers in these fields. Even the most politically committed of recent movements, critical discourse analysis (e.g. Fairclough 1992, 1995; Caldas Coulthard and Coulthard 1996), has had relatively little to say about advertising, choosing instead to concentrate its efforts upon political discourse and news – two areas which, like advertising, also seek to manipulate public opinion in the interests of establishment values, but lack its redeeming energy, playfulness and wit.[5]

It may be in part that the faltering of criticism stems partly from the increasingly secure position of ads in the contemporary political scene. Perhaps too it reflects some ambiguity in both public and academic attitudes, and a realisation that there is something more to advertising than mere commercial activity. In political terms, attacking advertising seems rather like shooting the messenger – or even the jester – rather than the king. In response to this realisation, an interesting new line of criticism is now beginning to emerge: a critique of the 'brand' – of which advertising is but one facet – and more importantly of the international corporate power which lurks behind it (Klein 2000).

Public attitudes are hard to assess, not least because most advertising research is notoriously partisan or uses quantitative methods where qualitative ones would have been more appropriate ('Who's really getting screwed?' asked one 1980s ad in the advertising press. It showed a couple making love on a sofa in front of a TV set – to which of course they are paying no attention – with the comment 'Current advertising research says these people are watching your ad'). Nevertheless, a pattern emerges, and is borne out by non-partisan research into attitudes such as that reported by O'Donahue (1997) or Myers (1999: 151–69). This pattern is a growing tolerance of ads, and acceptance, reflected in the consistent finding that the younger the respondents, the more positive they are in their attitude. The trend reported by Cinquin in 1987 is still in evidence today:

> 82% of the French from 10 to 24 years of age declare themselves unreservedly in favour of advertising. 60% of the French think that advertising is informative and entertaining rather than manipulative. 60% consider that it is close to art and 45% prefer advertising to political discourse ... 48% of the French less than 35 years of age would not object to the Coca Cola corporation installing a giant Coca Cola bottle on the Place de L'Etoile, close to the Arc de Triomphe.
>
> (Cinquin 1987: 490, 493)

Whether this should be a cause of complacency for marketing and corporations, or the condition for a resurgence of criticism we have yet to see. A new generation of critics may be less distracted by the tinsel and more focused on the economic system underneath.

9.6 New factors

Perhaps it is not ads which have changed but the related genres which configure around them, and the political order which this configuration reflects. The orders of discourse in a society change with its technology, especially its technology of communication. Periods of change understandably arouse insecurity and anger in those with interests in existing genres, because new ones disturb an existing way of classifying the world. This happens with major changes in modes and media. There have been attacks on writing, print, photography, film, television, computers, the Internet. There is also antagonism towards the genres which develop from these changes. In **chirographic** culture (i.e. one with writing but not print), few texts were considered worth the labour of copying. With the advent of printing, when more could be produced, new genres evolved, including the novel. But the novel was criticized as mere entertainment: immoral, trivial and fictional (Watt 1963: 36–61). Similarly, film (as a genre) dependent on film (as a technology) aroused antagonism in its early days.

New technologies bring the opportunity to reproduce both greater varieties and greater quantities of discourse. (The Internet is a startling example.) Advertising as it is today (rather than in 1950) – brief, disposable, multi-modal, often quite trivial – is very much the child of new printing technology, then television, and now the Internet. In earlier decades, it would have been unthinkable to devote print, or film, or computer time to such unimportant issues as the purported difference between one soap powder and another. Yet, although our society has the capability to produce on such a scale, there is also awareness of a new factor which should motivate reduction. Paper and other materials, in a world of diminishing resources, are always valuable, and there is a valid ecological argument against the quantity used. This, however, is a different issue from moral, aesthetic and political criticism.

Ads need not be perceived as a threat to other genres nor the harbingers of social disintegration. They are one among the many genres of contemporary society. In small doses – which is how most people take them – they are often entertaining, sometimes amusing, sometimes aesthetically pleasing, occasionally insightful and thought-stimulating; but many instances are also often trite, predictable, annoying or boring. (Precisely which ads belong to which category will vary between individuals and groups.) Many arguments about the artistic merit and social status of ads are surely circular. Ads have no special power to demand attention, and thus, for most people, they remain of peripheral interest. If in the future they become more important, this will presumably be because they deserve attention. If they become valuable, even according to values alien to us, they will be valued. For the moment, while they remain of interest as an active part of the totality of contemporary discourse, as individual works, they often seem no more than mildly entertaining. As such, there is no reason why they should be seen as a threat to an existing literary and artistic canon, and the judgements of our own and earlier generations which it reflects. There is no reason to suppose that future generations will suddenly cease to value more highly those other genres which seem to provide insight into life and increase understanding of it. Ads at present seem seldom to belong to that category.

They may however play a role beyond the commercial and the political which has escaped both critics and apologists – and which paradoxically links them not to changes in contemporary communications technology, commerce, and social and political organisation, but to more ancient and universal aspects of human behaviour and language use. It is to this, and to the social and psychological function and nature of ads in general, that we shall turn in the final chapter.

Exercises

1   What is your view of ads? If you are using this book as part of a course, can you divide your class by their attitude to ads? Is your view of ads affected by consideration of any of the following?

Cigarette ads aim to persuade people to use a drug which causes foetal abnormalities, bronchitis, cancer and death.

The late 1980s saw a marked increase in condom advertising. Condoms are believed to prevent the spread of AIDS.

The weeks leading up to Christmas are marked by an increase in toy advertising during children's programmes, drawing children's attention to toys which their parents may not be able to afford.

The weeks leading up to Christmas are marked by an increase in advertising to stop drinking and driving. Frequently links have been suggested between the effectiveness of these campaigns and falling casualties. The 'better' the ad, it is claimed, the greater the effect. One hard-hitting campaign in Australia was followed by a 37 per cent fall in road deaths in the seven weeks following the campaign. (However for a critical discussion of such claims, see Myers 1999, Chapter 12)

2   Many artists, writers and film directors have designed and written ads. For example: Several paintings by Toulouse-Lautrec were ads for the Moulin Rouge.

Salvador Dali wrote and appeared in an ad for Lanvin Chocolate. He bites into a bar of Lanvin with the words 'Je suis fou du chocolat Lanvin' and the ends of his very long moustache vibrate and curl upwards.

Rene Magritte (despite his condemnation of ads cited earlier) ran an advertising agency called *Dongo*, and produced many ads for it.

The novelist Fay Weldon is reputed to have written the words of an ad for eggs: 'Go to work on an egg.' The novelist Salman Rushdie is reputed to have authored the words of a cake advertisement 'Naughty but Nice'.

The Russian poet Vladimir Mayakovsky wrote an ad for biscuits.

Many influential film directors (Martin Scorsese, Frederico Fellini, Ken Loach, Peter Greenaway, Alan Parker, Ridley Scott) have also directed advertisements.

In all of these cases, should the advertisement be considered part of the artist's oeuvre? If not, why not?

3   Do you object to direct marketers compiling files of information about your socioeconomic status, purchasing preferences, Internet routes, personality, lifestyle, age etc? Are you happy to be assigned to a general category of consumer such as one of the following (used in direct marketing): 'Cosmopolitan'; 'House Sharers'; 'Upwardly Mobile'; 'Financially Active'; 'Golf Clubs' and 'Volvos'; 'Lager', 'Crisps and Videos'.

4   The following is an extract from a newspaper report (*International Herald Tribune*, September 16, 2000):

> A digital and media art exhibition here features not only museum pieces but also works shown on huge electronic screens on streets throughout the city and on walls and pillars in subway stations. The exhibition 'Media-City Seoul 2000' includes more than 60 pieces of interactive media art at the Seoul Metropolitan Museum downtown and two adjacent exhibition halls. Visual works by internationally known artists also appear randomly on 42 electronic Jumbotron screens throughout the city. (...) Works by (...) artists from around the world are inserted between advertisements and news briefings on the Jumbotron screens. A Yahoo! Korea commercial, for example, is followed by '102', a brief visual

presentation of scenes of Seoul by the French artist Dominique Gonzales-Foerster in which he stresses certain colors that to him characterise each scene. (...) People in Seoul seem to welcome the explosion of art into their everyday surroundings. On the sidewalk of a major intersection one recent evening, Lee Mi Ok, a 24 year old college student, and her boyfriend, Hong Sung Hee, a 28 year old office worker, seemed absorbed by the Jumbotron billboards, but uncertain whether they were seeing advertisements or art. 'We've been here for close on an hour, but I don't think I saw any works of art,' said Hong, adding, 'I don't think I'd be able to recognise them even if I saw them.'

What in your opinion is the likely cause of confusion: the medium of presentation, the situation, the kind of artworks and advertisements selected, or the knowledge and attitude of the observers?

5   Would you describe this book as pro-advertising or anti-advertising?

Further reading

The best way to follow this chapter is with a series of polemical readings both for and against advertising. Particularly useful are the chapters on advertising in Alvarado and Thompson (1990) *The Media Reader,* which deliberately sets out to provide a balance between proponents and opponents. Sean Brierley (1995) *The Advertising Handbook*, Chapter 12, gives a good summary of opposition to ads throughout the twentieth century (but is generally on the side of the advertisers). Greg Myers (1999) *Ad Worlds* (Part Three) includes informative discussion of the regulation and social effects of advertising.

More partisan offerings are:

Against

John Berger (1974) *Ways of Seeing*, Chapter 7.
Dwight Bolinger (1990) *Language: The Loaded Weapon*, Chapters 10 and 13.
M. Knight (1990) 'Is the micro macho? A critique of the fictions of advertising'.
Raymond Williams (1980) 'Advertising: the magic system'.
Naomi Klein (2000) *No Logo*.

For

R. White (2000) *Advertising*, pp. 252–65.
J. Wilmshurst and A. Mackay (1999) *The Fundamentals of Advertising*, Chapter 1.

10 Conclusion
The genre of the advertisement

10.1 Introduction

This chapter reassesses the issue with which we began: the nature of ads as a genre. Taking account of the analyses in the preceding nine chapters, it first attempts to extract from them features which are characteristic of the materials, language and participants of ads. It then makes further suggestions about ads' social and psychological function.

Let us begin with fourteen features suggested in the analysis so far. In keeping with what has been said earlier about the indeterminacy of definitions, and the impossibility of establishing clear boundaries between one genre and another, features are presented as prototypical of ads rather than as definitive components (see Chapter 1).

1 ads use a variety of substances, including some which are not used in communication elsewhere (e.g. soap, vapour)
2 ads are embedded in an accompanying discourse
3 ads are presented in short bursts
4 ads are multi-modal, and can use pictures, music and language, either singly or in combination, as the medium permits
5 ads, in their use of language, are multi-submodal, and can use writing, speech and song, either singly or in combination, as the medium permits
6 ads contain and foreground extensive and innovative use of paralanguage
7 ads foreground connotational, indeterminate and metaphorical meaning, thus effecting fusion between disparate spheres
8 ads make dense use of parallelisms, both between modes (e.g. the pictures and music have elements in common), and within modes (e.g. the words rhyme)
9 ads involve many voices, though they tend to be dominated by one
10 ads are parasitic: appropriating the voices of other genres, and having no independent existence
11 ads are often heard in many contradictory ways simultaneously

12   ads merge the features of public and private discourse, and the voices of authority and intimacy, exploiting the features which are common to these poles
13   ads make extensive use of intertextual allusion, both to other ads and to other genres
14   ads provoke social, moral and aesthetic judgements ranging from the most positive to the most negative (they are 'harmful' or 'beneficial', 'bad' or 'good', 'not artistic' or 'artistic').

As this list progresses it becomes more controversial. There is no clear dividing line between a feature which appears independent of individual or group opinion, and is thus apparently a feature of text, and one which depends upon the existing values and knowledge of the receiver, and is thus clearly open to dispute. But this is not surprising. Discoursal features arise, as we have seen, through the interaction of sender and receiver, and are therefore relative and variable. Even assuming an unlikely uniformity among the senders of ads, there is tremendous variation both within and between the people who receive them. It is impossible to be specific about discoursal features without also specifying the receiver (variation between individuals) or one way of hearing (variation within an individual). Advertising, or an individual ad, can thus be many contradictory things at once: precisely because judgement depends on factors which vary between individuals (such as attitudes to computer technology, economic growth, globalization, capitalism, patriarchy, art) and because the receptiveness of an individual will change with mood.

This book has adopted a metaphor of discourse as levels, and moved 'upwards' from substance through form to interaction. As we 'rise' through the levels, the issues become more and more controversial. There is certainly nothing like daylight on the surface. Thus while features 1–5 are relatively uncontroversial and 6–8 a little less so, features 9–14 are becoming more contentious. Look, for example, at feature 9. For some people, and for some ways of hearing, the apparent heteroglossia of ads is a complete sham, masking a noxious monologic discourse. In this view, there are not many voices in ads at all, but one voice, skilled in ventriloquism and mimicry. Where differences in receivers may yield opposite results only an area can be specified. One might say, for example, that 'ads provoke moral judgements', and this might be widely accepted. Saying that 'ads are immoral' or 'ads are moral' on the other hand, will be true only for some people. Perhaps the only features of ads on which everyone might agree is:

15   ads provoke controversy.

If discourse must always be linked to a particular sender, then this chapter, and this book as a whole, are no exception. Though written in an academic style, it too expresses the opinion of one person. By writing above about 'what this chapter does', I personified the text which you are now reading – a common device in contemporary culture with its tendency to reify texts and detach them from their senders. It might be preferable to say not that the text does something, but that I, the writer, and you, the reader, do things by means of this text. In the same way, it is not ads which do the things listed above, and have intentions and habits, but their senders and their receivers – although from another perspective senders and receivers gain their identity from interactions with texts. The notion of 'objective judgements', when pursued, may mean no more than 'assumptions which are shared by the majority', while 'subjective judgements' are how we describe more personal or idiosyncratic views. Yet although 'objectivity' in discourse, in the absolute sense of representing truths independent of observers, may be a positivist myth,[1] there persists a feeling (which I share) that there are *degrees* of objectivity and subjectivity. Thus, though no statement about advertising is uncontroversial, the remainder of this chapter (and of the book) could be described as a more speculative view of the nature and function of advertising than earlier chapters – though its purpose is to raise rather than answer the larger questions of advertising. It focuses upon five main areas: the restlessness of ads; their disposition to change and reverse any features which become typical; their uses of time and space; their social and psychological role (in particular their playfulness and its relation to poetry and display); and their value. It suggests a further eleven typical features which may be added to the fifteen above. Again, these features are proposed as prototypical, rather than definitive.

16 ads have the typical restless instability of a new genre
17 ads are a discourse on the periphery of attention
18 ads constantly change
19 ads follow a principle of reversal, causing them to change many features, as soon as they become established, to their opposite
20 ads seek to alter addressees' behaviour but this is understood by default, and need not occupy space or time
21 ads are identified by their position in an accompanying discourse, and need not use space or time to establish their identity as an ad
22 ads use their space and time in an attempt to give pleasure
23 ads use code-play
24 ads answer a need for display and repetitive language
25 ads are unsolicited by their receivers
26 ads, as verbal art, are detrimentally constrained by the need to obey the orders of their clients.

10.2 A restless discourse

Ads have the typical instability of a relatively new genre. (There is no fixed date at which we may say the modern soft-sell ad came into existence, but clearly what we have today is a different phenomenon from that of even fifty years ago.) Alluding to their frenetic brevity, Barthes aptly referred to the images of ads as 'restless'. This restlessness is not only internal to an individual ad, but also applies to advertising in general, its effect on receivers, and its relations to society and to other genres. The conventions of ads change fast, driven by an internal dynamic, by changes in society, and by changes in the genres on which they are parasitic or in which they are embedded. Virtually any statement about advertising becomes outdated as soon as it is made. Like parody and the novel, ads have no voice of their own (though this similarity does not necessarily imply that they are of equal value); they are a fluctuating and unstable mixture of the voices around them, constantly transmuting and re-combining, invading new media and technologies – so that at present any lasting characterization is impossible. Synchronically, there are too many exceptions. Diachronically, the rules are in flux.

This restlessness is characteristic of new genres, which, like volcanic lava, erupt through the hardened cold rock of older discourse, before themselves hardening as time progresses. Before they settle and cool, their shape is hard to define. What we need to decide is whether advertising is now – or indeed ever was – restless in this exciting and disruptive way. If it was, has it begun to cool and rigidify, making it easier to predict and to handle? Or has it perhaps never had an unpredictable dimension at all?

10.2.1 *The periphery of attention*

Another reason for this impression of restlessness is that ads, for many people, are either not at the centre of attention or do not hold attention for long. Ads come in short bursts. (This term while ordinally coined to describe television campaigns, aptly characterizes the effect not only of television ads, but also of those on magazine pages, Internet banners, and roadside hoardings; though it is possible for attention to linger on them, we tend to flick, click or drive past them fast, creating the effect of a short burst.) While they may momentarily amuse or attract, their nature changes under careful scrutiny – of the kind we have engaged in in this book. They are not intended to be studied in this way. Their brief is to gain and hold attention, fix a name with positive associations, and go. Yet many ads do not succeed in attracting attention at all. Those which do, do so only fleetingly. They are uninvited, embedded in another discourse (such as a television programme, newspaper article, mail delivery, or search engine site listing) which, from the receiver's point of view, is more important. For these reasons, ads often exist on the periphery of receiver attention.

To say this is not necessarily to criticize, for that is how ads are designed to be perceived. Unlike some other genres – such as legal codes, religious tracts, or poems – they are not expected to attract minute scrutiny. To subject them to intense analysis changes this nature (and is also very unsettling for the observer). In a sense, an ad ceases to be itself when it is scrutinized, and it is impossible to study an ad as it is usually perceived. To treat an ad as something at the centre of attention transforms it. This makes ads frustratingly resistant to dissection and criticism, which always seems to be taking ads more seriously than they were intended.

10.3 Constant change

In some ways, advertising is constantly changing. This is most evident in changes at the 'lower' levels of substance, surroundings, mode and paralanguage (dealt with in Part I), also to some degree at the level of text (dealt with in Part II) where there is ever more skilful use of poetic devices such as parallelism. It may be, however, that changes *only* take place at these 'lower' levels, and that the readiness for innovation there is compensation for an inability to change at 'higher' level of content ('what sort of world is portrayed') and overall intention ('what advertisers aim to do'). A classic instance of this debate in recent years relates to advertising on the Internet. In the view of some, it is only superficially different, having simply transferred old techniques to a new medium; in the view of others it is a radical and major new departure, using quite different semiotic techniques with quite radical social effects. Let us examine some of these issues level by level, looking at the less controversial 'lower' levels first.

Often, genres become – as it were – inseparably attached to particular media or modes. They appear reluctant to move into the novel substances made available by major new technologies such as writing, printing, the telephone, and the Internet. (University lectures for example often continue as though none of these technologies existed!). In advertising, on the other hand, new uses of substance are embraced with eagerness. In their relationship to their physical surroundings, ads constantly raid new territory. In the course of a very short history, they have colonised shop fronts, magazines, posters, film, radio, television, the telephone, the post, email, the World Wide Web. Consequently, they have appeared in new places: the street, the cinema, the sitting room, the mailbox, the roadside and the computer screen.

The relationship of ads to their accompanying discourse changes too. Within forty years they have shifted away from attempts to merge with accompanying discourses, to a tendency to keep separate, and then back again. On television, the sponsored television programmes of the 1950s gave way to the clearly delineated 'commercial break' to be followed by a partial move back to sponsorship from the 1980s. In magazines, advertorials merging comment and promotion, gave way to clearly labelled and separated advertisements, to be succeeded by increasing numbers of 'lifestyle articles', often mentioning particular products and services. On the Internet, the distinction between advertising and information is particularly hard to draw – as when, for example, search engines asked for sites relating to a particular city or country, invariably yield details of cheap flights to them.

Generally, there is pressure on advertisers to maintain the boundaries and keep themselves within a closed space. Ads are under considerable pressure to remain short, and other genres are well defended against encroachment. In some ways, however, the border has already been breached. Banner ads sit quite legitimately within other web pages in much the same way as television ads sit within programmes, or magazine ads are interleaved into articles. Trespassing outside these defined spaces can bring sharp reactions and quick retreat. In 1999, for example, there were strong objections to the revelation that a company called AutoNation had paid AltaVista to ensure that their website appeared first in response to any Web search using the word 'cars' (Durham 2000). Yet perhaps this war of attrition – constantly seeking to insinuate advertising into other discourse – is one which advertising will eventually win. The strategies open to advertisers are too many and too various to counter. Some television ads also try to break out of their enclosed space through intertextual allusion, or by creating stories which proceed from one commercial to the next. A case in point was the classic *Nescafe Gold Blend* ongoing love story, which not only developed from ad to ad as though it itself were a programme, but was also converted into a novel!

10.4 A principle of reversal

Ads not only change their features, but also reverse them. This tendency is so marked and persistent that it warrants description as a **principle of reversal.** According to this principle many features, once established as typical of ads, are liable to be replaced by their opposite. This can take place at any of the levels of discourse (except perhaps that of overall intention). Paradoxically, this fickleness is motivated presumably by the constancy of the advertisers' desire to attract attention. Features considered typical of ads are often pointedly abandoned, thus defeating expectation and arresting attention. Let us look first at three common assumptions about ads: that they are 'unrealistic'; that they always portray a bland and problem-free world; and that they necessarily eulogize a product, stressing its advantages, while ignoring, or distracting attention from, its disadvantages.

10.4.1 'Unrealism' in ads and its reversal

The notion of 'realism' is by no means straightforward. In ads, as in literature, an effect of realism derives partly from the manipulation of convention rather than from correspondence to the non-linguistic world. It may be caused by the inclusion of detail which by earlier conventions is omitted (Tomashevsky 1965; Jakobson 1978). Consider, for example, a fictional description of a male character in a novel, as perceived by a female character, at a first meeting. The whole event is fictional, in the sense that these two people do not exist and never came together in this place; yet it is also measurable against reality, in that the component details may be matched against the reader's own non-fictional and non-verbal experience. By current convention, saying that the man has rippling muscles and steel-blue eyes is regarded as 'unrealistic'; saying that he has bad breath and a fat beer-belly may be regarded as 'realistic'. Yet both kinds of men exist in the real world. (If the latter kind occur more frequently in a reader's experience, that does not make the former unreal.) The clichéd feel of the former description is partly a quality of the phrases 'rippling muscles' and 'steel blue eyes' rather than of the person – factual or fictional – to whom they refer. In a similar way, it is convention which makes coincidences seem 'unrealistic' in literature, because coincidences do actually happen in life. (Paradoxically, they occur less frequently in 'realistic' literature – because they are conventionally 'unrealistic' – than they do in real life.) The relation between 'realism' and reality, in other words, is anything but simple. In the modern world, 'realism' in art is generally considered to be a positive quality. This is a good example of something unsaid, a 'gap' which reveals a shared ideology (see Section 8.3.3). If we say a book is 'realistic', we do not need to add 'and I think realism is a positive quality'. We take for granted the widely held view that art and literature should be, as Hamlet says, 'a mirror up to nature'.[2] In the light of this view, the description of advertising as 'unrealistic' is taken to imply that it is automatically bad.

More pertinent perhaps than claims that the worlds in ads are 'unreal' – for so are those of science fiction – is the observation that they are often bland and problem-free. The families are happy; the days are sunny; the meals tasty; the Christmases snowy; the grannies kind; the roads uncongested; the countryside unspoiled; the farming traditional. The conventional nature of this 'unrealism' is borne out by the fact that all of the above occur. As we have already noted, the realism/unrealism distinction is a matter of convention rather than fact. A white-haired granny who rolls out home-made pastry and then sits in a rocking chair by a log fire is just as possible in the real world as a bad-tempered alcoholic granny who cooks tasteless meals. There are still green meadows and farmyards, as well as factory farms. The point is not so much that advertising is unrealistic, as that it generally avoids the truly controversial. That is why its portrayal of home life, for example, does not often feature single-parent families, or gay men and lesbians – but goes for the 'safe' option of a happy, heterosexual, married couple with not too many children.

If we criticize ads for this selectivity and avoidance of problems, we should remember that many respected art forms are open to the same criticisms. In ancient Greek sculpture, all young men are muscular, all young women shapely, all old men dignified. In pastoral poetry, just as in butter

ads, all rural life is idyllic. In Jane Austen's novels, all deserving unre-
quited love finds fulfilment.

What perhaps differentiates contemporary advertising from such ideal-
ism in art, is that the values it eulogises – unspoilt nature, traditional crafts,
social stability, cultural diversity – are exactly those same positive aspects
of life which are most threatened by the globalised growth-oriented
market economy of which advertising is so central a part.

10.4.2   Reverses in the worlds portrayed

From the 1980s onwards advertising has increasingly flirted with both the
'realistic' and the controversial. People with problems have made their
appearances alongside the 'normal', happy, healthy families (two parents,
two children) of the stereotypical ad. An ad for Bisto Chicken Gravy
showed not the usual happily married housewife feeding her growing son,
but a divorced father in a bedsit knocking up a quick meal for his child's
hasty visit. An Anadin ad showed a husband being unpleasantly aggressive
towards his wife, then calming down with the help of the product. It is still
the case, however, that the effect of these advertisements lies more in the
contrast they make with the 'norms' of advertising rather than in anything
intrinsic to their portrayal of such situations.

In ads campaigning to change behaviour, the images have kept pace
with this change. An ad against drinking-and-driving has shown in detail
the long term consequences of severe injury in a car crash: a paralysed
young man needing to be spoon fed by his mother. An ad urging middle-
aged men to eat more healthily showed a woman waking to find her
husband has died in bed beside her. A later version followed scenes of a
man eating, smoking and drinking, with close ups of his child's face after
he has suffered a heart attack.

Some ads have been shot from a real rather than a staged scene. A
Wranglers jeans ad included documentary footage of beggars and a
mugging in New York. An ad for Southern Comfort showed kerb crawlers
and pickpockets in the red light district of New Orleans. The distinction
between pictures of real and fictional scenes is, however, as Goffman
(1979: 10–23) and Barthes (1977d) have commented, more complex than
popularly supposed. A real scene may be used as fiction, or a fictional
scene presented as real. In such ads, though the photographs make use of
actual events, it seems that their function is to provoke an attractive aura
of streetwise excitement rather than reflect any independent reality. In
many ways, they seem more idealizing and 'unrealistic', than those cautionary, but nevertheless fictional, depictions of the effects of drunk
driving or an unhealthy diet.

The popular view that ads are uniformly anodyne and idyllic overlooks
the fact that, paradoxically, some of the most shocking and disturbing pictures are found in ads. Ads for charities use images which most indict the

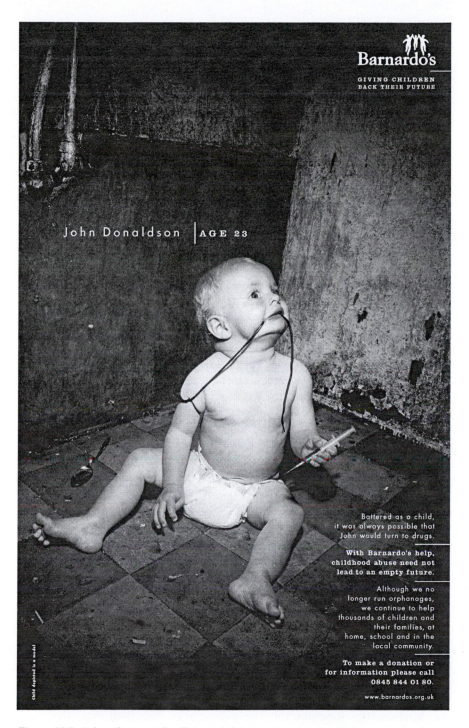

Figure 10.1 Advertisement for Barnardo's.

consumers of the rich world: the emaciated legs and distended stomachs of children on the verge of death; the homeless on the streets of rich cities; sufferers from diseases which can easily be cured. One advertisement for Amnesty International showed thirteen photographs of tortures, executions and beatings in thirteen different countries. One photograph showed soldiers casually carrying the parts of a child they have torn apart alive. Critics should remember that these images, as well as those of happy prosperous families, are brought to our attention by advertising agencies. They are 'realistic' in both senses: they depart from convention, and also inform us of a real situation. Against this, it may be said that opinion and behaviour in the rich world are too hardened to the plight of the poor and oppressed for such ads to have any effect. Yet, if anything might shift this entrenched complacency, it is such photographs. Of course, they appear only in a minority of ads, and only when agencies are paid to produce them. But if the credit for showing such pictures lies with the client rather than with the agency, then, by the same token, the blame for 'unrealistic' ads should surely lie with the client too. So, while the majority of ads show a world where all is well, others, albeit a minority, show the world as – for many of its inhabitants – it is. Such a reverse is typical of this restless discourse.

As we have seen, the 'lower' levels of ads all change with speed. The world to which they refer – whether real or fictional – also changes. At the simplest level, the realia of ads – clothes, cars, houses – keep pace with change. Yet, as fiction can influence the behaviour of real people, the relation between the fictional and real worlds is dynamic, with each affecting the other. Ads show a world in which toothpaste is used more often than tooth powder, because that world was influenced by the successful marketing of toothpaste. They show (in countries where they are still allowed to do so) a world in which men as well as women smoke tipped cigarettes, because – in the 1950s – a successful advertising campaign persuaded men that it was not 'effeminate' to do so.

To this it might be objected that such changes as these, brought about by advertising, are quite trivial. What matters is people; material objects are interesting only for their cultural and social significance. The connection between plain cigarettes and masculinity is arbitrary. Yet the objects of ads also symbolise and contribute to more important changes in personal and social relationships. The obedient housewife of the 1950s and 1960s becomes the sex object of the 1970s, the power-dressed executive of the 1980s, the super-fit woman of the 1990s – and in the 2000s perhaps a mixture of all of these. The patriarch the 1950s and 1960s becomes the vain Don Juan of the 1960s and 1970s, the selfish executive of the 1980s, the smug family man of the 1990s, the reconstituted (macho but sensitive!) man of the 2000s. These changes are captured in the physical settings of the kitchen, the supermarket, the boardroom, the bedroom, the open road, or the gym – and the objects within them. Questions arise of course about the degree to which these changes in the realia of advertising only follow, rather than lead, those in the world outside. Questions to which there is no simple answer.

10.4.3 Claims, techniques and their reverses

Further evidence of a principle of reversal is provided by the way ads mock advertising conventions. If an ad departs from expectation, it will attract attention and/or convince. Take, for example, the 'blonde on the bonnet' syndrome: the gratuitous use of conventionally attractive women in advertisements aimed at men (see Figure 5.5). One car ad actually used the phrase 'blonde on the bonnet' but shows not a bikini-clad girl, but an elderly judge in a wig. A related tendency is the attraction of attention by internal contradiction. An ad for Anderson & Lembke with the headline 'Why people don't read long copy ads' was followed by two pages of small print copy and no pictures. Standard claims for the product are also reversed. Sanatogen Cod Liver Oil 'tastes as awful today as it always did'. Stella Artois lager is 'Reassuringly expensive'. One classic example of such reversal was a series of advertisements for Eastern Airlines in the USA in 1990. In a bid to attract attention and win sympathy, they produced an ad which quoted genuine customer complaints, such as:

> Lack of professionalism.
> Bags don't get there when the planes get there.
> I don't feel it's a first class carrier right now.
> Mechanical problems.

The ad admits these are true but promises to try to improve! Apart from attracting attention, this strategy also skilfully manipulates the assumption that ads lie. The honesty of a part cunningly implies the honesty of the whole.

Probably the most famous shock tactic of this kind, in which the ad startles by doing things which are simply not expected in advertising, is the series of Benetton campaigns showing either shocking or controversial photojournalist images (a murder, an AIDS death, a soldier with a human bone etc., the faces of prisoners on death row). Figure 10.2 – a picture of an electric chair – is an example. While the publicity generated by such campaigns is immense – and their globalized distribution protects them from the effects of a ban in any one country (Falk 1997) – it is also surely shocking that the shock effect wears off so quickly. Perhaps the overall driving motive of such campaigns is in fact nothing new – but simply an astute loyalty to one of the oldest adages in the business: There is no such thing as bad publicity. The controversy generated by outrageous ads becomes itself an extension – free of charge – of the campaign. For example, the Wonderbra campaign (see Figure 3.1), by stirring up accusations of sexism, was estimated to have

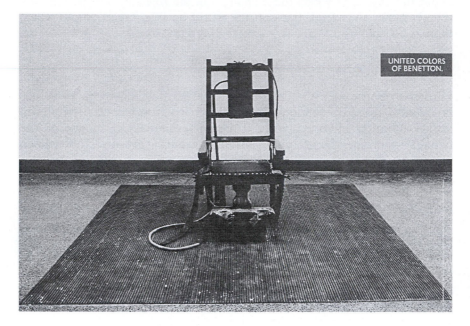

Figure 10.2 'Electric Chair': advertisement for United Colours of Benetton. Photograph by Lucinda Devlin.

generated extra publicity worth £50 million for an initial expenditure on the campaign of £500,000 (Brierley 1995: 50).

Such total reversals of expectations may make us wonder whether any feature of ads is stable other than their instability. Yet, though the method and the content may change, the desired effect remains the same: to influence behaviour in the way demanded, that is to say, by the paymaster. The apparent heteroglossia of ads (as discussed in Chapter 8) is an illusion. Different voices may appear. Some of them such as those of condemned prisoners on death row may be very unexpected. Yet no voice must ever override the dominant if disguised voice of the client.

10.5 Uses of time and space

The time and space available to an ad are usually very limited: a minute or less of television time, the area of a screen or poster, one or two pages of a magazine, a banner on a much larger Web page. They pass or are passed by quickly, flicked or clicked into oblivion. Even within that limited time and space, there are apparently further constraints of content and function. The advertiser, it seems, is obliged to serve a client and sell a particular product. The stereotypical ad is distinguished from other genres by its obligatory reference to a product, and its intention to make that product appeal to the addressee. It might also seem that an ad must take time and a space to identify itself as an ad, and such restraints could account for the predictability, uniformity and superficiality of many ads. An ad is a time and a space whose content – already hopelessly brief – is also predetermined.

The situation is, however, more complicated. Though time and space are indeed limited, there are a number of reasons why their use is not as predictable as might at first appear.

10.5.1 *Uses of time and space: seeking to change behaviour*

The notion that ads must always refer to a product (or service) is limited to ads which sell something: product ads (see Section 1.3). These are the majority of ads, it is true, but there is also a minority of non-product ads – warnings, health advice, political campaigns and charitable appeals – which do not fit into this category. A general characterization of ads will need to take these into account too.

If we view the ad as a genre advocating a change of behaviour, rather than as just referring to a product, then both kinds of ad can be accounted for. Product ads also refer to a change of behaviour: buying the product. Non-product ads (which are often conveniently ignored by the opponents of ads) encourage such changes of behaviour as not drinking and driving, wearing a condom, voting Green, sending money for famine relief, helping a political prisoner, even paradoxically (in ads for advertising control) reporting ads which are untruthful. Yet even in non-product ads (including those of which we approve) the argument that the content is predetermined still applies. An Amnesty International ad must tell you about the work of Amnesty International with the purpose of getting you to join or send money. So the claim that all ads advocate a change of behaviour makes little difference to the issue of whether the content of ads, and therefore their use of time and space, is determined. Ads may not always be obliged to refer to a product, but they *are* still obliged to refer, however obliquely, to a change of behaviour.

Yet the reference to a change of behaviour need neither occupy much time or space nor preclude other elements entirely; and it is not the case that, for the receiver who does not change his or her behaviour as suggested, there is nothing else in the ad at all.

Ads do not always refer to the advocated behaviour directly, though in the case of ads which encourage purchase, the identity of the product must be clear. Naming is often oblique, and demands some induction on the part of the receiver; but, as in riddles and lateral thinking problems, addressees derive pleasure from their own successful inferencing strategies and ability to decipher unusual ways of encoding the product name.

10.5.2 Uses of time and space: establishing the genre

Similarly, in contemporary ads, very little space is taken either for establishing that the text is an ad, rather than some other genre, or by any overt persuasion. Ads do not need to identify themselves as ads, for this is done, as it were, outside them, by their position within other genres. Once recognized as an ad, the intention to persuade the addressee is assumed. Product ads simply depict a scene, including the product, and/or the name of the product. Non-product ads often show only the effects of not adopting the advocated behaviour: accidents caused by drunkenness, people worried about AIDS, etc. They too do not need to say that their intention is to alter our behaviour.

10.5.3 Uses of time and space: opportunity and variety

Thus it takes little or none of the available time or space to refer to a product or desired behaviour; establishing the genre and the intention to persuade may take no space at all. Even where there is reference to one or more of these supposedly 'defining' features, they need not be at the centre of either the sender's or the receiver's attention. This frees the time or space of the ad – small as it is – for other uses. The obligatory core element – 'do this' (usually 'buy our goods') – is either external to the text or only a small proportion of it. Almost the entire time or space of the ad is left, to be used in any way which does not negate that central core.

The use of such vacant discoursal time and space says a great deal about the needs of the society from which it comes. In this respect it is revealing that ads of the 1950s and early 1960s filled this space with pseudo-scientific descriptions of newly available goods, that the ads of the late 1960s and 1970s used it to present an idyllic and idealized fictional world. But no particular use is definitive of this genre, and it would be a mistake to assume that the features of ads in one decade are features of advertising as a whole. As the reverses cited in Section 10.3 bear witness, the uses of this time and space have changed, are changing, and will probably go on changing. Yet, though these uses may not be defining of the genre, it is they, rather than the minimal core, which attract interest.

10.5.4 Uses of time and space: giving pleasure

But how do ads actually use this vacant time and space? The traditional critical view (derived from the advertising of the 1950s–70s) has been that it is used first to attract receivers' attention, then trick them into buying the product, appealing to greed, vanity, lust and fear, and suggesting that purchase will make the receiver like the people portrayed. For many ads, this characterization is as true as ever. Yet the time and space in contemporary ads is also used in other and more complex ways as well, and the general tendency is perhaps away from simple attention-grabbing and deception.

It is worth considering that ads, despite the belief of manufacturers and advertisers that they exist solely to promote goods, may do many other things as well, and that these other activities are extremely revealing about the needs of contemporary society. Debate about the morality of ads tends to focus on the use of time and space to sell. This, however, may be only a small part of ads' function and attractiveness.

Pateman (1985) and Thompson (1990) argue that many ads aim to give pleasure, and thus create a loose association between this pleasure and the advocated behaviour. If this is the case, then further questions arise about what exactly gives pleasure, and why. We might suppose that pleasure is an epiphenomenon, a side-effect of experience which, while not of imme-diate practical or social benefit, is yet in the long run biologically, socially or psychologically beneficial. In previous chapters we have analysed the ways in which the space of contemporary ads is used: to merge the public and private; to foreground elements of the means of communication through innovative use of paralanguage and language; to play with expec-tations. It seems that such features give pleasure and answer a need. We need to consider why.

10.5.5 Uses of time and space: code play

As we have seen in Chapters 2–6, ads indulge in **code play:** focusing atten-tion upon the substance and means of communication, rather than using these only to refer to the world. At the textual level they play with the sounds and rhythms, meaning and grammatical patterns. As has often been observed, such self-reflexive use of language is a common feature of poetry. The question arises as to whether some advertising merits being described as 'poetic', and whether, more generally, it has usurped some of the social and psychological functions of poetry.

Sadly, the discourse of poetry is in practice now often confined to a social minority. Even within that minority, it is frequently considered as a private and individual activity rather than as a public and collective one. It has also become synonymous with seriousness, and is valued only if it is felt to yield some insight of social or individual significance. In these cir-cumstances, some ads may answer a need for a light-hearted code play in the public domain, which, though once provided by poetry, is now no longer available to many people, either because they do not come into contact with poetry or because, when they do, they are encouraged to focus only upon its more serious aspects or manifestations.

'Useless' play with language – patterning and variation of no apparent meaning or purpose – is now often restricted to intimate discourse: lover talk, baby talk, grumbling, boasting, banter. Yet it is also reminiscent of public discourses of a kind associated with very different times and places than our own – riddles, rituals, spells and incantations. The diminishing importance of such discourse in our societies is evidence of a dislocation of public and private. Though there are other genres, such as graffiti, stand-up comedy and pop songs which bring code play into the public domain, they are often marginalized. Graffiti are regarded as irresponsible and criminal; stand-up comedy and pop songs are denied the status of poetry or drama (Cook 1996). Yet the code play of such marginalized 'low' discourses may answer a need. They fuse the public and private domains, and indulge in trivial public wordplay in a society dominated by notions of communication as the 'container' of facts or deep insights, or the performer of utilitarian practical and social functions. In literature code play is often valued only as the vehicle of psychological and social insight; in ads the means of selling and trade. Ads' apparently trivial uses of language, in other words, are given high status through their association with big business, trade and prosperity. It is as though we need a reason for the pleasure of code play, and cannot value it for itself. It reflects badly, I believe, on contemporary values, that we must give such reasons for this pleasure. Manipulation of the code, so widely enjoyed in all cultures, must in contemporary society often be justified in terms of something else. In ads the excuse is commerce!

But this view, far from answering all problems, leads on to others. Why is code play so pleasurable, and why does it resurface in new genres when it is undervalued or marginalised in others, or denied to a section of the community? What is its function? On the psychological level, it may be that code play has cognitive benefits of which we are only vaguely aware, providing us with a readiness for complex change and innovation which is essential to human survival (Cook 1994a, 2000). It may also be typical of language which functions as a means of display.

10.5.6 Uses of time and space: display and ritual boasting

As described in Chapter 7, Goffman (1979) has suggested that ads frequently make use of verbal and other communicative behaviour reminiscent of 'display' and ritual boasting between contestants (both animal and human). The purpose of display is to establish identity, to act out a version of the relationships which exist within society. As such, it may be, on occasion, a kind of talking-to-oneself in public, as much for the benefit of the sender as of the receiver, whose reception of it may be almost incidental. Although often associated with aggression, it is often a substitute for violence, a means of avoiding rather than initiating conflict, and though it may originate in competitiveness, this origin is often eclipsed by the intricacies of composition, which become a substitute purpose in themselves. It is an aspect of behaviour neglected by functional views of language, which tend either to ignore it, conflate it with the phatic function, or regard it as an ephemeral feature in infancy. A reason for this neglect is perhaps the incompatibility of its apparent uselessness with descriptions which classify all uses of codes in terms of their social or practical usefulness. Yet its ubiquity and persistence suggest that it is both an important and a needed activity, even if we cannot explain why; there is good reason to agree with Goffman that ads, in contemporary society, partly answer this need. They are an activity absorbing an amount of effort, talent and attention, far in excess of their proclaimed purpose.

Because display is in essence talking for the sake of talking, it leads to the use of language and other semiotic systems in ways which are repetitive and predictable, or – if innovative – seem to play with substance and code for no purpose other than to attract attention. It may also involve, as does talking to oneself, the dramatisation of points of view as different voices – a feature which the discourse of display shares with that of the novel.

In advertising, the repetition of the same texts, over and over again, is a feature which is so obvious that it is often neglected. A regular television watcher may see the same ad tens of times or more, a magazine reader will see the same print ad again and again. This distinguishes ads from genres whose texts are generally received only once, and aligns them with those which are frequently received, such as prayers and liturgies, favourite works of literature, songs, children's rhymes and stories, and jokes. A difference between these texts and those of ads, however, is that the repetition of ads is not sought out, but forced upon us. One reason for the dislike of ads is this unsolicited intrusiveness.

This repetition of certain genres is a universal feature of human societies.[3] They unite the most private and the most public spheres. Prayers, for example, are said not only at children's bedsides, at deathbeds, at moments of crisis and loss, but also in public congregation. The words of songs are also repeated in the most private and public circumstances.[4] Such repetition perhaps induces a sense of security and community, and is a means of establishing or confirming (if only to oneself) identity within the society to which the text belongs (because everyone within the society knows the same text). Repetition also allows the comfort of speech, without the burden of invention. In many contemporary societies, especially those in which rote knowledge of prayers or poetry and songs has declined, such widely shared texts are hard to find. Ads, by constantly repeating themselves, bid to answer this need. Yet participation of the receiver in these repetitions of ads is passive. It is the purchase of the product which is active participation!

10.6 Aesthetic value judgements

The rapidly changing uses of the available space in ads, and its employment for purposes other than those of the manufacturer, has dismayed and confused critics. The problem remains, however, as to whether the existence of the mercenary central core (even if it is unstated or only briefly mentioned) debars ads in perpetuity from achieving the status and acclaim of the arts. The trivial issue of ads' mixture of modes and media is not a barrier to such a judgement. Though literature, music and painting operate in one single mode, there are other forms of art, such as song, opera or film, which mix the modes of language, music and image, in similar ways to ads. Yet although they represent fictional situations and scenes, and demand the same technical skills as other arts, many people still feel that they do not have such profound importance, or give such sustained pleasure.

The reason for this cannot be explained away as arising from their short length: one page in a magazine or at most sixty seconds of television time. Many paintings and poems are as brief in space or time, and the simultaneous use of writing and pictures, in conjunction with speech and music on television, gives ads, like opera or film, dimensions which create concentrations of meaning which the linear nature of language, or the static nature of still photography and painting, find difficult to emulate.

Neither can the relation of ads to the arts be explained away by defining different genres in purely formal terms. (Saying, for example, that poetry is language presented in lines when written or keeping to a rhythm when spoken; that painting is coloured marks on a two-dimensional surface, etc.) Such formal definitions dodge the key issue of value at the heart of any designation as 'artistic'. Poetry, for example, in the contemporary view, is not just any piece of lineated or rhythmic language. It is valued language of this kind. Indeed, value seems to outweigh all other criteria, for there are instances without these formal features which are still described as poetry.

It is this emphasis on value which for many people excludes ads from admission into the canons of art. The value of art, moreover, especially in literature, is often associated with opposition to or detachment from the dominant values of society. In comparison with literature, ads accept and glorify the dominant ideology while literature often rejects and undermines it. The simple fact that ads answer the brief of their clients accounts for the common perception that, while art is a vehicle of honesty, advertising is more likely to be a vehicle of deceit.

Yet the notion that art is rebellious and honest is not universal. The kind of relationship which ads have to their patrons, and their service to their patrons' ideology, is by no means unknown in the arts, especially in music and painting. In music this is usually considered unimportant. Handel's and Mozart's compositions are not considered compromised by their jobs as court musicians. In pictorial art, the situation is more complex. Take, for example, Western European portraiture and religious painting of the Renaissance. Such paintings have many of the features often detrimentally attributed to ads. The creators (often a team rather than an individual) worked under patronage, with strict instructions from their employer. They both expressed and were limited by the general dominant ideology of their society. A receiver who objects to that ideology (dogmatic religion, hereditary privilege, inequality) might object to such paintings. They propagate those values, just as ads propagate certain political, economic and social means of organization. The strength of that ideology has been softened by time and the diminution of their patrons' power, but that may also happen to ads. Yet it is not, for many people, the expression of beliefs imposed from outside (even though the painter may well have shared them) which is valued. As in advertisements, there was space in these paintings, around the central obligatory core, for other purposes, and they are not *merely* evangelical, or flattering of their patrons. Consequently, they are not *only* valued for the purposes for which they were commissioned. Yet, for some people, the ideological purpose of such creative activity overweighs all other considerations (Berger 1972; Klein 2000). For others it is relatively unimportant. It may be that in ads the ideological content is salient because it is contemporary. Perhaps it will soften as time progresses, enabling receivers to turn to elements outside the central mercenary core – though it may also be that, when they do, they will find nothing there to value.

Yet whereas music, and to some degree the pictorial arts, may maintain their integrity under patronage, it is harder for the verbal arts to do so. It is in the nature of language to commit its user to a point of view more unequivocally than pictures and music, and whereas painters and composers may survive the constraints of patronage it is harder for the speaker or writer to do the same. Consequently, there is a stronger link between the creator's independence and the right to dissent in literature than in the other arts. For this reason, the verbal creations of advertising, though often skilful and clever, seem unable to attract the same positive evaluation which would lead them to be classed as literary. Ads may have usurped some of the functions of literature, and in particular poetry, but there is good reason to regret this. Poetry and novels, being more disinterested and free, fulfil these functions more fully. If there is some need for code-play and display in our society, there is cause to deplore the fulfilment of this need in a commercial arena permeated by competitive consumption.

Yet the very quantity of advertising in our society, the skill and effort which goes into its creation, the complexity of its discourse, and its impact on its receivers, are enough to make it interesting. Advertising can focus and redefine ideas about language, discourse, art and society, and in this respect its study is well worthwhile.

Notes

1 Introduction: the genre of the advertisement

1 I follow the applied linguistics use of the term (see Widdowson 1973, 1975, 1979, 1984a; Brown and Yule 1983; Cook 1989, 1994a; McCarthy 1991; McCarthy and Carter 1994). This is not the same as the definition of discourse given by Foucault as 'practices that systematically form the object of which they speak' (1972: 49), although there are overlaps. For an excellent exposition of differences between approaches to this term see Pennycook 1994.
2 *Campaign* 21 December 1990: 33–4.
3 George Lakoff (1987: 145) argues that this view of prototype representations as an aid to recognition has since been abandoned by Rosch. Prototypes, he claims, are used in reasoning rather than recognition.
4 For the AMD Athlon processor.
5 The general approach to grammatical analysis follows Quirk *et al.* (1985), and the simplified version of this approach set out in the course book by Leech *et al.* (1982).

2 Substance and surroundings

1 By the pan-European organisation Adlink.
2 A logo is a name or initial in a distinctive typeface (see page 96 for examples).
3 Directed by Luhrmann 1996, with Leonardo DiCaprio and Claire Danes; shown on ITV, 6 August 2000.
4 Gold Award, Campaign Direct Awards, June 2000.
5 Silver Award, Campaign Direct Awards, June 2000.

3 Pictures, music, speech and writing

1 This differs from the usual use in linguistics, where it is limited to language and used to refer to the choice of speech or writing.
2 'Sprite' is a registered trademark of the Coca-Cola Company.
3 This body replaced the Independent Broadcasting Authority in January 1991.
4 At the time this ad was made, Wrigley's controlled 88 per cent of the UK market (*Campaign* 23 November 1991) and similar proportions elsewhere.
5 An idea 'borrowed' from Man Ray's 1921 sculpture *The Gift* which is also an iron with spikes.
6 Homophones are words with the same pronunciation but different spellings and meanings, e.g. *herd*, *heard*.

4 Language and paralanguage

1 This is not to say that this is necessarily the order of the psychological processing of language.
2 The book *Cours de linguistique générale* was in fact written by two students of de Saussure, Bally and Sechehaye, from lecture notes.
3 Many words which seem onomatopoeic to speakers of one language do not seem so to speakers of another, even when those languages belong to the same family (e.g. Russian '*ga*' and English '*honk*' for the noise of a goose). On the other hand, there are sometimes striking similarities between distant languages (the Japanese for '*miaow*' is '*nyao*'). Although de Saussure believed in the phenomenon of onomatopoeia, he marginalized its importance; for discussion, see Derrida (1974: 106–10; 1976); Culler (1983: 189).
4 This at least is the traditional view of metaphor. For an alternative view see Lakoff and Johnson 1980: 106–10.
5 In Peirce's terminology, an arbitrary sign is termed a 'symbol'.
6 Adam Lury, the originator of a number of successful and innovative campaigns, sets out his ideas on advertising in Lury (1994). Trevor Beattie is the originator of the fcuk campaign (Figure 4.4) and of the first Wonderbra campaign.
7 In a lengthy court case between Elizabeth Taylor and her 'ex lover' Henry Wynberg over who branded the perfume, one of its features was said to be its 'distinctive heart shaped bottle'. (*The Independent*, December 1990.)
8 For further analyses of this advert, see Cook 1994a: 161–73.
9 *Campaign*, May 2000

5 Words and phrases

1 A collocation is a frequent occurrence of one or more words together, e.g. 'natural goodness'.
2 A homonym is a word with the same form but different meanings, e.g. 'bank' (of a river) and 'bank' (for money); 'coke' (the drink), and 'coke' (the fuel).
3 *Voices*, broadcast by Channel 4 (UK, 1988).
4 Belk (1987) reports that in a survey of 248 American adults asked to grade items on a continuum between 'self' and 'not self', cars (for men) and perfumes (for women) ranked higher than any other products, with the former ranking higher for the subjects than their own bodily organs and religion!
5 Ford, as is well known, takes its name from its manufacturer Henry Ford. The Buick is called after David D. Buick, a Detroit plumber who entered the automobile business in 1899 and ended up bankrupt.

6 Prosody, parallelism, poetry

1 The 1985 campaign comprised two ads: the first, 'Launderette', showing a young man stripping down to his boxer shorts in a launderette; the second, 'Bath', showing a young man wearing his Levis in the bath so that they would shrink to fit him. Their success was spectacular. UK sales of 501s rose from 80,000 pairs to around 650,000 in one year (Sebag-Montefiore 1987).
2 BBC Radio 4, *Front Row*, April 6, 2000.
3 Here, as in Chapter 1, I have slightly adapted Jakobson's original terminology.
4 They are sometimes distinguished by the terms 'deviance' and 'deviation' respectively (Leech and Short 1981: 55–7). For an excellent discussion of the phenomenon and its terminology see Wales (1989: 116).
5 Although the use of the verb 'go' as the reporting verb in reported speech (e.g. And she goes, 'That's mine you know.') is common in adult speech too (Yule 1995).

7 Connected text

1 This does not imply that people in pre-literate cultures remember discourse verbatim. Contrary to popular belief, stories and myths handed down by word of mouth may undergo considerable change as they pass from speaker to speaker and generation to generation (Lord 1960; Buchan 1972; Ong 1982: 59–61). But recitations do make extensive use of parallelism.

2 Halliday uses this phrase to characterize what he calls the Personal Function in the language of a child, but it is equally pertinent to adult discourse too.

3 Some analysts would describe 'yet' as a sentence connector (e.g. Leech, Deuchar and Hoogenraad 1982: 50)

4 Though written as a separate orthographic sentence, 'Creating the softness of silk against the gentle crispness of chocolate shell.' is a non-finite relative clause which postmodifies the noun phrase in the preceding orthographic sentence.

8 Narrative voices

1 Writing is not necessarily non-reciprocal nor speech reciprocal, but there is an affinity between speech and reciprocity, writing and non-reciprocity.

2 The numbers of people involved is one reason for high costs. 'Last Stick', for example, cost $5.5 million to make *(Campaign* 23 November 1990).

3 There are of course considerable differences between the uses of T and V forms in different languages. Correspondingly, motives for choice in advertisements may vary. Russian ads, for example, frequently use the V form 'vy' , in reaction against the 'ty' of communist slogans.

4 I do not make use here of the customary distinction in linguistics between the semantic meaning of an utterance (its encoded denotation which is not context dependent) and its pragmatic force (what it is intended or taken to do by particular people in a particular context). In keeping with Bakhtin's belief that the former cannot be divorced from the latter, I use the term 'meaning' to encompass both.

5 Bakhtin's theories have elements in common with Firthian linguistics (Firth 1957), Vygotsky's theories of language acquisition (Vygotsky 1962), Pragmatics (see Levinson 1983), Reader Response Theory (see Freund 1987) and Deconstruction (see Culler 1983).

6 I follow the view of Bakhtin's most authoritative translators and biographers, Clark and Holquist (1984), that Bakhtin, and not his friend Volosinov, was the author of the books *Freudianism: a Critical Sketch* and *Marxism and the Philosophy of Language.*

7 This view of the self as primarily social has a long tradition in Russian thought (Cook 1994c). It is also evident in the work of the Russian psychologist Vygotsky (1886–1934) who, in developing a theory of child development, suggested that the child first enters into and participates in communicative behaviour without understanding, then gradually internalizes this behaviour, to create his or her 'self'.

8 For a discussion of Bakhtin's attitudes to Marxism see Clark and Holquist (1984: 295–341).

9 An example is Jonathan Swift's *Gulliver's Travels.*

10 An example is Henry James's *The Turn of the Screw.*

11 An example is Edgar Allan Poe's *The Facts in the Case of M. Valdemar.*

12 For a summary of the critical debate see Leech and Short (1981: 339).

13 In an earlier novel, *Northanger Abbey*, she had made a much more explicit use of the voice of one particular Gothic novel, Anne Radcliffe's *The Mysteries of Udolpho.*

14 The characters, played by Mel Geidroyc and Susan Perkins from the comedy duo Mel and Sue, would be recognised immediately as comedians by many viewers.
15 See also 6.2.4, and Chapter 6, note 1.
16 *Campaign*, 24th March 2000.

9 Ways of hearing

1 Though this is true of linguistics, it is not so in the sociology of communication (Goffman 1981), pragmatics (Levinson 1988) or literary theory (Freund 1987).
2 According to *The Independent* (November 1990) Boursicot's seven-hour compilation film *The Night of the Ad Watchers* made the audience react with criticism and ridicule. O'Donahue (1997), in her survey of young adult attitudes to ads, reports an interview with one young man who expressed a more positive attitude to the idea of the film. Interestingly, however, his interest was hypothetical, as he had not actually seen it.
3 *France-Soir* Expos Special: 'Art Pub', November 1990: 3.
4 Such as Sturgess's *Christmas in July* (1940), or Tashlin's *Will Success Spoil Rock Hunter?* (1957).
5 The tabloid press, however, is noted for its wit, especially in punning headlines, and other uses of language reminiscent of ads (Cook 1996). In critical discourse analyses, however, this playfulness tends to be treated as only a minor and distracting phenomenon (e.g. Fowler 1991: 44–5).

10 Conclusion: the genre of the advertisement

1 For discussion of this point see, for example, Hudson (1972), Chalmers (1982), Barnes, Bloor and Henry (1996).
2 *Hamlet*: III: ii: 27
3 This applied to both literate and pre-literate societies. (The word 'text' is used here to refer to a stretch of spoken or written language.) It does not imply, however, that people in pre-literate cultures remember discourse verbatim. Nevertheless, 'the same texts' are repeated, if not in the sense understood in literate societies where the technology of writing makes word for word repetition possible. (See also Chapter 7, note 1.)
4 This alternation between public and private is also evident in the current cult of the celebrity, where there is intense interest in the private lives of the most public figures: royalty, politicians, film stars, singers etc.

Bibliography

Aitchison, J. (1994) *Words in the Mind: An Introduction to the Mental Lexicon* (2nd edition), Oxford: Basil Blackwell.

Althusser, L. (1971) *Lenin and Philosophy and Other Essays*, trans. B. Brewster, London: New Left Books.

Alvarado, M. and Thompson, J. (eds) (1990) *The Media Reader*, London: British Film Institute.

Argyle, M., Alkema, F. and Gilmour, R. (1971) 'The communication of friendly and hostile attitudes by verbal and non-verbal signals', *European Journal of Social Psychology* 1: 385–402.

Argyle, M., Salter, V., Nicholson, H., Williams, M. and Burgess, P. (1970) 'The communication of inferior and superior attitudes by verbal and non-verbal signals', *British Journal of Social and Clinical Psychology* 9: 222–31.

Bakhtin, M.M. (1968) *Rabelais and His World,* trans. H. Iswolsky, Cambridge, Massachusetts: MIT Press. (Original Russian version 1940.)

Bakhtin, M.M. (1984) *Problems of Dostoevsky's Poetics*, trans. C. Emerson, Manchester: Manchester University Press. (Original Russian version 1929.)

Barnes, B., Bloor, D. and Henry, J. (1996) *Scientific Knowledge: a Sociological Analysis*, London: Athlone.

Barthes, R. (1973) *Mythologies*, trans. A. Lavers, London: Paladin. (Original French version 1957).

Barthes, R. (1977a) 'The rhetoric of the image', in Barthes, R., *Image, Music, Text*, trans. S. Heath, London: Fontana: 32–51. (Original French version 1964.)

Barthes, R. (1977b) 'The death of the author', in Barthes, R., *Image, Music, Text*, trans. S. Heath, London: Fontana: 142–9. (Original French version 1968.)

Barthes, R. (1977c) 'The grain of the voice', in Barthes, R., *Image, Music, Text*, trans. S. Heath, London: Fontana: 179–90. (Original French version 1972.)

Barthes, R. (1977d) 'The photographic message', in Barthes, R., *Image, Music, Text*, trans. S. Heath, London: Fontana: 15–32. (Original French version 1961.)

Barthes, R. (1985) *The Fashion System*, trans. M. Ward and R. Howard, London: Cape. (Original French version 1967.)

Belk, R.W. (1987) 'Identity and the relevance of market, personal and community objects', in J. Umiker-Sebeok (ed.), *Marketing and Semiotics*, Amsterdam: Mouton de Gruyter.

Berger, J. (1972) *Ways of Seeing*, London: BBC and Penguin.

Bernstein, D. (1974) *Creative Advertising*, London: Longman.

Bernstein, L. (1976) *The Unanswered Question*, Cambridge, Massachusetts: Harvard University Press.

Bloomfield, L. (1935) *Language*, London: George Allen and Unwin. (First published in 1933.)

Bolinger, D. (1975) *Aspects of Language* (2nd edition), New York and Chicago: Harcourt Brace Jovanovich.

Bolinger, D. (1980) *Language: The Loaded Weapon*, London: Longman.

Bonney, B. and Wilson, H. (1990) 'Advertising and the manufacture of difference', in Alvarado, M. and (Thompson, J. eds), *The Media Reader*, London: British Film Institute. (First published in 1983.)

Brierley, S. (1995) *The Advertising Handbook*, London: Routledge.

Brown, D. (1991) *Human Universals*, New York: McGraw Hill.

Brown, G. and Yule, G. (1983) *Discourse Analysis*, Cambridge: Cambridge University Press.

Brown, P. and Levinson, S. (1987) *Politeness: Some Universals in Language Usage*, Cambridge: Cambridge University Press.

Buchan, D. (1972) *The Ballad and the Folk,* London: Routledge & Kegan Paul.

Caldas Coulthard, C. and Coulthard, M. (eds) (1996) *Texts and Practices: Readings in Critical Discourse Analysis*, London: Routledge.

Cameron, D. (2000) *Good to Talk? Living and Working in a Communication Culture*, London: Sage.

Cameron, L. (1991) 'Off the beaten track: a consideration of the implications for teachers of recent developments in the study of metaphor', *English in Education* 25(2): 4–15.

Carey, P. (1982) *Bliss*, London: Pan (Picador).

Carroll, J. (1995) *Evolution and Literary Theory*, Columbia: University of Missouri Press.

Carter, R. (1998) *Vocabulary: Applied Linguistic Perspectives* (Second Edition), Routledge: London.

Carter, R. and McCarthy, M.J. (1995) 'Grammar and the spoken language', *Applied Linguistics* 16(2): 141–58.

Chalmers, A.F. (1982) *What Is This Thing Called Science?*, Milton Keynes: Open University Press.

Chandler, D. (forthcoming 2002) *Semiotics: The Basics*, Earlier version available HTTP: http://www.aber.ac.uk/media/Documents/S4B. London: Routledge.

Chomsky, N. (1965) *Aspects of the Theory of Syntax*, Cambridge, Massachusetts: MIT Press.

Chomsky, N. (1995) *The Minimalist Program*, Cambridge, Massachusetts: MIT Press.

Cinquin, C. (1987) 'Homo Coca-Colens: from marketing to semiotics and politics', in J. Umiker-Sebeok (ed.), *Marketing and Semiotics*, Amsterdam: Mouton de Gruyter.

Clark, E. (1988) *The Want Makers: Lifting the Lid off the World Advertising Industry*, London: Hodder & Stoughton.

Clark, K. and Holquist, M. (1984) *Mikhail Bakhtin*, Cambridge, Massachusetts: Harvard University Press.

Collins Concise Dictionary Plus (1989) London and Glasgow: Collins.

Cook, G. (1986) 'Text, extract and stylistic texture', in Brumfit, C. and Carter, R. (eds), *Literature and Language Teaching*, Oxford: Oxford University Press.

Cook, G. (1988) 'Stylistics with a dash of advertising', *Language and Style* 21(2): 151–61.

Cook, G. (1989) *Discourse*, Oxford: Oxford University Press.

Cook, G. (1990) 'Transcribing infinity: problems of context presentation', *Journal of Pragmatics* 14(l): 1–24.

Cook, G. (1994a) *Discourse and Literature*, Oxford: Oxford University Press.

Cook, G. (1994b) 'Repetition and knowing by heart: an aspect of intimate discourse', *English Language Teaching Journal*, 48.2: 133–42.

Cook, G. (1994c). 'Contradictory voices: a dialogue between Russian and Western European linguistics', in Sell, R. and Verdonk, P. (eds) *Literature and the New Interdisciplinarity: Poetics, Linguistics, History*, Amsterdam: Rodopi.

Cook, G. (1996) 'Language play in English', in Maybin, J. and Mercer, N. (eds), *Using English: from Conversation to Canon*, London: Routledge with the Open University.

Cook, G. (2000) *Language Play, Language Learning*, Oxford: Oxford University Press.

Cronin, A. (2000) *Advertising and Consumer Citizenship: Gender, Images and Rights*, London: Routledge.

Culler, J. (1975) *Structuralist Poetics*, London: Routledge & Kegan Paul.

Culler, J. (1983) *On Deconstruction*, London: Routledge & Kegan Paul.

Davis, H. and Walton, P. (eds) (1983) *Language, Image, Media*, Oxford: Basil Blackwell.

Derrida, J. (1974) *Glas*, Paris: Galilee.

Derrida, J. (1976) *Of Grammatology*, trans. G. Spivak, Baltimore, Maryland: Johns Hopkins University Press. (Original French version 1967.)

Dimter, M. (1985) 'On Text Classification', in van Dijk, T. (ed.), *Discourse and Literature*, Amsterdam: Benjamins.

Dissanayake, E. (1988) *What is Art For?*, Seattle: University of Washington Press.

Douglas, T. (1984) *The Complete Guide to Advertising*, London: Macmillan.

Dreyfus, H.L. (1987) 'Misrepresenting human intelligence', in Born, R. (ed.), *Artificial Intelligence: The Case Against*, Beckenham: Croom Helm.

Durand, J. (1987) 'Rhetorical figures in the advertising image', in Umiker-Sebeok, J. (ed.), *Marketing and Semiotics*, Amsterdam: Mouton de Gruyter.

Durham, T. (2000) Review of R. Rogers (ed.) *Preferred Placement: Knowledge Politics on the Web*, Akademie editions Jan van Eyk, *Times Higher Educational Supplement*, 14 September 2000.

Ellis, A. and Beattie, G. (1986) *The Psychology of Language and Communication*, London: Weidenfeld & Nicolson.

Eysenk, M.W. and Keane, M.T. (1990) *Cognitive Psychology*, Hove: Lawrence Erlbaum.

Fairclough, N. (1989) *Language and Power*, London: Longman.

Fairclough, N. (1992) *Discourse and Social Change*, Cambridge: Polity.

Fairclough, N. (1995) *Media Discourse*, London: Edward Arnold.

Falk, P. (1997) 'The Benetton-Toscani effect: testing the limits of conventional advertising', in Nava, M., Blake, A., MacRury, I., Richards, B. (eds), *Buy this Book: Studies in Advertising and Consumption*, London: Routledge.

Firth, J.R. (1957) *Papers in Linguistics 1934–51*, Oxford: Oxford University Press.

Fish, S. (1980) *Is There a Text in this Class?*, Cambridge, Massachusetts: Harvard University Press.

Fitzgerald, F. Scott (1967) *The Great Gatsby*, London: Heinemann. (First published in 1926.)

Fontana Dictionary of Modern Thought (1988 edition) Bullock, A., Stallybrass, O. *et al.* (eds), London: Fontana.

Forceville, C. (1996) *Pictorial Metaphors in Advertising*, London: Routledge.

Foucault, M. (1972) *The Archeology of Knowledge and the Discourse on Language*, New York: Pantheon.

Foucault, M. (1979) 'What is an author?', trans. J.V. Harari, in Harari, J.V. (ed.) *Textual Strategies: Perspectives in Post-Structuralism* (reprinted in Lodge, D. (ed.) (1988) *Modern Criticism and Theory: A Reader*, London: Longman). (Original French version 1969.)

Fowler, R. (1991) *The Language of the News*, London: Routledge.

Frances, M. (1989) 'Women in advertising', *Woman*, November: 56–9.

Freund, E. (1987) *The Return of the Reader*, London: Methuen.

Fuentes, C. (1987) *The Old Gringo*, trans. M. Sayers Peden and the author, London: Pan (Picador). (First published in Spanish in 1985.)

Geis, M.L. (1982) *The Language of Television Advertising*, New York: Academic.

Gell, A. (1977) 'Magic, perfume, dream', in Lewis, I.M. (ed.), *Symbols and Sentiments: Cross-Cultural Studies in Symbolism*, London.

Gibbs, R. (1994) *The Poetics of Mind: Figurative Thought, Language, and Understanding*, Cambridge: Cambridge University Press.

Ginsberg, A. (1956) *'Howl' and Other Poems*, San Francisco, California: City Lights.

Glucklich, A. (1997) *The End of Magic*, New York: Oxford University Press.

Godard, A. (1998) *The Language of Advertising*, London: Routledge.

Goffman, E. (1979) *Gender Advertisements*, London: Macmillan. (First published in 1976.)

Goffman, E. (1981) *Forms of Talk*, Oxford: Basil Blackwell.

Goldman, R. (1992) *Reading Ads Socially*, London: Routledge.

Gombrich, E.H. (1977) *Art and Illusion* (5th edition), London: Phaidon.

Grice, H.P. (1975) 'Logic and conversation', in Cole, P. and Morgan, J.L. (eds), *Syntax and Semantics*, Vol. 3, *Speech Acts*, New York: Academic Press. (First published in 1976.)

Halle, M. (1989) 'On theory and interpretation', in Fabb, N., Attridge, D., Durant, A. and MacCabe, C. (eds), *The Linguistics of Writing*, Manchester: Manchester University Press.

Halliday, M.A.K. (1975) *Learning How to Mean*, London: Arnold.

Halliday, M.A.K. (1994) *An Introduction to Functional Grammar* (2nd edition), London: Edward Arnold.

Halliday, M.A.K. and Hasan, R. (1976) *Cohesion in English*, London: Longman.

Hartley, J. (1994) *Designing Instructional Text* (3rd edition), London: Kogan Page.

Hodge, R. (1985) 'Song', in van Dijk, T. (ed.) *Discourse and Literature*, Amsterdam: Benjamins.

Holbrook, M.B. (1987) 'The study of signs in consumer esthetics: an egocentric review', in Umiker-Sebeok, J. (ed.), *Marketing and Semiotics*, Amsterdam: Mouton de Gruyter.

Hoshino, K. (1987) 'Semiotic marketing and product conceptualization', in Umiker-Sebeok, J. (ed.) *Marketing and Semiotics*, Amsterdam: Mouton de Gruyter.

Hudson, L. (1972) *The Cult of the Fact*, London: Jonathan Cape.

Ind, N. (1997) *The Corporate Brand*, Basingstoke: Macmillan Business

Jakobson, R. (1960) 'Concluding statement: linguistics and poetics', in Sebeok, T.A. (ed.), *Style in Language*, Cambridge, Massachusetts: MIT Press.

Jakobson, R. (1978) 'On realism in art', trans. K. Magassy, in Matejka, L. and Pomorska, K. (eds) *Readings in Russian Poetics*, Ann Arbor, Michigan: Michigan University Press. (Original Russian version 1921.)

Joyce, J. (1956) *Dubliners*, Harmondsworth: Penguin. (First published in 1914.)

Kafka, F. (1961) *Metamorphosis and Other Stories*, trans. W. Muir and E. Muir, Harmondsworth: Penguin. (Original German version 1933).

Kehret-Ward, T. (1987) 'Combining products in use; how the syntax of product use affects marketing decisions', in Umiker-Sebeok, J. (ed.), *Marketing and Semiotics*, Amsterdam: Mouton de Gruyter.

Klein, N. (2000) *No Logo: No Space, No Choice, No Jobs, Taking Aim at the Brand Bullies*, London: Flamingo.

Knight, M. (1990) 'Is the micro macho? A critique of the fictions of advertising', in Day, G. (ed.), *Readings in Popular Culture: Trivial Pursuits?*, London: Macmillan.

Kress, G. and van Leeuwen, T. (1996) *Reading Images: the Grammar of Visual Design*, London: Routledge.

Lakoff, G. (1987) *Women, Fire and Dangerous Things: What Categories Reveal about the Mind*, Chicago, Illinois: Chicago University Press.

Lakoff, G. and Johnson, M. (1980) *Metaphors We Live By*, London and Chicago, Illinois: University of Chicago Press.

Lakoff, R. (1973) 'The logic of politeness: on minding your p's and q's', in *Proceedings of the Ninth Regional Meeting of the Chicago Linguistic Society*.

Langer, S. (1967) *Mind: An Essay on Human Feeling, Vol. 1*, Baltimore, Maryland and London: Johns Hopkins University Press.

Lawrence, D.H. (1949) *The Rainbow*, Harmondsworth: Penguin. (First published in 1915.)

Lawrence, D.H. (1960) *England My England*, Harmondsworth: Penguin. (First published in 1922.)

Leech, G.N. (1966) *English in Advertising*, London: Longman.

Leech, G.N. (1969) A *Linguistic Guide to English Poetry*, London: Longman.

Leech, G.N. (1981) *Semantics* (2nd edition), Harmondsworth: Penguin.

Leech, G.N. (1990) 'What is a text: the case of Kentucky Fried Chicken', paper given at the annual Conference of the Poetics and Linguistics Association (PALA), University of Amsterdam, September.

Leech, G.N., Deucher, M. and Hoogenraad, R. (1982) *English Grammar for Today: a New Introduction*, Macmillan in association with the English Association.

Leech, G.N. and Short, M.H. (1981) *Style in Fiction*, London: Longman.

Lévi-Strauss, C. (1969) *The Raw and the Cooked*, trans. J. Weightman and D. Weightman, New York: Harper & Row. (Original French version 1964.)

Levinson, S.C. (1983) *Pragmatics*, Cambridge: Cambridge University Press.

Levinson, S.C. (1988) 'Putting linguistics on a proper footing: explorations in Goffman's concept of participation', in Drew, P. and Wooton, A. (eds) *Erving Goffman: Exploring the Interaction Order*, Cambridge: Polity Press.

Lewis, R. and Rolley, K. (1997) '(Ad)dressing the dyke: lesbian looks and lesbian looking', in Nava, M., Blake, A., MacRury, I. and Richards, B. (eds), *Buy This Book: Studies in Advertising and Consumption*, London: Routledge.

Lord, A. (1960) *The Singer of Tales*, Cambridge, Massachusetts: Harvard University Press.

Lury, A. (1994) 'Advertising moving beyond stereotypes', in Keat, R., Whiteley, N. and Abercrombie, N. (eds), *The Authority of the Consumer*, London: Routledge.

Lyons, J. (1977) *Semantics* (2 vols), Cambridge: Cambridge University Press.

Macherey, P. (1978) *A Theory of Literary Production*, London: Routledge & Kegan Paul. (Original French version 1922.)

McCarthy, M. (1991) *Discourse Analysis for Language Teachers*, Cambridge: Cambridge University Press.

McCarthy, M. and Carter, R. (1994) *Language as Discourse: Perspectives for Language Teaching*, London: Longman.

McLuhan, M. (1964) 'Keeping upset with the Joneses', in *Understanding Media*, London: Routledge & Kegan Paul.

Morley, D. and Robbins, K. (1995) *Spaces of Identity: Global Media, Electronic Landscapes and Cultural Boundaries*, London: Routledge.

Morris, D. (1977) *Manwatching: A Field Guide to Human Behaviour*, London: Cape.

Morris, D. *et al.* (1979) *Gestures: Their Origins and Distribution*, London: Cape.

Myers, J. and Simms, M. (eds) (1989) *The Longman Dictionary of Poetic Terms*, London: Longman.

Myers, G. (1994) *Words in Ads*, London: Arnold.

Myers, G. (1999) *Ad Worlds: Brands, Media, Audience*, London: Arnold.

Nash, W. (1998) 'The biro and the word processor', in Nash, W. *Language and Creative Illusion*, London: Longman.

Nava, M., Blake, A., MacRury, I. and Richards, B. (eds) (1997) *Buy this Book: Studies in Advertising and Consumption*, London: Routledge.

O'Donahue, S. (1997) 'Leaky boundaries: intertextuality and young adult experiences of advertising' in Nava, M., Blake, A., MacRury, I. and Richards, B. (eds), *Buy this Book: Studies in Advertising and Consumption*, London: Routledge.

Olson, C. (1950) 'Poetry New York', in Allen, D. (ed.) *The New American Poetry*, New York: Grove Press.

Ong, W.J. (1982) *Orality and Literacy*, London: Routledge.

Packard, V. (1956) *The Hidden Persuaders*, Harmondsworth: Penguin.

Pateman, T. (1985) 'How is understanding an advertisement possible?', in Davis, H. and Walton, P. (eds), *Language, Image, Media*, Oxford: Basil Blackwell.

Peirce, C.S. [1931–58] *Collected Papers 1931–1958* (8 Vols), Cambridge, Massachusetts: Harvard University Press.

Pennycook, A. (1994) 'Incommensurable discourses?', *Applied Linguistics* 15(2): 115–38.

Quirk, R., Greenbaum, S., Leech, G.N. and Svartvik, J. (1985). *A Comprehensive Grammar of the English Language*, London: Longman.

Reddy, M. (1978) 'The conduit metaphor', in Ortony, A. (ed.) *Metaphor and Thought*, Cambridge: Cambridge University Press.

Romaine, S. (1998) *Communicating Gender*, Oxford: Basil Blackwell.

Rosch, E. (1977) 'Human categorization', in Warren, N. (ed.) *Advances in CrossCultural Psychology, Vol. 1*, New York: Academic Press.

Saussure, F. de (1974) *Course in General Linguistics*, trans. W. Baskin, London: Fontana. (Original French version 1915).

Searle, J. (1975a) 'Indirect speech acts' in P. Cole, and J.L. Morgan (eds) *Syntax and Semantics, Vol. 3, Speech Acts*, New York: Academic Press.

Searle, J. (1975b) 'A taxonomy of illocutionary acts', in Gunderson, K. (ed.), *Language, Mind and Knowledge*, Minnesota Studies in the Philosophy of Science Vol. 7, Minneapolis, Minnesota: University of Minnesota Press.

Sebag-Montefiore, H. (1987) 'The bottom line', *Sunday Times*, 1 February.

Shklovsky, V. (1974) *Mayakovsky and His Circle*, trans. L. Feiler, London: Pluto. (Original Russian version 1940.)

Sinclair, J. McH. (1966) 'Taking a poem to pieces', in Fowler, R. (ed.), *Essays on Style and Language*, London: Routledge & Kegan Paul.

Sterne, L. [1759–67] *Tristram Shandy*, London.

Stobart, P. (ed.) (1994) *Brand Power*, Basingstoke: Macmillan.

Swales, J. (1990) *Genre Analysis*, Cambridge: Cambridge University Press.

Talbot, M. (2000) ' "It's good to talk"? The undermining of feminism in a British Telecom advertisement', *Journal of Sociolinguistics* 4(1): 108–20.

Tanaka, K. (1994) *Advertising Language: a Pragmatic Approach to Advertisements in Britain and Japan*, London: Routledge.

Tannen, D. (1984) *Conversational Style: Analyzing Talk among Friends*, Norwood, New Jersey: Ablex.

Tannen, D. (1989) *Talking Voices: Repetition, Dialogue and Imagery in Conversational Discourse*, Cambridge: Cambridge University Press.

Thomas, J. (1995) *Meaning in Interaction: an Introduction to Pragmatics*, London: Longman.

Thompson, J. (1990) 'Advertising's rationality', in Alvarado, M. and Thompson, J. (eds), *The Media Reader*, London: British Film Institute.

Tomashevsky, B.V. (1965) 'Thematics', in Lemon, L.T. and Reis, M.J. (eds), *Russian Formalist Criticism: Four Essays*, Lincoln, Nebraska: University of Nebraska Press. (Original Russian version 1922.)

Turner, F. 1992. 'The Neural Lyre: poetic meter, the brain and time', *Natural Classicism: Essays on Literature and Science*, Charlottesville: University of Virginia Press.

Umiker-Sebeok, J. (ed.) (1987) *Marketing and Semiotics*, Amsterdam: Mouton de Gruyter.

Usunier, J.-C. (1999) *Marketing Across Cultures* (3rd edition), New York: Prentice Hall.

van Leeuwen, T. (1999) *Speech, Music, Sound*, London: Macmillan.

Vestergaard, T. and Schrøder, K. (1985) *The Language of Advertising*, Oxford: Basil Blackwell.

Volosinov, V.N. (1973) 'Freudianism: a critical sketch', trans. I. Titunik, in *Freudianism: A Marxist Critique* (written by M.M. Bakhtin), New York: Academic Press. (Original Russian version 1927.)

Volosinov, V.N. (name used by M.M. Bakhtin) (1986) *Marxism and the Philosophy of Language*, trans. L. Matejka and R. Titunik, Cambridge, Massachusetts: Harvard University Press. (Original Russian version 1929.)

Vygotsky, L.S. (1962) *Thought and Language*, trans. E. Haufmann and G. Vakar, Cambridge, Massachusetts: MIT Press. (Original Russian version 1934.)

Wales, K. (1989) A *Dictionary of Stylistics*, London: Longman.

Walker, S. (2001) *Typography and Language: Prescriptions and Practices*, London: Longman Pearson.

Watt, I. (1963) *The Rise of the Novel*, London: Peregrine. (First published in 1957.)

Weber, J-J. (ed.) (1996) *The Stylistics Reader: from Roman Jakobson to the present*, London: Arnold.

Werth, P.W. (1976) 'Roman Jakobson's verbal analysis of poetry', *Journal of Linguistics* 12: 21–73.

White, D. (1988) Entry on advertising, in Bullock, A., Stallybrass, O. *et al.*, *Fontana Dictionary of Modern Thought* (First edition), London: Fontana.

White, R. (1988) *Advertising: What It Is and How To Do It* (2nd edition), London: McGraw Hill.

White, R. (2000) *Advertising* (4th edition), London: McGraw Hill.

Widdowson, H.G. (1972) 'On the deviance of literary discourse', *Style* 6: 292–308.

Widdowson, H.G. (1973) 'An applied linguistic approach to discourse analysis', unpublished Ph.D. Thesis, Department of Linguistics, University of Edinburgh.

Widdowson, H.G. (1975) *Stylistics and the Teaching of Literature*, London: Longman.

Widdowson, H.G. (1979) *Explorations in Applied Linguistics*, Oxford: Oxford University Press.

Widdowson, H.G. (1984a) *Explorations in Applied Linguistics 2*, Oxford: Oxford University Press.

Widdowson, H.G. (1984b) 'Reference and representation as modes of meaning', in *Explorations in Applied Linguistics 2*, Oxford: Oxford University Press.

Widdowson, H.G. (1992). *Practical Stylistics: an Approach to Poetry*, Oxford: Oxford University Press.

Williams, R. (1980) 'Advertising: the magic system', in *Problems in Materialism and Culture*, London: Verso. (First published in 1960.)

Williams, R. (1983) *Keywords* (2nd edition), London: Collins Fontana.

Williamson, J. (1978) *Decoding Advertisements*, London and Boston, Massachusetts: Marion Boyars.

Wilmshurst, J. and Mackay, A. (1999) *The Fundamentals of Advertising*. Oxford: Butterworth Heinemann.

Wittgenstein, L. (1968) *Philosophical Investigations*, trans. G.E.M. Anscombe, Oxford: Blackwell. (First published in German, 1953.)

Wolfson, N. (1988) 'The bulge: a theory of speech behaviour and social distance', in Fine, J. (ed.), *Second Language Discourse: A Textbook of Current Research* Norwood, New Jersey: Ablex.

Wolfson, N. (1989) *Perspectives: Sociolinguistics and TESOL*, Cambridge, Massachusetts: Newbury House.

Yule, G. (1995) 'The paralinguistics of reference; representation in reported speech' in Cook, G. and Seidlhofer, B. (eds), *Principle and Practice in Applied Linguistics: Studies in Honour of H.G. Widdowson*, Oxford: Oxford University Press.

Index